1-2-3: Tips, Tricks, and Traps

1-2-3: Tips, Tricks, and Traps

Dick Andersen
Douglas Ford Cobb

Que Corporation
Indianapolis, Indiana

Library of Congress Catalog No.: LC 84-60135

ISBN 0-88022-110-0

123® is a registered trademark of Lotus Development Corporation.

VisiCalc® is a registered trademark of VisiCorp.

WordStar® is a registered trademark of MicroPro International Corporation.

Volkswriter™ is a trademark of Lifetree Software, Inc.

89 88 87 86 85   12 11 10 9 8

Interpretation of the printing code; the rightmost double-digit number is the year of the book's printing; the rightmost single-digit number, the number of the book's printing. For example, a printing code of 87-4 shows that the fourth printing of the book occurred in 1987.

Dedication

To Dr. James Mackie, without whose loving guidance this book and many other wonderful things would not have been possible

R.A.

To my brother Steve

D.F.C.

Editorial Director
David F. Noble, Ph.D.

Editor
Jeannine Freudenberger, M.A.

Managing Editor
Paul L. Mangin

About the Authors

Dick Andersen

Dick Andersen is Director of the consulting firm, Advanced Micro/ Mainframe Solutions. He holds a B.A. from the University of California, Berkeley, and an M.A. from Graduate Theological Union, Berkeley, California. Mr. Andersen has been connected with the computer industry for 17 years; he has served as consultant to many Fortune 1000 companies and has extensive experience in developing and presenting seminars and training sessions in 1-2-3, mainframe data base systems, micro/mainframe connection, and other related topics.

Douglas Ford Cobb

Douglas Ford Cobb received his B.A., magna cum laude, from Williams College and his M.S. in accounting from New York University's Graduate School of Business Administration. He has worked for Arthur Andersen & Co. and was president of Cobb Associates, Inc., a Boston-based microcomputer consulting firm. Mr. Cobb has worked for Que Corporation as general manager of the company's business software products. He coauthored *Spreadsheet Software: From VisiCalc to 1-2-3*; *Using 1-2-3*; *1-2-3 Tips, Tricks, and Traps*; and *1-2-3 for Business*, all published by Que Corporation. He is president of The Cobb Group, Inc., a microcomputer information firm in Louisville, Kentucky.

Table of Contents

Acknowledgments

The authors wish to thank Tom Perkins and Sharon Sears of Que Corporation for their help with this book. A special thanks to Jeannine Freudenberger, Tim Russell, Jonathan Mangin, and Dennis Sheehan for all those figures.

Introduction

Why This Book Is Unique

By the time you pick up this book, many good books about 1-2-3 will be on the market. 1-2-3 has been the hottest-selling microcomputer software around for months; so, naturally, authors and publishers want to jump on the bandwagon.

So what's different about *1-2-3: Tips, Tricks, and Traps*? Unlike most of the Lotus books you'll see, this is a nitty-gritty, how-to book, full of Tips, Tricks, and Traps aimed directly at the practical problems you encounter when you try to use 1-2-3. The authors of this book have been working with 1-2-3 since late 1982—writing about 1-2-3, teaching seminars, and developing 1-2-3 applications.

In *1-2-3: Tips, Tricks, and Traps*, you won't get a lot of verbiage or general descriptions of 1-2-3's capabilities. What you will get is concise, hard-hitting, practical suggestions about how best to use 1-2-3. Although *1-2-3: Tips, Tricks, and Traps* includes thorough explanations of many 1-2-3 concepts, the authors assume that you know most of the basics. However, *1-2-3: Tips, Tricks, and Traps* is not just for advanced Lotus users. Far from it. Even beginning users will run up against problems for which existing reference and tutorial materials may not be much help, but for which *1-2-3: Tips, Tricks, and Traps* is just right.

Here are some of the situations in which you'll reach for this book:

When you've tried to do something apparently simple, you've gotten an unexpected result, and you're sitting there scratching your head.

When it looks as if "you can't get there from here" with 1-2-3, but you think there ought to be a way.

When you know how to get the job done, but you're sure there has to be a quicker and easier solution.

Here, chapter by chapter, are some of the topics covered in *1-2-3: Tips, Tricks, and Traps*:

Chapter 1: Worksheet Design

What to do when you get the dreaded "memory full" message.

How to avoid wiping out parts of your worksheet with the **/W**orksheet **I**nsert and **D**elete commands.

Chapter 2: Data Entry

How to cut in half the time for entering dates and other functions.

How to use the numeric keypad and move the cursor at the same time on an IBM PC.

Chapter 3: Using the Worksheet

How to use the **/W**orksheet **W**indow command.

How not to get confused by the **/W**orksheet Title command.

Chapter 4: Recalculation

How to recalculate a small group of cells without waiting for the whole worksheet to recalculate.

What to do when "ERR" shows up unexpectedly.

How to overcome circular references.

Chapter 5: "What If" and Sensitivity Analysis

How to design your worksheets to make "what if" analysis easy.

How to get "floating labels" in your line and bar charts.

Chapter 13: Data Base

What to do when you are trying to Extract a few records from a data base and you get the whole data base instead.

How to save /Data Query definitions and recall them instantaneously.

How to keep data base subtotals up-to-date automatically.

1-2-3: Tips, Tricks, and Traps answers all these questions and more. No matter how much you know about 1-2-3, you'll find many new ideas and techniques in this book.

How to Use This Book

What are Tips, Tricks, and Traps? A Tip is a helpful hint that tells you a better way to use a 1-2-3 command or function. Tips will let you do things you may have thought you could not do, or help you do what you want more quickly, more easily, or more safely. Tricks go a bit further than Tips, usually combining several techniques into an innovative solution to a 1-2-3 problem. A Trap is a different animal: it focuses on a situation where you're likely to get into trouble with 1-2-3. The discussion under the heading of a particular Trap usually tells you both how to avoid the trap and what to do when you encounter it. Many of the Traps in this book are followed by Tricks that offer solutions.

Some of the chapters in *1-2-3: Tips, Tricks, and Traps* have several subsections; others have only one. Each subsection is composed of a long list of Tips, Tricks, and Traps on that particular topic. The Tips and Traps in many subsections are progressive; earlier Tips lay the groundwork for later ones. Therefore, you may sometimes want to read straight through this book the way you would through an ordinary book. However, each Tip and Trap is designed primarily to stand on its own, and we expect that you will usually read one or only a few at a time. We believe that people already have enough books that they must sit down and read from cover to cover. What they need is one that helps them go directly to what they need to solve their immediate problems.

You will often find that a particular entry does not refer to other entries even though the material in other Tips and Traps may be relevant to the one you're reading. We've done it this way because we'd rather not clutter the text with many references to other sections. We've included a thorough index in this book. If you want to find all the important references to a particular topic, please use the Index.

We've used examples that are as simple as possible, with small amounts of data. This means that if you have any doubts about how something really works, you can enter the data from our example yourself in a few minutes and try it out. That should be your by-word in working with Lotus 1-2-3: TRY IT OUT! By trying things immediately instead of wondering about them, you'll learn many of the program's remarkable subtleties.

Remember this: *1-2-3: Tips, Tricks, and Traps* is a practical, how-to book. We hope you'll always have it by your side while your computer is running and Lotus is loaded.

A Word on Macros

You'll find that many of the Tips throughout the book include complete keyboard macros that make a particular job much quicker and easier. If you're not familiar with the concept of keyboard macros and how they work, you may want to start by reading the chapter on macros in *Using 1-2-3* or the macros section of the basic skills chapter in the 1-2-3 Manual.

Although it may take a little time to learn how to work with macros, you won't regret it. Macros will save you so much time in the long run and give you so much pleasure when they work that you'll soon join the growing numbers of Lotus macro aficionados.

The macros in this book are mostly short, simple ones that expedite limited but important tasks. This is the easiest and safest type of macro to create and to use. Ezra Gottheil of Lotus Development Corporation refers to these simple, focused macros as "golden macros."

Learning More about 1-2-3

Que Corporation is the leading publisher of books and periodicals relating to Lotus 1-2-3. No matter what your 1-2-3 interest may be, Que has a book or periodical for you.

Books

If you are new to 1-2-3 and need a comprehensive 1-2-3 tutorial, try *Using 1-2-3* by Douglas Cobb and Geoffrey T. LeBlond. This is the most popular book ever about 1-2-3. More than 400,000 users have relied on this book to teach them about their 1-2-3 program. You can find the book in your bookstore or computer store, or you can order directly from Que.

A second book, *1-2-3 for Business*, by Douglas Cobb and Leith Anderson, presents fourteen 1-2-3 worksheets. This book contains practical applications of many of 1-2-3's commands and functions.

Periodicals

Absolute Reference: The Journal for 1-2-3 and Symphony Users is a monthly newsletter published by Que especially for 1-2-3 and Symphony users. *AR* offers tips on how to use Lotus software, columns that discuss the programs' commands and functions, reviews of 1-2-3 and Symphony-related products, and special features designed to help 1-2-3 and Symphony users to get the most from their software. You can order *AR* with the convenient form at the back of this book.

Seminars

Seminars are available for those who would like personal instruction from the authors on Lotus 1-2-3. These seminars can be given either publicly or "in house." For more information, write

Que Corporation
7999 Knue Road
Indianapolis, IN 46250

A Final Word

This edition of *1-2-3: Tips, Tricks, and Traps* is based primarily on Release 1A of 1-2-3. However, those who have not upgraded from Release 1 will find that 99 percent of the material covered applies equally to that first release.

Conclusion

We hope our Tips, Tricks, and Traps will help you to work more wonders with the magic of Lotus 1-2-3. But don't forget: Don't just read. TRY IT OUT!

1
Worksheet Design

Planning and Documenting the Worksheet

1 Tip: When you're planning a complex worksheet, draw a map showing the layout of the various areas and keep this map updated.

A map of a worksheet looks something like Figure 1. The map helps you plan efficient memory use from the beginning of your project, reminds you where you can use /**W**orksheet **I**nsert and **D**elete safely, and tells you where space is available if you need to add new areas of information.

A worksheet map also provides basic documentation for anyone else who may later need to modify your worksheets. You might even include the map somewhere in the worksheet itself.

2 Tip: When building your model, make all your assumptions explicit.

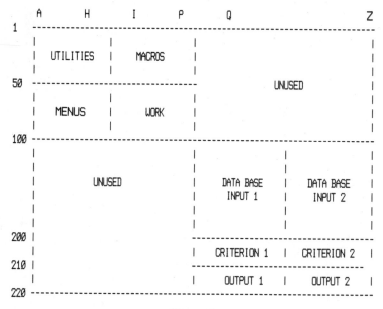

Figure 1

This may sound obvious, but consider the time that can be saved by making your assumptions explicit. Suppose we create a simple @NPV function:

B5: @NPV(.11,A2..E2)

This function computes the net present value of the values in the range A2..E2 at a discount rate of 11%. Now suppose you want to change the discount rate. To change the rate with the formula entered as shown, you must {Edit} the cell, move the cursor ten cells to the left, change the rate, and press {Enter}. This change is not too easy, even when the {Tab} key is used to move the cursor. But suppose you enter the formula in this fashion:

B5: @NPV(A5,A2..E2)

To change the discount rate in this case, just move to cell A5 and enter the new rate. Making the assumption for the discount rate explicit by entering it in a separate cell makes the process of changing the assumption simpler and more efficient.

This same technique can be used with growth rates in financial forecasts, for the key term in @VLOOKUP and @HLOOKUP functions, and in dozens of other ways.

3 **Tip:** Document in one area all the assumptions of your model.

Often you make certain assumptions in constructing a 1-2-3 model. If these assumptions are not clear (to you or to others) when the model is used, confusion can result. It's a good idea to pick a special area where you put information about the assumptions. You can also include special cautions and instructions in the same area.

For example, in a sales projection model, you may use different percentage growth factors for different years. Your model may also be based on other assumptions. A natural place to document all assumptions is the area where you place the variable growth factors you will be changing when you do your "what if" analysis. (See Figure 2.)

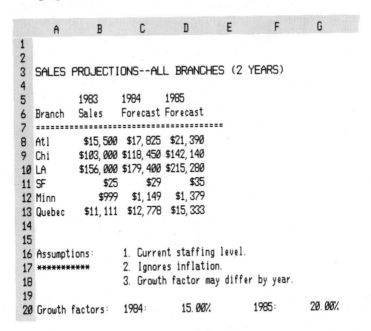

Figure 2

4 **Tip:** Use named ranges in formulas and in macros, whenever possible, to make your worksheets easier to understand.

You can use /**R**ange **N**ame **C**reate or **L**abels to give sensible names to ranges you use in formulas and in macros. For example, if you are adding a column of sales figures, you can assign the name "ALL_SALES" to that column and then refer to it in a formula: @SUM(ALL_SALES). This convention makes the purpose of the function clearer. Using range names also means that you don't need to change the formula or the macro if the boundaries of the range change. (This topic will be addressed again in the Tips that deal with keyboard macros.)

5   **Tip:** Document named ranges with comments in the worksheet.

If you place a label giving the name next to a named range, you'll find it easier to identify that range later. If the range is one cell, you can then use the /**R**ange **N**ame **L**abels command to name the range. This is the practice we've followed with all the macros in this book. For example, look at Figure 3. This figure shows two keyboard macros, \X and \C. Notice that the names for the macros have been entered in column A. The /**R**ange **N**ame **L**abels **R**ight **A1..A7** command automatically names the macros according to the labels in column A.

	A	B	C	D	E
1	\X	/fxfSALES_XT		Extract to file SALES_XT	
2		SALES_REPORT~		Extract range SALES_REPORT	
3					
4					
5					
6					
7	\C	{Goto}SALES_REPORT~		Go to range SALES_REPORT	
8		/fcceSALES_XT~		Combine file SALES_XT	
9					

Figure 3

The only problem with this approach is that it's not always easy to find an inconspicuous place for the label. Still, you should put the labels in where you can.

6   **Tip:** Keep a printed copy of the formulas you use in a model.

A printout of the formulas is useful for reference and permanent documentation of all your detailed assumptions. There are three ways to do it:

1. Use /**P**rint **P**rinter **O**ptions **O**ther **C**ell-Formulas to print all formulas. (Figure 4 shows a listing created with this command.) The limitation of this method is that you don't see the formulas in the cell positions they occupy on the worksheet.

```
C8:  (C0) +B8+B8*$GROWTH84
D8:  (C0) +C8+C8*$GROWTH85
C9:  (C0) +B9+B9*$GROWTH84
D9:  (C0) +C9+C9*$GROWTH85
C10: (C0) +B10+B10*$GROWTH84
D10: (C0) +C10+C10*$GROWTH85
C11: (C0) +B11+B11*$GROWTH84
D11: (C0) +C11+C11*$GROWTH85
C12: (C0) +B12+B12*$GROWTH84
D12: (C0) +C12+C12*$GROWTH85
C13: (C0) +B13+B13*$GROWTH84
D13: (C0) +C13+C13*$GROWTH85
```

Figure 4

2. Use /**R**ange **F**ormat to format as **T**ext all cells containing formulas. Widen all the columns so that the entire formulas will display. (The /**W**orksheet **C**olumn-width **S**et command does this.) You can then print the entire range that contains the formulas. If you use the {PrtSc} key, you'll get the column and row borders printed, too, so that you can easily see what formula is in what cell. This method not only shows formulas in their natural positions but also uses less paper than the first method. (See Figure 5.)

3. Use a good print-formatting utility, like DocuCalc, to print the formulas in their relative locations and to document graph names, range names, and other important information about your worksheet.

7 Tip: When planning a large model, create a safe area in the upper-left corner of the worksheet; this area will be unaffected by the /**W**orksheet **I**nsert and **D**elete commands.

```
         I      J      K         L        M      N
 1
 2
 3  SALES PROJECTIONS--ALL BRANCHES (2 YEARS)
 4
 5         1983   1984      1985      1986
 6  Branch Sales  Forecast  Forecast  Forecast
 7  =============================================
 8  Atl    15500 +J8+J8*$C17  +K8+K8*$C17  +L8+L8*$F$17
 9  Chi   103000 +J9+J9*$C18  +K9+K9*$C18  +L9+L9*$F$17
10  LA    156000 +J10+J10*$C19 +K10+K10*$C19 +L10+L10*$F$17
11  SF        25 +J11+J11*$C20 +K11+K11*$C20 +L11+L11*$F$17
12
13
14
15
16  Growth factors:  1984-1985              1986
17        Atl        15.00%    ALL          15.00%
18        Chi        10.00%
19        LA         12.00%
20        SF         20.00%
```

Figure 5

The /**W**orksheet **I**nsert and **D**elete commands are convenient for inserting or deleting entire rows and columns. However, the commands are also dangerous. It's easy to delete rows, for instance, that you think you're not using and later discover that they contained important information that was off the screen at the moment.

Place information you want to protect from this kind of disaster in a safe area in the upper-left corner of the worksheet. Then you can insert and delete to your heart's content in the area diagonally below and to the right of the safe area and not be afraid of affecting any vital information. Divide this safe area into subareas for different purposes. Figure 1 shows subareas for macro utilities (generalized macros that can be reused), macros, menus, and work cells. You may prefer a different layout for your own purposes.

One reason for dividing your safe area into subareas is that you need different column widths for different kinds of entries—macros, for instance—in contrast to certain data areas. Subdivisions can also help you keep track of things by keeping all your macros together and all your menus together.

The areas in the worksheet that we have called unused are not completely unused because they can be temporary work areas when you are not using /**W**orksheet **I**nsert or **D**elete in the main part of the worksheet.

8   Trap: A safe area may use too much memory.

The problem with the safe area described in the previous Tip is that the unused spaces in the worksheet use memory even though the cells in these areas are blank. If you build large models and have a limited amount of memory, this can be a problem. The Tips on the following pages give you insight into this problem and some solutions for it.

Managing Memory

9   Tip: To save memory, define your models so that the active area of the worksheet is as small as possible.

The active area of a 1-2-3 worksheet is a rectangle with its upper-left corner at cell A1 and its lower-right corner at the intersection of the farthest right column that contains an entry or a formatted cell and the lowest row that contains an entry or a formatted cell. In the sample worksheet in Figure 1, the active area is the range A1..Z220.

The size of the active area is significant because 1-2-3 uses some RAM (random-access memory) for every cell in the active area, whether or not there is anything in the cell. Every blank cell in the active area uses about 4 bytes; therefore, 1,000 blank cells (the number of cells in a 10-column-by-100-row area) consume approximately 4,000 bytes.

For an illustration of the use of memory by blank cells in the active area, take an empty worksheet; move the cursor to cell IV2048, the last cell in the worksheet; and try to make an entry. When you press {Enter}, 1-2-3 will beep and return the message "Memory full." You may wonder how a single entry can fill 1-2-3's memory. With 2,048 rows and 254 columns, the 1-2-3 worksheet has over 500,000 cells. Making an entry in cell IV2048 causes the entire worksheet to be active, so 1-2-3 assigns about four bytes to every empty cell, for a total of at least 2,000,000 bytes. No wonder 1-2-3 won't accept the entry.

In most cases the loss of even several thousand bytes will not cause too great a problem. However, if you have a limited amount of RAM, every byte counts. Therefore, it is best to do all your work in a compact rectangle in the upper-left part of the worksheet grid. If memory is tight, avoid blank cells.

A large safe area, like the one discussed previously, results in large unused areas that can use up a lot of memory unnecessarily. If you use a safe area, keep it as small and compact as possible, and locate it in the upper-left corner of the worksheet. This practice avoids creating large areas of memory-using blank cells.

10   Trap: If you inadvertently increase the size of the active area, you may use up memory unnecessarily.

If you use or format a cell or range outside the part of the worksheet that you really need, you increase the size of the active area and waste memory. Even one mistake can use up a great deal of memory. For example, suppose you build a worksheet that contains a 1,000-record-by-10-field data base. The bottom cell in the active area is cell J1001. If, by accident, you format cells K1001 and L1001 with the /**R**ange Format command, you have added 2,002 cells to the active area and have lost over 4,000 bytes!

Be careful, especially when formatting, not to activate cells that you don't need.

11   Tip: Monitor your memory use frequently.

The /**W**orksheet Status command tells you at any time how much memory you have left. Use this command to monitor your memory use. Every time you add a new area to your worksheet or erase or delete a large area, use the /**WS** command both before and after the action. You'll start to get a feel for how much memory you use and how much you free up in the activities you commonly perform.

You can always find out the size of the active area. Pressing the {End} and {Home} keys in sequence moves the cursor to the last cell, the lower-right cell, in the active area. From there, you can easily discover any unneeded rows or columns.

12   Trap: Deleting or erasing large portions of the worksheet recovers only small amounts of memory.

The /**Worksheet** **D**elete **R**ow or **C**olumn command and the /**R**ange **E**rase commands do not affect the size of the active area and so do not recover the memory allocated to the cells in the ranges that are erased or deleted. If the deleted or erased cells contain large numbers or complex formulas, some memory can be recovered; but the active area is not changed.

To test what we mean, build the simple worksheet shown in Figure 6. Use the command

· /**Worksheet** **D**elete **R**ow **A3**

to delete the third row. Then press {End} and {Home}. The cursor jumps to cell D3. 1-2-3 still considers row 3 part of the active area even though you have just deleted it from the model. 1-2-3 will continue to allocate four bytes to every cell in row 3.

	A	B	C	D	E
1	1	2	3	4	
2	2	3	4	5	
3	3	4	5	6	
4					

Figure 6

13 **Trick:** If you run out of memory or want to reduce the memory used by a model, you can reclaim some memory through a /**F**ile **X**tract followed by a /**F**ile **R**etrieve.

When you get the dreaded "Memory full" message, the chances are good that you have inadvertently overextended the current active area. Perhaps you have accidentally made an entry into a cell or formatted a cell that is far removed from the area you're really using.

First, find out the current size of your active area by pressing the {End} and {Home} keys in sequence. This action takes you to the lower-right corner of the active area.

If the active area of the worksheet is significantly larger than the area you're actually using, do the following:

1. Make a backup copy of your current worksheet with the /**F**ile **S**ave command so that you can recover your work if something goes wrong.

2.   Execute a /**W**orksheet **S**tatus to see how much memory is currently available.

3.   Do a /**F**ile **X**tract **F**ormulas on the part of your worksheet that you are really using.

4.   Do a /**F**ile **R**etrieve on the file to which you've just **X**tracted.

5.   Check your memory availability again with /**W**orksheet **S**tatus to see how much you've reclaimed.

As an alternative, you can

1.   Use the {End} and {Home} keys to move to the lower-right corner of the active area.

2.   Use the /**W**orksheet **D**elete command to remove any unneeded rows and columns from the worksheet.

3.   Save the entire file by the command /**F**ile **S**ave.

4.   Retrieve the file with /**F**ile **R**etrieve.

As 1-2-3 saves the file, any blank rows at the bottom or any blank columns at the right edge of the active area are removed from the active area, thus reducing the memory requirements of the model. You can use this technique at any time to reduce the amount of memory used by a model.

14 **Tip:** You can save memory by getting rid of areas you're no longer using and by compacting the ones that remain.

This seems obvious, but sometimes the obvious escapes us. By *compacting*, we mean getting all your work into as compact a rectangle as possible in the upper-left corner of the worksheet. When you've done this, do a /**F**ile **X**tract on the area you want to keep, followed by a /**F**ile **R**etrieve of that **X**tracted file. See the previous Tip for more details on how to /**F**ile **X**tract the active area.

15 **Tip:** You may save memory by swapping worksheet areas in and out of memory.

If you have certain sections of a spreadsheet that you use only part of the time, you can save them to disk by /**F**ile **X**tract and then bring them back as needed with /File Combine Copy. This way you may be able to use the same memory at different times for different purposes.

This procedure can be a bother if you must do it often, but you can make it easier by setting up Xtract and Combine macros. (See Figure 3 for an example of /File Xtract and Combine macros.)

16   Tip: Speed up swapping with a hard disk or a RAM disk.

The previous Tip discusses swapping areas of the worksheet in and out of memory as a strategy for minimizing memory usage. The trouble with swapping on a floppy-disk system is that reads and writes are slow. They are especially slow with 1-2-3 because its worksheet files are unusually large compared to other spreadsheet programs. However, reads and writes are several times faster if you use a hard-disk system.

You can speed up the swapping even more by using a RAM disk. A RAM disk is an area of memory that you have fooled the operating system into thinking is a disk drive. You can read and write to this area of memory as if you were reading from and writing to a file; the operating system does not know the difference.

RAM disk software is commonly available free when you buy a RAM expansion board from certain manufacturers. Be advised, however, that this software may make a patch to the standard operating system. Therefore, you should find out from the vendor whether the RAM disk software will run with 1-2-3 or with any other software you wish to use.

You can swap things in and out of the RAM disk area very quickly. This speed comes at a price, however. Any RAM memory you designate as a RAM disk will be unavailable to your 1-2-3 worksheet. RAM disks work best when your computer has memory beyond what 1-2-3 can use directly. For instance, Release 1 of 1-2-3 could address 544K of memory on the IBM PC. If you have this release and also have more than 544K of RAM in your computer, then you can perhaps benefit by using some of the excess for a RAM disk.

2

Data Entry

Entering Formulas

17 **Tip:** You can often enter formulas most quickly and safely when you are in POINT mode.

One of the cleverest features of 1-2-3 is the program's ability to specify ranges just by the user's pointing out their boundaries with the cursor keys. We can enter formulas, define functions, and specify Print and other command ranges with the POINT mode. The Point method not only saves time, but also prevents mistakes because we don't have to worry about entering, for instance, A12 when we mean to enter A122.

Figures 7 through 11 show how the process works. Suppose we want to enter the formula +K7*K8 in cell K9. We first position the cursor on K9 and enter a plus to let 1-2-3 know we're going to enter a formula. This activates the VALUE mode (see the upper-right corner of Figure 7). The second line of the control panel in Figure 7 shows the plus that we've just entered (upper-left corner).

```
K9: (C0)                                              VALUE
+

              I         J         K         L         M         N
  1
  2                     January Grain Sales
  3                     ====================
  4
  5                     Cotton    Corn      Oats      Barley
  6                     --------  --------  --------  --------
  7  Unit Price          $12.32    $5.50    $18.21    $15.47
  8  Unit Sales          12,100    5,000    22,438    25,018
  9  Total Sales $
 10
 11
```

Figure 7

Next we move the cursor up two cells to K7 by pressing the ↑ key twice.
The mode indicator in the upper-right corner of the screen changes from
"VALUE" to "POINT"; moving the cursor has placed us in POINT
mode. The entry +K7 now appears on the second line of the control
panel in the upper left. Because we're now in POINT mode, 1-2-3
assumes that the cell the cursor is now on (K7) will be the next part of
the formula. Figure 8 shows this situation.

```
K7: (C2) 12.32                                        POINT
+K7

              I         J         K         L         M         N
  1
  2                     January Grain Sales
  3                     ====================
  4
  5                     Cotton    Corn      Oats      Barley
  6                     --------  --------  --------  --------
  7  Unit Price          $12.32    $5.50    $18.21    $15.47
  8  Unit Sales          12,100    5,000    22,438    25,018
  9  Total Sales $
 10
 11
```

Figure 8

Now we enter an asterisk to let 1-2-3 know we want to multiply the +K7 times something; this puts us back in VALUE mode again, and the asterisk now appears in the control panel after the +K7. See Figure 9.

```
K9: (C0)                                        VALUE
+K7*

        I        J        K        L        M        N
 1
 2                       January Grain Sales
 3                       ===================
 4
 5                       Cotton   Corn     Oats     Barley
 6                       -------- -------- -------- --------
 7  Unit Price            $12.32   $5.50  $18.21   $15.47
 8  Unit Sales            12,100   5,000  22,438   25,018
 9  Total Sales $
10
11
```

Figure 9

To finish the formula, we need to point to cell K8, so we move the cursor up one cell with the ↑ key. Figure 10 shows how the screen appears. We're back in POINT mode again, and K8 has been added to the formula in the upper-left corner of the screen.

```
K8: (,0) 12100                                  POINT
+K7*K8

        I        J        K        L        M        N
 1
 2                       January Grain Sales
 3                       ===================
 4
 5                       Cotton   Corn     Oats     Barley
 6                       -------- -------- -------- --------
 7  Unit Price            $12.32   $5.50  $18.21   $15.47
 8  Unit Sales            12,100   5,000  22,438   25,018
 9  Total Sales $
10
11
```

Figure 10

Now that we've completed the formula, we press {Enter}. 1-2-3 returns us to the READY mode and evaluates the formula we just entered, as Figure 11 shows. We don't strike {Enter} until we have finished entering the formula. If we press {Enter} before we have what 1-2-3 considers to be a complete formula, we'll just get a beep.

```
K9: (C0) +K7*K8                          READY

        I       J       K       L       M       N
 1
 2                  January Grain Sales
 3                  ===================
 4
 5                  Cotton  Corn    Oats    Barley
 6                  ------- ------- ------- -------
 7  Unit Price       $12.32   $5.50  $18.21  $15.47
 8  Unit Sales       12,100   5,000  22,438  25,018
 9  Total Sales $   $149,072
10
11
```

Figure 11

18   Tip: When you enter formulas in POINT mode, the {Abs} key helps
              you enter absolute references.

Let's look again at the example discussed under the previous Tip (Figures 7 through 11). We entered the formula K7*K8 in K9. This is a relative cell reference, but suppose we want an absolute cell reference so that we can /Copy the formula elsewhere without 1-2-3's adjusting the cell references.

We can enter absolute references in POINT mode by using the {Abs} key. Suppose we have the situation shown in Figure 8. We've entered a plus sign and moved the cursor to cell K7, thus placing us in POINT mode. If we now press the {Abs} key, 1-2-3 turns the relative reference K7 into an absolute reference $K$7 (see Figure 12).

If we press the {Abs} key a second time, the formula in the control panel becomes K$7, a mixed reference (see Figure 13). If we press the {Abs} key a third time, we'll get the other possible mixed reference, $K7. A fourth press gives the relative K7, and a fifth time gives the same as the first, $K$7.

```
K7: (C2) 12.32                              POINT
+$K$7
```

```
         I       J       K       L       M       N
 1
 2                     January Grain Sales
 3                     ====================
 4
 5                     Cotton  Corn    Oats    Barley
 6                     ------- ------- ------- -------
 7  Unit Price         $12.32  $5.50   $18.21  $15.47
 8  Unit Sales         12,100  5,000   22,438  25,018
 9  Total Sales $
10
11
```

Figure 12

```
K7: (C2) 12.32                              POINT
+K$7
```

```
         I       J       K       L       M       N
 1
 2                     January Grain Sales
 3                     ====================
 4
 5                     Cotton  Corn    Oats    Barley
 6                     ------- ------- ------- -------
 7  Unit Price         $12.32  $5.50   $18.21  $15.47
 8  Unit Sales         12,100  5,000   22,438  25,018
 9  Total Sales $
10
11
```

Figure 13

19 Trap: You'll get puzzling results if your formula begins with a cell reference or range name and you forget to start with a plus sign.

Suppose you're entering the formula +K7*K8 in K9. If you forget the plus at the beginning, 1-2-3 will think you're entering a label, not a formula. Figure 14 shows a formula entered without the plus sign. The tipoff here should be that 1-2-3 does not evaluate the formula immediately and display the evaluated result, as is always the case if 1-2-3 accepts the entry as a formula (unless the cell is formatted as Text).

K9: (T) K7+K8

```
         I       J       K       L       M       N
 1
 2                   January Grain Sales
 3                   ===================
 4
 5                   Cotton  Corn    Oats    Barley
 6                   ------- ------- ------- -------
 7  Unit Price        $12.32   $5.50  $18.21  $15.47
 8  Unit Sales        12,100   5,000  22,438  25,018
 9  Total Sales   +K7*K8
10
11
```

Figure 14

If you use POINT mode to enter formulas, as suggested under the previous Tip, you'll avoid this trap because you won't even be able to get into POINT mode until you enter the plus.

The same caution applies to entering range names at the beginning of formulas. If you want to enter the formula +TOT/100, where "TOT" is a range name, the plus at the beginning is essential. Otherwise, 1-2-3 interprets "TOT/100" as just another label, not as a formula.

20 Tip: You don't have to use the {Enter} key to "lock in" an entry in 1-2-3.

Whenever you make an entry in a cell in the 1-2-3 worksheet, you must press a key to let 1-2-3 know that the entry is finished. You'll usually use the {Enter} key for this purpose, but there are several other ways to "lock in" the entry as well. Among the keys that will lock in an entry are {Home}, →, ←, ↑, ↓, and {Window}.

Entering Labels

21 **Tip:** You don't need to enter a label prefix before a label that begins with a space.

In some spreadsheets, including VisiCalc and SuperCalc, you need to type a label prefix to start entering a label that begins with a space. This is not the case in 1-2-3. To enter a label that begins with a space, simply enter the space, type the label, and then press {Enter}.

22 **Trap:** Entering a space creates a label that can overwrite the contents of a cell.

The problem with the previous Tip is that it is possible to erase a formula inadvertently simply by positioning the cursor over a cell, entering a space, and then pressing {Enter} or one of the cursor keys. 1-2-3 interprets those keystrokes as a label entry consisting of one space. This label will overwrite anything else in the cell.

You'd be surprised at how easy it is to do this. Be careful and protect all your important cells.

Using the Cursor Keys

23 **Tip:** The {Shift} key lets you use the IBM PC numeric keypad and the cursor movement keys at the same time.

One drawback of the IBM PC keyboard is that when you turn {Num Lock} on to activate the numbers on the numeric keypad, you disable the cursor keys. It's a bother to enter a number on the numeric keypad and then have to turn {Num Lock} off to get the cursor keys to work.

Holding the {Shift} key down temporarily toggles the {Num Lock} condition. If you have {Num Lock} on to enter numbers from the keypad, you can hold the {Shift} key down and strike any cursor key you wish. When you release the {Shift} key, you're back in Numbers mode again.

24 **Trick:** You can automate the cursor movement after a numeric keypad entry with a simple macro.

The macro in Figure 15 makes numeric keypad use easier. This macro can be activated by holding down the {Alt} key and the K key simultaneously.

	AA	AB	AC	AD	AE
1	\K	{?}	Accepts numeric entry		
2		{down}	Moves cursor down one cell		
3		/xg\K~	Loops back to beginning		
4					

Figure 15

The macro assumes that you have turned on {Num Lock} before activating the macro. It begins by using the {?} input command to halt the macro until a number is entered from the keyboard. This version of the macro lets you jump automatically to the next cell down after entering from the numeric keypad and pressing {Enter}. If you were to change {down} to {right} in the macro, you'd automatically jump to the next cell to the right after entry.

The /XG command in the third line causes the macro to loop and repeat itself. Because this simple version of the macro has no counter or other brake, the only way to stop it is to exit the macro forcibly. The standard way to exit is to press {Ctrl}{Break}. (For more on macros and the /XG command, see the chapter on macros.)

Speeding Up Entry

25 Tip: To speed up entry of a long series of similar items, use the **/D**ata **F**ill command to fill in a series of regularly spaced numbers or dates.

Frequently, when creating a new worksheet, you are required to enter a series of consecutive or evenly spaced numbers in a row or column. 1-2-3's /**D**ata Fill command can make this task quick and simple.

Suppose, for example, you want to enter the series of numbers 1, 2, 3, and so on to 10 in cells A1 to A10. Issue the /**D**ata Fill command. The Fill range is A1..A10; the Start value is 1; the Step value is 1; and the

Stop value is 10. When you press {Enter}, cells A1 to A10 are instantly filled with the numbers from 1 to 10.

26 **Tip:** You can use **/D**ata **F**ill to enter a series of dates in the worksheet.

Another use of **/D**ata **F**ill is to fill in a series of dates. In 1-2-3 dates are entered by either the @TODAY function or the @DATE function and are stored as the number of days since 12/31/1899. Because dates are just numbers to 1-2-3, you can supply dates as responses to the **/D**ata Fill prompts.

Figure 16 shows an example of this Tip at work. This column of dates was entered by supplying the following answers to the following **/D**ata Fill command prompts:

Prompt	Answer
Fill Range	**K5...K19**
Start	**@TODAY**
Step	**1**
Stop	**@TODAY+14**

```
      I      J     K      L     M      N
 1
 2
 3                Date   Amount
 4                ===================
 5                30673
 6                30674
 7                30675
 8                30676
 9                30677
10                30678
11                30679
12                30680
13                30681
14                30682
15                30683
16                30684
17                30685
18                30686
19                30687
20
```

Figure 16

Because this column of dates has General format, the dates are displayed in their pure number form. Figure 17 shows the same dates with the format changed to Date-1.

```
        I       J       K       L       M       N
1
2
3               Date        Amount
4               ========== ========
5               23-Dec-83
6               24-Dec-83
7               25-Dec-83
8               26-Dec-83
9               27-Dec-83
10              28-Dec-83
11              29-Dec-83
12              30-Dec-83
13              31-Dec-83
14              01-Jan-84
15              02-Jan-84
16              03-Jan-84
17              04-Jan-84
18              05-Jan-84
19              06-Jan-84
20
```

Figure 17

27   Tip: Think of the **S**top value and the **F**ill range as two separate braking systems on the **/D**ata **F**ill command.

The Fill range and the Stop value can be thought of as two separate limits on the /**D**ata Fill function. For example, consider the following cases.

Case 1	*Case 2*
Fill range: **A1..A10**	Fill range: **A1..A100**
Start: **1**	Start: **1**
Step: **1**	Step: **1**
Stop: **100**	Stop: **10**

These two cases both fill the range A1 to A10 with the numbers 1 through 10. In Case 1 the Stop value is 100, indicating that the Fill should continue until the value 100 is reached. However, the Fill range includes only 10 cells, so only 10 cells are Filled despite the higher Stop value. In Case 2 the Fill range includes 100 cells, but the Stop value allows only 10 cells to be Filled. The result of Case 2 is the same as the result in Case 1.

28 **Tip:** You can use a macro to help you quickly fill in a series of similar functions, formulas, or labels.

Figure 18 shows a macro to fill in a series of random dates in a column. The macro enters the first part of the function—"@DATE("—and the closing ")" so that you can concentrate on entering only the year, month, and day. The dates in Figure 19 were entered with this macro. In doing so, the user had to enter only the following:

>   83,11,11 {Enter}
>   83,5,5 {Enter}

Everything else was supplied by the macro. Like the keypad macro shown in Tip 24, this macro must be stopped by holding down the {Ctrl} and {Break} keys simultaneously.

```
          I      J        K      L      M      N      O      P
21
22  \D    @DATE(   Enter the constant beginning part of date function.
23        (?)      Accept year, month, day and Return.
24        )~       Fill in end of function and Enter.
25        {down}   Jump down to next cell in column.
26        /xg\D~   Loop back and start entering next date.
27
```

Figure 18

```
          I      J        K      L
1
2
3         Date     Amount
4         ========= =========
5         11-Nov-83
6         05-May-82
7
8
```

Figure 19

The same general technique can be used to speed up entry of a series of similar formulas or labels. Code the label or value you need into a macro; then use that macro to enter the label or value into a cell instantly.

Ensuring Accuracy and Clarity

29   Tip: Use range protection to ensure that essential areas of the worksheet are not inadvertently changed.

1-2-3 assumes that all cells on the worksheet are protected unless they are explicitly unprotected by the /**R**ange Unprotect command. However, all cells act as if they are unprotected unless you enable protection on the worksheet as a whole with the /**W**orksheet **G**lobal **P**rotection **E**nable command.

Safe operating practice calls for you to enable global protection and to unprotect only those cells in which you need to enter or update data. Every other cell should be left protected. This way you make it unlikely that you or anyone else will inadvertently change an important formula, constant, or macro.

Unfortunately, you can't use /**W**orksheet **I**nsert or **D**elete with protection enabled; if you try, you'll get a "Protected Cell" message, and the insert will fail. Inserts and deletes are sometimes useful, but they are dangerous because you can unknowingly mess up a part of the worksheet that's off the screen. One way around this limitation is to place your insertion under control of a macro. Using a macro makes you think twice about inserting or deleting. A macro also disables protection immediately before insertion or deletion and enables it again immediately after.

Figure 20 shows one version of a delete macro. It's actually three macros and a menu: a startup macro (\D) that displays a menu forcing you to confirm the deletion; a DEL macro to disable protection, delete, and then turn protection back on; and a DONT macro to get you out without doing a delete.

	I	J	K	L	M	N	O
82	\D	/xmDEL_MENU~			Execute delete menu.		
83							
84	DEL_MENU	Delete	Don't		Delete menu.		
85		Delete row	No-don't delete!				
86		/xgDEL~	/xgDONT~				
87							
88	DEL	/wgpd			Disable protection for delete.		
89		/wdr~			Delete current row.		
90		/wgpe			Enable protection again.		
91		/xq~			Quit.		
92							
93	DONT	/xq~			No delete, so quit.		
94							

Figure 20

30 **Tip:** Use **/R**ange Input to restrict data entry further.

The **/R**ange Input command limits the movement of the cursor to unprotected cells within a specified range. By leaving unprotected the cells that require data entry, you can restrict the movement of the cursor to only the data entry cells. In addition, while **/R**ange Input is in effect, you can only enter data (in unprotected cells in the range specified), request help (with the {Help} key), edit (with the {Edit} key), or recalculate (with the {Calc} key). You can use the {Backspace} key to correct mistakes, and you can cancel an entry that you're in the middle of by pressing {Esc} once. All other function keys and all commands are disabled while the **/R**ange Input command is in charge. To end the **/R**ange Input session, press {Enter} or {Esc} without first typing or editing an entry.

Figure 21 shows a special input area where we've given the range I111..M111 the name "INPUT_RANGE." Figure 22 shows a macro that issues a **/R**ange Input on this range, copies the new input record to the next available area in a data base, and resets the next available record when the copy is finished. (We don't show here the subroutine macro that does this last job.)

31 **Tip:** For clarity use range names in formulas or in situations where the actual cell addresses may change.

We've given the "Amount" column in Figure 23 the name "ITEMS." Not only does this help us to recognize what it means when we see it in a

```
          I      J      K      L      M      N
106
107                  CHECK REGISTER INPUT AREA
108                  *************************
109
110  CHECK   NAME            DATE   AMOUNT
111
112
```

Figure 21

```
          I        J        K        L        M      N        O
121  \I      /ri INPUT_RANGE~                  Activate Range Input.
122          /c INPUT_RECORD~NEXT_DB_RECORD  Copy new input to data base.
123          {goto}NEXT_DB_RECORD~            Reset next data base record.
124          /rndNEXT_DB_RECORD~
125          {down}/rncNEXT_DB_RECORD~~
126
127
```

Figure 22

formula (such as the one shown in Text format on the totals line), but it also means that if we move the totals line down and add items to the end of the list, we don't have to change the formula. All we have to do is redefine the range name "ITEMS" to include the additional rows.

```
        I        J        K
1 Item      Amount
2 --------  --------   |
3 Salt        $0.39 |
4 Cereal      $1.19 |<=ITEMS
5 Bread       $1.25 |
6 Oranges     $1.57 |
7 --------  --------   |
8 TOTAL    @SUM(ITEMS)
9
```

Figure 23

32 Tip: Use parentheses to make clear the precedence of operations in a formula.

In 1-2-3 the different elements of formulas are evaluated from left to right unless other considerations intervene. These "other considerations" have to do primarily with what we refer to as rules for "precedence of operations." For instance, the formula 10 + 20 * 100/ 10 evaluates as 210 because the multiplication operation and the division operation take precedence over the addition operation (100/ 10 = 10, then 10 * 20 = 200, then 200 + 10 = 210).

The formula (10 + 20) * 100/ 10, however, uses parentheses to say, "Add 10 and 20 before you perform the next operation." The result is that the expression evaluates as 300 because the 20 and 10 are added to give 30 before the multiplication and division are performed. The parentheses have changed the precedence of operations.

1-2-3's rules on precedence of operations are shown in Figure 24. Operations with larger precedence numbers are performed first unless overridden by parentheses. Operations of equal precedence are performed from left to right. It's easy to slip up here. The safest approach is this: When the user could have the slightest doubt about precedence of operations rules in a formula, use parentheses to make clear the order of operations you want.

Operator	Description	Precedence Number
^	Exponentiation	7
-	Negative	6
+	Positive	6
*	Multiplication	5
/	Division	5
+	Addition	4
—	Subtraction	4
=	Equal	3
<	Less than	3
<=	Less than or equal	3
>	Greater than	3
>=	Greater than or equal	3
<>	Not equal	3
#NOT#	Logical not	2
#AND#	Logical and	1
#OR#	Logical or	1

Figure 24

Editing

33 Tip: You can use the {Home}, {End} and Tab keys while in EDIT
mode.

When you've pressed the {Edit} key and gone into the EDIT mode on a
cell in the worksheet, you can move immediately to the first character in
the cell by pressing {Home}. Similarly, you can go immediately to the
space after the last character in the cell by hitting {End}. The two Tab
keys ({Tab} and {BackTab}) move the edit cursor through the cell's
contents five spaces at a time in the indicated direction. These keys can
be very useful when you need to change a long character string.

34 Trap: The {Abs} key does not always work as you might expect
when 1-2-3 is in the EDIT mode.

Suppose you want to change the formula

     A5: +A1+A2

to

     A5: +$A$1+A2

by editing the cell. You might think that you can move the cursor to cell
A5, press {Edit}, press {Home}, and press {Abs}. Unfortunately, the
{Abs} key doesn't work that way. {Abs} converts a formula to an
absolute reference only when you are in the POINT mode.

35 Trap: Pointing in the EDIT mode can be tricky.

The POINT and EDIT modes don't always work together perfectly.
Because the ← and → keys are used in the EDIT mode to move from
character to character in the entry being edited, they lose some of their
power to move the cursor from cell to cell. Naturally, this limitation on
the ← and → keys restricts the use of Pointing while Editing is under
way.

It is not impossible to Point while Editing, but you must follow a few
simple rules. First, you can point from only the last position in the entry.
For example, in the formula

     A5: +A1+A2

1-2-3 will not allow you to Point to alter A1 to A4, to change A2 to A3,
or to create the formula

A5: +A1+A3+A2

However, you can create the formula

A5: +A1+A2+A3

by pointing because the cell reference created by pointing falls at the end of the entry.

The second rule is that while you are editing, all pointing must begin with an ↑ or ↓ key. Because the ↑ and ↓ keys do not take on special meaning in the EDIT mode, they retain their ability to move the cursor between cells. Once you have begun Pointing with the ↑ or ↓ keys, all the other cursor keys are restored to their normal pointing functions.

When Pointing from the EDIT mode, you sometimes need several keystrokes to accomplish simple tasks. For example, suppose you want to change the formula

A4: +A3

to

A4: +A3+B4

by pointing. First, position the cursor on cell A4 and press {Edit}. The edit cursor will appear at the end of the entry just after the 3. Type a + sign. Next, point to cell B4 by striking ↑ → ↓ or ↓ → ↑. Finally press {Enter} to lock in the change. Notice that three keystrokes were required to point to the cell one space to the right.

36   Tip: Use EDIT mode to turn labels into numbers.

1-2-3 distinguishes between labels and numbers by using a label-prefix character (', ", ^, or \) to mark all label entries. This character is stored as the first character of a label cell; although the character does not show in the cell, the character is displayed as the first character in the control panel at the top of the screen when the cursor rests on a cell containing a label.

To convert a numeric label cell into a value, {Edit} the cell; press {Home}, which takes the cursor to the label-prefix character at the beginning of the cell; then press {Del} to delete the label-prefix character. Deleting the label-prefix character turns the label into a number when you press {Enter}.

There are many ways you can use this Tip. For example, if you use /File Import Text to load some numeric information into the 1-2-3 worksheet from a word processor or some other program that can write only a text file, the numbers are imported as numeric labels. By using this Tip, these numbers can be converted to 1-2-3 values that can be manipulated with 1-2-3's functions and commands.

You can quickly perform this transformation for a whole row or column with a simple macro. Figure 25 shows one version of such a macro. This version assumes that you're transforming a row from left to right, that the cursor is resting on the first cell in the row when you start the macro, and that you've entered @NA in the cell immediately to the right of the last cell you want to transform. To execute the macro, press {Alt} N. This macro performs the {Edit}{Home}{Del} function on each cell. After a cell is converted, the {right} command moves the cursor one cell to the right and the whole process repeats.

	I	J	K	L	M	N	O
41	\N	/rncHERE~~			Name current cell.		
42		/xi@isna(HERE)~/xgEND~			@NA loop ender present?		
43		{edit}{home}{del}~			Change to number.		
44		/rndHERE~~			Delete range name.		
45		{right}			To next cell in row.		
46		/xg\N~			Loop back to check next cell.		
47	END	/rndHERE~~			Delete range name before quitting.		
48		/xq~			Quit.		
49							

Figure 25

Why do we put the @NA function in the cell to the right of the last cell to be transformed? Line 2 of the macro checks for the @NA as a "loop ender." There are other ways of ending a macro loop, but this is one of the simplest. For more on loops and ways to end them, see the chapter on macros.

37 **Tip:** You can use {Edit} to turn numbers into labels.

The process here is the reverse of that described in the previous Tip. To transform a value cell into a label, {Edit} the cell, use the {Home} key to move to the first character in the cell, and enter a label prefix. Any 1-2-3 label prefix (', ", or ^) can be used.

Again, you can perform this task automatically with a macro like the one shown in Figure 26. This macro differs from the one in Figure 25 only in that the macro here inserts the label character instead of deleting it.

	I	J	K	L	M	N	O
49							
50	\L	/rncHERE~~			Name current cell.		
51		/xi@isna(HERE)~/xgENDL~			@NA loop ender present?		
52		{edit}{home}'~			Change to label.		
53		/rndHERE~~			Delete range name.		
54		{right}			To next cell in row.		
55		/xg\L~			Loop back to check next cell.		
56	ENDL	/rndHERE~~			Delete range name before quitting.		
57		/xg~			Quit.		
58							

Figure 26

There are several reasons for transforming numbers into labels. One is the situation in which you have a series of data base field names that you've entered as numbers, for example, the years 1980, 1981, 1982, etc. It's convenient to enter a regular series of numbers like this using the /Data Fill command, but /Data Fill can enter only numbers, not labels; and data base field names must be labels. If you have the numbers-into-labels macro, enter the years with /Data Fill and then transform them into labels with the macro. This kind of transformation is also sometimes handy in macro programming.

38   Tip: Use the {Edit} and {Calc} keys together to turn formulas or functions into pure numbers.

Many earlier spreadsheet programs had an option on the /Copy command that allowed you to turn formulas into pure numbers as you copied the original entry or entries. This capability is useful when you want to "freeze" the current value(s) of a formula or group of formulas. Unfortunately, 1-2-3 does not have such an option in Releases 1 and 1A. A roundabout way of accomplishing this transformation, however, is to use the {Edit} and {Calc} keys together to transform the contents of a formula or function cell into a pure number and then press {Enter} to make the change permanent.

These keys used together cause the formula in the current cell to be recalculated and replace the formula in the cell with the current numeric value of the formula. No other cells in the worksheet are recalculated.

Sometimes you may want to turn a formula into a number. For example, you may want to date your worksheet to have in the worksheet a record of when the worksheet was last saved. Unfortunately, you cannot simply place the @TODAY function in a cell, save the worksheet, and retrieve it. If you retrieve the worksheet on a different day, the @TODAY function is reevaluated and the old value that you want to retain is lost.

You need some way to freeze the old date value so it doesn't change on the next retrieval. Using {Edit} and {Calc} together followed by {Enter} is a simple way to lock in the current date value. The macro in Figure 27 accomplishes the job and maintains today's date in a cell named "NEW_DATE." If the worksheet were saved on 12-23-83, these two fields would display as follows after you press {Alt} T and before you saved:

    SAVE_DATE   NEW_DATE
    23-Dec-83   23-Dec-83

When the fields are retrieved from the disk on 12-25-83, however, they look like this:

    SAVE_DATE   NEW_DATE
    23-Dec-83   25-Dec-83

```
         I      J           K        L      M      N      O
62
63 \T   {goto}SAVE_DATE~    Enter @TODAY in both the
64      @TODAY~              Save Date cell and the
65 \    /C~NEW_DATE~         New Date cell.
66      {edit}{calc}~        Change the Save Date to a pure number.
67
```

Figure 27

39 Trick: To debug a long formula, convert it to a label and /Copy it to another cell.

Have you ever entered a long and complex formula, pressed {Enter}, and watched the message "ERR" appear on the screen? You know there's an error in the formula, but you don't know where it is. Using the {Edit} key, you set out to debug the formula.

One way to debug a long formula is to break it into pieces to isolate the error. To do this, you might {Edit} the cell, use the {Del} key to eliminate all but the part you want to test, and then press {Enter}. If the error is in the section being tested, the ERR message remains on the screen. If the error is in a different part of the formula, the message disappears. This technique allows you to find the error more quickly than if you try to debug the whole formula at once.

This method has a couple of problems, however. The Editing process destroys the formula you are trying to debug. One way around this problem is to /Copy the formula to another cell and Edit it there. But /Copying the formula alters any relative cell references in the formula and defeats the purpose of the /Copy.

To overcome these problems, convert the formula into a label before you /Copy it. Simply {Edit} the cell, move the cursor to the first character in the formula by pressing {Home}, and enter a label prefix character. The formula is instantly converted into a label.

Now /Copy this label to another cell for debugging. Because the entry is now a label, no reference is changed by the /Copy. When the /Copy is complete, move the cursor to the new cell, {Edit} the contents, and remove the label prefix. The formula is now a formula again, and you can proceed to break it into pieces to debug it.

After you find the error, erase the new copy of the formula, move to the cell containing the old copy, erase the label prefix, and make the required changes.

3

Using the Worksheet

Getting Around the Worksheet

40   **Tip:** Assign range names to important areas so that you can jump to them directly.

If you use the /**R**ange **N**ame **C**reate command to assign names to key areas, you can use the {GoTo} key, followed by the range name, to move immediately to that area. For instance, {GoTo} SALES takes you to the range you've named "SALES." If you've also assigned a name to the area you just left, you can return to it immediately. This Tip can be equally useful in macros.

This method can also save cursor movements when you are going to areas a long way from the cursor's current location. Moving, for instance, to a totals line at the end of a long data base can be a one-step operation. If you assign the name "TOTALS" to that row, you can {GoTo} TOTALS any time you want.

41   **Tip:** If a named range covers more than one cell, jumping to the named range will position the cursor in the upper-left corner of that range.

If you create a name for the range A1..C15, pressing {GoTo} RANGE-NAME will make the cursor jump to cell A1. The cursor always jumps to the upper-left corner of a named range.

42   Tip: Use the cursor-control keys with the {End} key to move quickly across many cells.

Pressing the {End} key, followed by one of the four cursor-arrow keys while you are in READY mode or POINT mode, causes the cursor to move as follows:

1. If the cursor is on a blank cell, the cursor moves in the arrow's direction to the first nonblank cell or to the edge of the worksheet.

2. If the cursor is on a nonblank cell, the cursor moves in the arrow's direction to the last nonblank cell before a blank cell or to the edge of the worksheet.

This feature is handy for moving quickly to the end of a column or row of entries. Figure 28 shows a column of sales figures. To begin, assume that the cursor is resting at the top of the column. Pressing {End} and then ↓ moves the cursor immediately to the last entry in the column, cell B9. This method is a good way to go directly to a totals column on the far right or to a totals row at the bottom of your worksheet.

```
        A         B        C        D
1
2                 1983
3    Branch      Sales
4    ---------  ---------
5    Atl         $15,000
6    Chi        $103,000
7    LA         $156,000
8    SF              $25
9    Total      $274,000
10
```

Figure 28

43   Tip: The {End} key can be used to find the end of a row or the bottom of a column of discontinuous entries.

Suppose column C in your worksheet is partially filled with numbers and labels, and you want to find the last cell in the column. Normally, you might use the {End} ↓ combination to move quickly to the bottom of the column. In this case, however, the gaps in the column will hinder the {End} ↓ combination.

Consider the following Trick, however. Assuming that column D is blank, move the cursor to any cell in column D. Now press {End} ↓. The cursor will jump to cell D2048, the last cell in column D. Now press the ← to move the cursor back into column C. Finally, press {End} ↑. The cursor will jump to the last cell in column C that contains an entry.

44 Trick: When working with empty or discontinuous ranges of cells, use adjacent full ranges to help move the cursor to the correct locations.

Using the {End} key with an adjacent full range can be particularly helpful in macros because it is impossible for a macro to "see" directly where a column begins and ends. Although you usually use the {End} key only to go to the end of a row or column that has no empty cells, there is a way you can go to the end of even an "empty" row or column.

Suppose that you want to assign a name to the range B8..B12 in your worksheet; suppose also that cell B9 is blank and that the cursor is in cell B8. To name the range, you must issue the /**R**ange **N**ame **C**reate command and point to the range B8..B12. What you just learned about the {End} key might lead you to use the {End} ↓ combination to point to the range. But pressing {End} ↓ moves the cursor only to cell B10. Pressing {End} ↓ again moves the cursor finally to cell B12. You could have moved the cursor to B12 almost as quickly just by pressing ↓ four times.

Fortunately, there is a better way. Assuming that there are no blank cells in the range A8 to A12, you can use this range as a crutch to help you point to the range B8 to B12. After the /**RNC** command is issued, you can point to the range B8..B12 by pressing ←, {End} ↓, and then →. These commands move the cursor from B8 to A8, and then from A8 to A12, and finally from A12 to B12. At the conclusion of this series, the proper range is marked. You used the continuous range in column A to help you overcome the limitations created by the blank cell in column B.

45 Tip: {End} followed by {Home} always takes you to the end of your current active area.

If the active area in the current worksheet covers the range A1..Z100, pressing {End}{Home} causes the cursor to jump to cell Z100. (See the first chapter for a discussion of the significance of the active area.)

46 **Tip:** The tab keys always move you 72 spaces to the left or right regardless of the widths of the columns.

Without the row numbers on the left side of the 1-2-3 screen, the screen is exactly 72 characters wide. The {Tab} key is designed to move the cursor exactly 72 characters, or one screen, to the right; {Back Tab} moves the cursor 72 spaces to the left. When the columns in your worksheet are 9 characters wide (the default width), the {Tab} key moves the cursor exactly 8 columns. However, if some or all of the columns are wider or narrower than the default, then the cursor will move more or less than 8 columns.

47 **Tip:** Construct simple macros to jump any number of cells at once.

Figure 29 shows a macro that causes the cursor to move three cells to the right. You activate this macro simply by pressing {Alt} and the J key simultaneously. You can create any number of simple macros like this one to move the cursor in almost any way you wish.

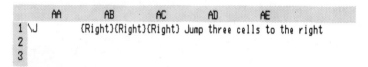

Figure 29

Using Windows

48 **Tip:** Use **/W**orksheet **W**indow to display widely separated areas of the same model on the screen at once.

You can split your screen into two separate areas with the **/W**orksheet **W**indow command. This command has two options: **H**orizontal and **V**ertical. After the screen has been split, you can move the cursor back and forth between the windows by means of the {Window} key (F6 on the IBM PC). You may also give each window its own set of frozen titles with the **/W**orksheet **T**itle command. Two windows are often an advantage when you are doing "what if" analysis and the input area for your assumptions is far from the area where you view the results.

Windowing is also useful when you need to make long jumps with the cursor across a large worksheet. If two widely separated sections of the worksheet are visible on the screen at the same time, you can make a big jump instantly by pressing the {Window} key instead of moving the cursor a long distance or using the {GoTo} key.

49   **Trap:** The way the {Window} key works depends on whether the windows are synchronized or unsynchronized.

When the two windows you've created are unsynchronized, the cursor jumps to the last cell it occupied in the other window. For example, suppose you split the worksheet as shown in Figure 30 and then position the cursor in cell A5 in the left window. Now press {Window}. The cursor appears in cell D5 in the second window. Next, move the cursor down two cells to cell D7. Press {Window} again, and the cursor pops up in cell A5 in the first window. If you press {Window} again, the cursor jumps to cell D7 in the second window.

If, on the other hand, the windows are synchronized (the default condition), the {Window} key has a different effect. In the same example, pressing {Window} when the cursor is in cell D7 in the second window causes the cursor to jump to cell A7 in the first window. If you move the cursor from there to cell B4 in the first window and press {Window} again, the cursor jumps to cell D4. Moving the cursor to cell E1 and pressing {Window} moves the cursor to cell B1. The cursor always stays in the same row when it moves between synchronized vertical windows; and the cursor always returns to the column containing the cell that the cursor occupied the last time it was in the window being jumped to.

If the windows are split horizontally instead of vertically, pressing {Window} causes the cursor to return to a cell in the opposite window. That cell is defined by both the column the cursor is currently in and the row the cursor was in, the last time the cursor was in the opposite window.

If all of this is a bit confusing, don't worry. Just try a few examples so that you can understand the difference between the two situations.

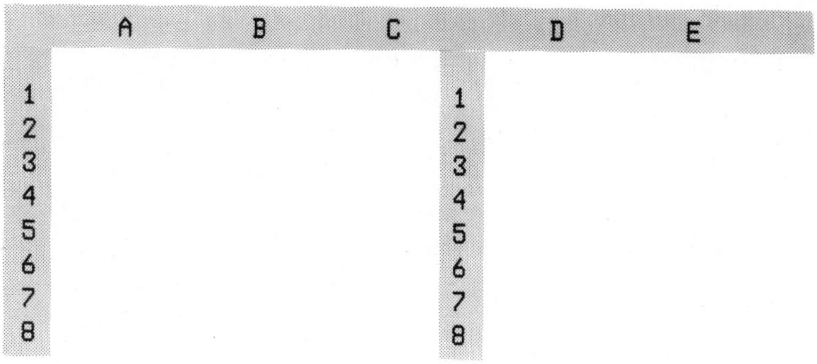

Figure 30

50   Trap: When you issue the **/W**orksheet **W**indow **C**lear command, the entire new worksheet retains the global formats and column widths of the top or left window.

If you decide to modify the format of the worksheet while the screen is split, and you want to retain the formats after the windows are cleared, be sure that you make your modifications in the top or left window. Otherwise the changes will be lost. This happens even if the cursor is in the right or bottom window when you issue **/WWC**.

51   Tip: Use **/W**orksheet **W**indow to display messages.

During macro execution you can split the screen to display messages in a second window without disturbing what is going on in the main window. You can display error messages, instructions, warnings, help text, etc. By displaying the messages in a separate window, you do not force the user to leave the current work area. If you wish, you can have the macro do a **/W**orksheet **W**indow **C**lear when you no longer need the split screen.

Another way of displaying messages from a macro is to use the menu-generating facility and make your messages part of a menu. See the Tips that cover macros for an example.

Using Titles

52   Tip: Use the **/W**orksheet **T**itles command to lock rows or columns containing important labels on the screen.

1-2-3 models are frequently more than one screen wide or deep. Sometimes when the cursor is in the lower-right portion of a worksheet that has expanded beyond the edge of the screen, the column headers in the upper rows and the row labels in the left columns disappear from the screen. It is hard to remember exactly what information is contained in each row or column when these labels are not visible. One way around this problem is to use the /Worksheet Titles command to freeze several rows, columns, or both on the screen. The /WT command has three options: Horizontal, Vertical, and Both. The Horizontal option locks any number of rows on the top of the screen. Vertical locks columns on the left edge of the screen. Selecting Both causes a specified number of both rows and columns to be locked on the screen.

53   Trap: Once the /Worksheet Titles command has been issued, it is difficult to move the cursor into the locked area to edit or add a label.

Once you have defined titles on the screen with the /Worksheet Titles command, 1-2-3 treats the row immediately below the last horizontal title row and the column immediately to the right of the last vertical title column as the borders of the worksheet. It is impossible to move the cursor into the titles area just by using the cursor keys.

For example, suppose you define both horizontal and vertical titles for a worksheet with the cursor on cell B2. In other words, assume that row 1 and column A are both locked on the screen. If you try to move the cursor into the titles area with the cursor keys, the cursor will stop moving when it reaches row 2 or column B. The highest cell you can reach with the cursor keys in this situation is B2.

54   Tip: Use {GoTo} to move the cursor to the titles area.

When you have frozen your titles, you cannot move the cursor into the titles area with the cursor keys. You can, however, use {GoTo}, F5, to go directly to a cell address or range name in the titles area. You can then edit any cell in this area.

55   Tip: Titles are not a barrier to 1-2-3's POINT mode.

Another exception to the rule that you cannot move the cursor into the titles area involves the POINT mode. When you are defining a cell with the POINT mode, the cursor can move freely into the titles area.

56   Trap: A {GoTo} or a Point into the titles area results in a double
          display of title lines.

Figure 31 shows what happens when you use {GoTo} to enter the titles
area. You get a confusing situation because title lines are displayed on
the screen twice. Do not be dismayed. You still have only one copy of
those titles, despite what the screen shows. Go ahead and edit the titles.
Then get rid of the double display. For horizontal titles, press {PgDn},
then {PgUp}; for vertical titles, press the right arrow key, then the left
arrow key.

```
        A         B         C         D         E
 1  Date of   Customer            Amount
 2  Receipt   Name                Due
 3  -------------------------------------
 1  Date of   Customer            Amount
 2  Receipt   Name                Due
 3  -------------------------------------
 4  11-Nov  Murphy,  J.        $23.45
 5  13-Nov  Feinberg, R.       $12.12
 6  15-Nov  Peebles, P.       $145.00
 7  17-Nov  Flint, F.          $18.54
 8  19-Nov  Grover, G.        $235.67
 9  21-Nov  Cleveland, C.      $18.18
10  23-Nov  Alexander, A.      $10.00
11
```

Figure 31

57   Tip: Use the {Home} key to take you to the cell adjacent to the titles
          area.

When you've turned on titles in a particular window, the {Home} key no
longer takes you to A1; it takes you to the top left of the area
immediately below and to the right of your titles.

Manipulating the Worksheet

Copying the Contents of a Range to Another Range

58 Tip: To make one or more copies of a range without automatic adjustment of a cell address reference, make that address an absolute reference.

The distinction that 1-2-3 makes between relative and absolute cell references can be confusing. To understand this distinction, first remember that the distinction applies primarily to the /Copy command and to the /Data Sort command (considered by 1-2-3 to be an implicit /Copy). 1-2-3 also expects an absolute reference in a criterion range if the reference is to a cell outside the data base. Here we're concerned only with the /Copy command.

Let's look at an example. Figure 32 shows projected sales for four branches for three years. The assumed growth percentages are shown in the assumptions area below the projection. We'll look at the 1986 projection first. The formula in M8 (which displays as a formula instead of a number because the cell is formatted as Text) shows that the 1986 sales projection for Atlanta is equal to the 1985 projection (in L8) increased by the percentage in N17. In the formula in M8, N17 is expressed as an absolute reference, $N$17, because we're going to copy the formula down the column into the cells for the other cities. When we do so, we want the reference to L8 to be automatically adjusted—first to L9, then to L10, etc. But we do not want the reference to N17 to be adjusted because the rule for 1986 is that we use the same growth factor for all branches. Figure 33 shows the results of this first /Copy.

The situation for 1984 and 1985 is different. Here we have a unique growth factor for each branch. Therefore, when we copy the formula in K8 down the column, we want the row to be adjusted. That is why the 17 part of $K17 in cell K8 is relative. Figure 34 shows the results of this second /Copy.

```
          I        J        K          L          M          N
 1
 2
 3   SALES PROJECTIONS--ALL BRANCHES (3 YEARS)
 4
 5            1983     1984       1985       1986
 6   Branch   Sales    Forecast   Forecast   Forecast
 7   =========================================================
 8   Atl       15500  +J8+J8*$K17            +L8+L8*$N$17
 9   Chi      103000
10   LA       156000
11   SF           25
12
13
14
15
16   Growth factors:    1984-1985                1986
17           Atl          15.00%       ALL        15.00%
18           Chi          10.00%
19           LA           12.00%
20           SF           20.00%
```

Figure 32

```
          I        J        K          L          M          N
 1
 2
 3   SALES PROJECTIONS--ALL BRANCHES (3 YEARS)
 4
 5            1983     1984       1985       1986
 6   Branch   Sales    Forecast   Forecast   Forecast
 7   =========================================================
 8   Atl       15500  +J8+J8*$K17            +L8+L8*$N$17
 9   Chi      103000                         +L9+L9*$N$17
10   LA       156000                         +L10+L10*$N$17
11   SF           25                         +L11+L11*$N$17
12
13
14
15
16   Growth factors:    1984-1985                1986
17           Atl          15.00%       ALL        15.00%
18           Chi          10.00%
19           LA           12.00%
20           SF           20.00%
```

Figure 33

```
      I        J         K              L           M         N
  1
  2
  3  SALES PROJECTIONS--ALL BRANCHES (3 YEARS)
  4
  5           1983      1984           1985        1986
  6  Branch   Sales     Forecast       Forecast    Forecast
  7  ====================================================================
  8  Atl        15500  +J8+J8*$K17                 +L8+L8*$N$17
  9  Chi       103000  +J9+J9*$K18                 +L9+L9*$N$17
 10  LA        156000  +J10+J10*$K19               +L10+L10*$N$17
 11  SF            25  +J11+J11*$K20               +L11+L11*$N$17
 12
 13
 14
 15
 16  Growth factors:    1984-1985                  1986
 17          Atl          15.00%         ALL               15.00%
 18          Chi          10.00%
 19          LA           12.00%
 20          SF           20.00%
```

Figure 34

But why is the $K part of $K17 absolute? Because after we get all our formulas for 1984 entered in column K, we want to copy the entire column over to column L. If we had K17 (relative reference) instead of $K17 (absolute reference to the column) in K8, the K would be adjusted to an L, which is not the reference we want. This $K17 reference is an example of a mixed absolute-relative reference. Figure 35 shows the results of using /Copy to copy column K to column L.

59 Trap: Overlapping From and To ranges on a **/C**opy can cause erratic results.

Overlapping sometimes gives the results you want, but don't count on it. Check your results carefully after every such /Copy.

60 Tip: Sometimes using overlapping From and To ranges can save time and effort.

Suppose you want to create a rectangular range in which each cell contains the same formula. For example, you have entered the formula

   A1: A25*.01

```
       I       J        K          L          M          N
 1
 2
 3  SALES PROJECTIONS--ALL BRANCHES (3 YEARS)
 4
 5          1983    1984        1985        1986
 6  Branch  Sales   Forecast    Forecast    Forecast
 7  ========================================================
 8  Atl        15500 +J8+J8*$K17   +K8+K8*$K17   +L8+L8*$N$17
 9  Chi       103000 +J9+J9*$K18   +K9+K9*$K18   +L9+L9*$N$17
10  LA        156000 +J10+J10*$K19 +K10+K10*$K19 +L10+L10*$N$17
11  SF            25 +J11+J11*$K20 +K11+K11*$K20 +L11+L11*$N$17
12
13
14
15
16  Growth factors:    1984-1985                 1986
17          Atl        15.00%         ALL         15.00%
18          Chi        10.00%
19          LA         12.00%
20          SF         20.00%
```

Figure 35

into cell A1 and want that same formula to appear in every cell in the range A1..E8. The best way to /Copy that formula into the range is to use overlapping From and To ranges:

/Copy **A1** {Enter} **A1..E8** {Enter}

If you don't use overlapping From and To ranges, you need to use two different /Copy operations to fill the rectangle: one to fill the rectangle B1..E8; and the other to fill the range A2..A8.

61   Trap: Copying to a protected cell with protection enabled has no effect.

The result of copying to a protected cell with protection enabled is that each cell in the To range retains its previous contents. You can use this fact as a trick in macros. You can control whether or not something is copied to a particular protected range simply by enabling and disabling protection. However, this technique results in somewhat obscure macro code, so we don't recommend it unless there is no better alternative.

62 **Trap:** Near the edges of the worksheet, copying a formula may give meaningless results.

If cell F20 contains the formula +$B$5*@SUM(E10..F18), /Copying from F20 to A1 produces the following:

+$B$5*@SUM(IV2039..A2047)

When the 1-2-3 relative address routine reaches the edge of the worksheet, 1-2-3 performs the adjustment as if that edge wrapped around and connected with the opposite edge.

63 **Trap:** Unexpected results can occur when one corner of the From range is absolute or partly absolute and the other is relative or partly relative.

The 1-2-3 relative address routine handles the two corners of a range independently.

If D15 contains @SUM($B$10..D14), when we copy it to each of the following target cells, we get different results:

To H15:	@SUM($B$10..H14)	(a rectangle)
To B26:	@SUM($B$10..B25)	(a column)
To K11:	@SUM($B$10..K10)	(a row)
To B11:	@SUM($B$10..B10)	(a single cell)

When mixed absolute and relative addresses are involved, things get wilder still. For example, if the formula in C15 were @SUM(A$10..C14), copying it to H15 would give @SUM(H$10..H14), a column instead of a rectangle as in the previous example.

64 **Tip:** You can create more than one copy of a column range or a row range with one /Copy command.

Suppose that A10 contains the value 100 and B10 contains the formula A10*10, and you want to copy this row range to rows 11 through 13. You first supply the From range, A10..B10. Then supply A11..A13 as a To range. The results are as follows:

	A	B
10	100	+A10*10
11	100	+A11*10
12	100	+A12*10
13	100	+A13*10

When 1-2-3 asks you for the To range, you supply only the first cell of each row to which you want to copy. 1-2-3 figures out the rest of it. The same principle applies to copying a column range to more than one column. Supply a To range consisting of the first cell in each column to which you want to copy.

Using the /Move Command

65   Trap: 1-2-3's **/M**ove command doesn't work like VisiCalc's **/M**ove command.

1-2-3 users who have experience with VisiCalc know that VisiCalc's /Move command is a two-step command. After the user enters the From and To ranges, the command first inserts a row at the To address and then moves the contents of the row being moved to the newly inserted row.

In 1-2-3 there are several important differences. First, in 1-2-3 you can move any rectangular range, not just a single row. More important, the /Move command does not insert cells at the To address before moving the contents of the From address. Instead, the From contents simply overwrite the To range. Any data in the To range is lost.

If you are an experienced VisiCalc user, be very careful to avoid this error.

66   Tip: Don't expect the same kind of automatic address adjustment from a **/M**ove as from a **/C**opy.

When you move a cell with /Move, its relative addresses are not adjusted just because you have moved it. However, both relative and absolute addresses will be automatically adjusted if you move any cells to which the addresses refer.

Let's try some things with the example in Figure 32 to illustrate these points. If we move the formula in M8 to M9, it remains exactly the same because the /Move—unlike the /Copy—makes no adjustment in a cell's formula just because it is moved. But suppose we move the range K8..M8 to K9. The results are shown in Figure 36. This time we get automatic adjustment of the L8+L8 part of the formula that was in M8.

L8+L8 has now become L9+L9. Because L8 itself was part of the range that was moved, all references to it are automatically adjusted to point to its new location, L9.

	I	J	K	L	M	N
1						
2						
3	SALES PROJECTIONS--ALL BRANCHES (3 YEARS)					
4						
5		1983	1984	1985	1986	
6	Branch	Sales	Forecast	Forecast	Forecast	
7	==					
8	Atl	15500				
9	Chi	103000	+J8+J8*$K17		+L9+L9*$N$17	
10	LA	156000				
11	SF	25				
12						
13						
14						
15						
16	Growth factors:		1984-1985		1986	
17		Atl	15.00%	ALL		15.00%
18		Chi	10.00%			
19		LA	12.00%			
20		SF	20.00%			

Figure 36

What happens to an absolute reference to a cell that is moved? Suppose we move the growth factor in N17 to N18; what happens to the reference to $N$17 in M8? Figure 37 shows us that it is adjusted to $N$18.

The bottom line is this: The /**M**ove command makes no distinction between absolute and relative references. What's more, the /**M**ove command never adjusts any reference unless the cell that is referenced is moved; then 1-2-3 adjusts all these references, both absolute and relative. The practical effect of these rules is that most of the time you get the results you really want. But be careful. Always check the results of a /**M**ove carefully to make sure things turned out the way you expected.

67   **Trap:** Moving a cell into another cell that has formula references to it results in those references being assigned the value of ERR.

```
        I        J        K             L            M           N
  1
  2
  3  SALES PROJECTIONS--ALL BRANCHES (3 YEARS)
  4
  5          1983     1984          1985         1986
  6  Branch  Sales    Forecast      Forecast     Forecast
  7  ================================================================
  8  Atl      15500 +J8+J8*$K17                  +L9+L9*$N$18
  9  Chi
 10  LA      156000
 11  SF          25
 12
 13
 14
 15
 16  Growth factors:     1984-1985                1986
 17          Atl         15.00%          ALL
 18          Chi         10.00%                       15.00%
 19          LA          12.00%
 20          SF          20.00%
```

Figure 37

Suppose that A5 contains the reference M16*10. If we move Q22 to M16, 1-2-3 changes the reference in A5 to ERR*10, which displays as ERR. Before you execute a /Move, check to see whether any cells in the To range are referenced in formulas elsewhere on the worksheet.

68   Trap: A /Move that results in moving one of the corners of a named range or a function range may give unexpected results.

The general rule is that if the upper-left or lower-right corner of a named range moves, the definition of the range name changes accordingly. In such a case, 1-2-3 will make three kinds of adjustments:

1. To the remembered definitions of the affected range, for example, a range specified previously to a /Print command

2. To formulas that refer to that range

3. To remembered definitions and formulas of range names that are synonymous with the one whose corner was

moved. *Synonymous* here means "completely over-lapping."

These changes are called *implicit changes to range names.*

The greatest complications here arise when you have overlapping ranges. Be very careful to check the results of a /**M**ove that affects them. Figure 38 shows a group of overlapping ranges before and after a move. The changed definitions of the ranges "ALL," "ONE," and "TWO" make sense according to the rule. However, the new definitions of "PLUS" and "LAP" are surprising. These are the two ranges that partially overlapped the range moved. We would expect "PLUS" to change to P11..O16 because its upper-left corner was moved and its lower-right corner was not; we would also expect "LAP" to change to O16..P15 for the same reasons. The results are opposite from this, and the reason is not clear.

Before Move of Range ALL to P11	After Move of Range ALL to P11
1 ALL = O11..O15	ALL = P11..P15
2 ONE = O11	ONE = P11
3 TWO = O12	TWO = P12
4 PLUS = O11..O16	PLUS = O11..P16
5 LAP = O15..O16	LAP = O15..P16

Figure 38

69 Trap: /**M**oving a cell to a corner of a named range may change the range's definition.

This is a subtle trap that can result in confusion. Suppose we have a data base named "SALES" that covers the range A10..G100. If we move cell A1 to A10, the range name "SALES" changes to a new definition, A1, a single cell. The old definition of A10..G100 is gone. Apparently 1-2-3 considers that each unnamed cell has an implicit range name definition that covers that one cell. So when the cell is moved, that definition goes with it and becomes the new definition of the previously named target cell in the To range.

This should further underscore what we have already stated. Be extremely careful when using the /**M**ove command in areas where you have named ranges.

70   Trap: /Moving a cell to the corner of a range that has been remembered by a command results in that range's being forgotten by that command.

This Trap is similar to the previous one. To understand it better, consider the following example. If you define a graph with an A range of A1..A10, and then /Move cell B5 to cell A1, the A range will be forgotten by the command. The same thing will occur if you move the top-left cell of a data range.

Avoiding Problems with the /Range Name Command

The following Tips and Traps will help you avoid unexpected results when you change the definition of existing range names.

71   Tip: Changing the definition of a range name changes the definition of all its synonyms.

Range names that share the same two corners are considered synonyms. This means that when you change the definition of one, 1-2-3 changes the definition of the other(s) automatically. For example, if you have the range names "CITY" and "CITIES" that both cover the range A5..A10, redefining "CITY" as A5..A6 redefines "CITIES" the same way. (There's an interesting wrinkle here. If you use /Range Name Delete to delete "CITY," any formulas that previously referred to "CITY" now refer to its synonym, "CITIES.")

72   Trap: Changing the definition of a range name from one that refers to a single-cell range to one that refers to a multiple-cell range does not alter formulas referring to that range name.

For example, we give the range name "ONECELL" to A77 and enter the formula +ONECELL+14 in cell B1. Later we use /Range Name Create to change the definition of "ONECELL" to A77..A82. The result is that 1-2-3 removes the range name from the formula in B1; the formula remains +A77+14 and is no longer displayed in the control panel as +ONECELL+14.

See the section in the 1-2-3 Manual, "Direct Changes to Range Names," on which this example is based.

73 Trap: Changing the definition of a single-cell range name changes all formulas that refer to that cell.

Suppose A5 contains 10, A6 contains 20, and A7 contains +A5*10. We then assign the range name "HERE" to A5. The result is that 1-2-3 adjusts the formula in A7 to +HERE*10. For the moment, that really changes nothing; the formula still evaluates as 100, as it did before.

But suppose we use **/R**ange **N**ame **C**reate to change the definition of "HERE" to cover cell A6. The result is that the formula in A7, which was previously adjusted to +HERE*10, evaluates as 200 because it is now implicitly +A6*10. 1-2-3 has pulled a fast one on us here because we would not expect this change. This can be especially troublesome in macros, where we often have occasion to change range name definitions.

There is, however, a simple rule for avoiding this type of problem. Always use **/R**ange **N**ame **D**elete to delete a range definition before redefining it with **/R**ange **N**ame **C**reate. If we do that, the formula in A7 goes back to +A5*10 before we create the new definition of "HERE"; and the result is that A7 still evaluates as 100 when we're done.

Avoiding Problems with /Worksheet Insert and Delete

74 Trap: Deleting or inserting a row or column may cause problems in parts of the worksheet not currently visible.

Worksheet inserts and deletes can be extremely dangerous, chiefly because they affect entire rows or columns throughout the whole worksheet. As a result, it's easy to wipe out—or place empty lines in the middle of—areas not currently visible on the screen. You can wipe out vital data or make important macros inoperable. (Inserting a line in the middle of a macro causes it to terminate at that point because the 1-2-3 macro processor interprets a blank cell as the end of the macro.)

Be very careful when using /**W**orksheet **I**nsert or **D**elete. In some cases you can insert by /**C**opying out everything below where you want the insert to go and then /**C**opying everything back one line farther down. (Admittedly, this is a bother and takes time; and you don't always have enough memory for the copy.) Sometimes you can do an indirect insert by entering data on the first empty line at the end of a range and then sorting the whole range to get the added line where you want it.

You can fake a delete of a row by doing a /**R**ange **E**rase on the range you want to delete and then sorting to get this empty row to the bottom of the area after temporarily placing a very large value in the primary key field. If your data area is defined as a data base, executing a /**D**ata **Q**uery **D**elete with the proper key will delete only that part of the row found within the data base. (But be careful in setting up your criterion in the criterion range, or you may delete more records than you want to.)

Of course, there are situations where the /**W**orksheet **I**nsert, in particular, is very handy. It may be the only practical way to cause existing range names to expand their definitions automatically. This ability can be particularly useful in macros.

See the "Data Base" chapter for more details on /**I**nserts and /**D**eletes.

75   Trap: /**W**orksheet **I**nsert and **D**elete can cause range name definitions to be adjusted mysteriously.

1-2-3 follows the same rules on implicit changes to range names here as it does with the /**M**ove command. See the section "Using the /**M**ove Command," as well as the section in the 1-2-3 manual, "Implicit Changes to Range Names." Briefly, what happens is that inserts or deletes in the middle of a named range either expand or shrink the range name definition. Usually, such an alteration of the definition is exactly what you want.

76   Trap: Deleting a cell referred to in a formula will cause ERR to be substituted for the reference.

This is similar to what happens when a cell that's a target of a /**M**ove has formula references to it. Before you delete a row or column, try to make sure none of its cells is referred to elsewhere.

4

Recalculation

Using Manual Recalculation

77 Tip: Use **/W**orksheet **G**lobal **R**ecalculation **M**anual when doing data entry.

In the default Automatic mode of recalculation, 1-2-3 recalculates the whole worksheet every time you press {Enter}. If you maintain Automatic Recalculation while doing data entry on a medium-to-large worksheet, you'll spend a great deal of time waiting for unnecessary recalculations between entries.

To avoid these delays, use the /Worksheet Global Recalculation Manual command to change from Automatic to Manual mode of recalculation. In Manual mode the worksheet recalculates only when you press {Calc} (F9 on the IBM PC). Because the worksheet does not recalculate after every {Enter}, data entry is not delayed. When all the data is entered, press {Calc} once to update the worksheet.

If you're controlling data entry through a macro, you can have the macro set recalculation to Manual before it does anything else.

55

78 Trick: With Manual Recalculation on, you can always recalculate selected cells by going into and out of EDIT mode on those cells.

Suppose you have a large worksheet on which you're doing data entry. Cell C5 contains the formula

C5: (A5*G2)/A5

You've set recalculation to be manual to avoid time-consuming recalculation after every entry; but because recalculation is manual, the worksheet is not updated after each entry.

Now suppose you want to see the impact on cell C5 of a change to cell A5, but you don't want to take the time to {Calc} the entire sheet. All you have to do is move the cursor to cell C5, press the {Edit} key, and then press {Enter}. 1-2-3 will recalculate C5—and only C5—instantly.

79 Trap: Remember that updating cell C5 with {Edit} has no effect on any cells that depend on C5.

You can get into trouble if you don't remember that recalculating a cell by {Edit}ing it updates only that one cell. For example, if cell D5 contains the formula

D5: +C5

cell D5 continues to display the old value of C5 until the sheet is {Calc}ed or until cell D5 is {Edit}ed.

80 Trap: If you press the {Calc} key after the {Edit} key when you are updating a single cell, you convert the formula in the cell into a value.

If you strike {Edit} {Calc} {Enter} instead of {Edit} {Enter} in the previous example, 1-2-3 replaces the formula in C5 with a pure number equal to the current value of the formula, and you lose the formula. There are times when you may want to do this, but be sure not to do it by accident.

81 Trick: You can use /Copy to recalculate a range of cells without recalculating the whole worksheet.

When you have finished /Copying a cell or a range of cells in Manual Recalculation mode, 1-2-3 recalculates any formulas in the range copied to. This recalculation is rapid because the program does not recalculate the whole worksheet in the process. (By the way, the /**M**ove command functions differently; 1-2-3 does not recalculate at all on a /**M**ove in Manual mode.)

You can use this fact to recalculate a small range quickly without having to wait for a large worksheet to recalculate. For example, look at Figure 39.

	A	B	C	D	E
1	SALES PROJECTIONS				
2			Jan	Feb	Mar
3	Unit Price	$12.95			
4	Unit Sales		10,000	10,000	7,000
5					
6	Total Sales		$129,500	$129,500	$90,650
7					

Figure 39

This figure shows a small part of a large sales projection model for a single product. The unit price of the product is entered in cell B3, and the expected monthly sales in cells C4, D4, E4, and so on. Cells C6 to E6 all contain similar formulas. For example, cell C5 is defined as

C6: (C2) +$B$3*C4

Suppose that you want to evaluate the impact on monthly dollar sales of a $.75 increase in the price of the product being evaluated. Because this worksheet takes several minutes to recalculate, you want to recalculate only the "Total Sales" row. Figure 40 shows the worksheet after the price has been changed but before row 6 has been recalculated.

	A	B	C	D	E
1	SALES PROJECTIONS				
2			Jan	Feb	Mar
3	Unit Price	$13.70			
4	Unit Sales		10,000	10,000	7,000
5					
6	Total Sales		$129,500	$129,500	$90,650
7					

Figure 40

To recalculate row 6 only, move the cursor to cell C6 and issue the command

/Copy **C6**{Enter}**C6..E6**{Enter}

Notice that the To range in this Copy includes cell C6, which is also the From range. This is one of those cases where overlapping From and To ranges is an advantage. After the Copy is complete, the worksheet looks like Figure 41.

	A	B	C	D	E
1	SALES PROJECTIONS				
2			Jan	Feb	Mar
3	Unit Price	$13.70			
4	Unit Sales		10,000	10,000	7,000
5					
6	Total Sales		$137,000	$137,000	$95,900
7					

Figure 41

Row 6 now reflects the change in price; and because we used the /Copy Tip, the whole process took only a few seconds.

82   **Tip:** Sometimes you can reduce recalculation time by using a RAM disk.

RAM disk software, which comes free with many memory expansion boards for the IBM PC, fools the operating system into thinking that part of RAM (random-access memory) is a disk drive. You can use this facility to keep parts of a large worksheet out of normal memory and on a simulated disk in this RAM disk portion of RAM. You can read and write from this RAM disk area quickly because 1-2-3 can work directly from memory instead of having to go to a physical disk.

A RAM disk allows you to keep portions of a large worksheet in the RAM disk area and use /File Combine to bring them into standard memory only when you really need them. This capability may result in a smaller basic worksheet and considerably faster recalculation time.

83   **Trap:** If you make any changes to the data in the RAM disk area, those changes will be lost when you turn off the machine unless you've also written those same changes to an actual disk.

84 **Tip:** Learn to watch for the "CALC" indicator when you're in Manual
          Recalculation mode.

When you're in Manual Recalculation mode and have changed one or
more cells without recalculating, 1-2-3 displays the "CALC" indicator
in the lower-right corner of the screen. (See Figure 42 for an example.)
It's a good idea to get used to looking for this message. You can be in
trouble if you think your calculations are up to date when they're not,
especially if you want to print a report.

```
15
16
17
18
19
20
                                                    Calc
```

Figure 42

85 **Trap:** In Manual Recalculation mode, your worksheet may not be
            up to date after a **/F**ile **C**ombine.

In Automatic Recalculation mode, a /File Combine results in an
automatic recalculation of the worksheet. However, in Manual mode,
no recalculation takes place after a /File Combine. This may be fine,
but you should keep in mind these points:

1. If the file you're Combining was Saved or Xtracted
    without having been recalculated, it will not be up to date
    until you recalculate.

2. If existing areas of the worksheet into which you're
    Combining another worksheet contain cells referring to
    the Combined area, these formulas will not be up to date
    until the sheet is {Calc}ed.

In this last case, however, the "CALC" prompt will appear in the
lower-right corner of the worksheet after the Combine operation is
ended.

86   Trap: In Manual Recalculation mode, your worksheet may not be up to date after a **/F**ile **R**etrieve.

This is similar to the case discussed under Trap 85. If you save a worksheet without recalculating it, the worksheet will still not be up to date if you do a /File Retrieve on it in the Manual Recalculation mode. However, the "CALC" prompt will appear in the lower-left corner of the worksheet after the file is loaded.

87   Tip: Maintain natural recalculation as the default.

1-2-3 differs from most other spreadsheet programs in providing a natural recalculation option. Most other spreadsheet programs provide recalculation by either row or column only. The row and column methods, however, can lead to wrong answers if your worksheet contains forward references. The designers of 1-2-3 provide a recalculation alternative that overcomes the problem of forward references: the natural order option. In natural mode 1-2-3 locates the most fundamental cell in the worksheet, the cell on which the greatest number of other cells depend. 1-2-3 recalculates that cell first; then the program finds the next most fundamental cell, and recalculates it; and so on, until the worksheet is completely recalculated. This method ensures that forward references are not a problem. (For a discussion of forward references and natural recalculation, see *Using 1-2-3*, pp. 119-120.)

There may be special situations in which you want to recalculate by row or column, for example, when you're running a converted VisiCalc model that depends on row/column recalculation, but generally you'll be much safer if you keep 1-2-3 in its default natural mode.

Dealing with Circular References

88   Trap: If you see the "CIRC" indicator in the lower-right corner of the screen, you have a circular reference in your worksheet.

Circular reference describes two cells that depend on each other for their meaning. For example, the following three cells

        A1: +C1
        B1: 100
        C1: A1*B1

constitute a circular reference. Because cell A1 depends on cell C1, which depends on cell A1, this sheet contains a circular reference.

When 1-2-3 tries to recalculate a sheet containing one or more circular references, it cannot find the "toe hold" it needs to recalculate the sheet; and the worksheet will not be correct even after the recalculation is complete.

89 Tip: Most models that contain circular references can be recalculated accurately using the iterative mode of recalculation.

One way to overcome circular references is to recalculate the worksheet a number of times. During each recalculation, the difference between the actual values in the cells and the correct values for those cells gets smaller. After a certain number of calculations, the difference becomes insignificant. (*Using 1-2-3* describes one such problem on pp. 121-122.)

To take care of such situations, 1-2-3 lets you set the recalculation iteration count to more than one (one is the default). If you set the iteration count to five, for instance, the entire worksheet will be recalculated five times each time you press {Calc} or change an entry (in Automatic mode).

1-2-3 assumes that you will use an iteration count greater than one only if you have a circular reference in one or more formulas in your model. Therefore, the iteration count is always equal to one unless you specifically reset it with the /**W**orksheet **G**lobal **R**ecalculation **I**terative command. An iteration count of up to 20 can be specified, and 20 recalculations will solve the circular references in nearly any worksheet. In fact, in most cases a count of only 5 or 10 is sufficient.

90 Trap: In most cases the "CIRC" message indicates that there is a formula error in your worksheet.

Although there are times when you want to create circular references, in most cases the message "CIRC" in the lower-right corner of the screen signals a formula error.

These errors can arise for a number of reasons. One frequent cause is an @SUM range that includes the cell containing the @SUM function. For example, the formula

    C15: @SUM(C2..C15)

is a circular reference because cell C15 is defined by referring to itself.

91 **Trap:** Finding a circular reference in a 1-2-3 worksheet can be very difficult.

Although 1-2-3 can tell you that a circular reference exists in a worksheet, it cannot tell you where that reference is. For that reason, if you are working with a large worksheet, the appearance of the "CIRC" indicator can be a reason to scream.

The best way to deal with circular references is to prevent them from occurring in the first place. Even when working with a big worksheet, recalculate often. Recalculating brings any circular references to light and often reduces the number of steps you need to retrace to find your error. In addition, save your worksheets frequently. If you can't find the circular reference, you can always start over with a recent version of the worksheet that you know is clean.

There are several ways to try to find circular references, but none is foolproof. First, you can return to the last cell or cells you worked on before you made the change to the worksheet and see if the circular reference is there. If it is, you're in luck. Otherwise, check other cells that you've changed recently.

92 **Trick:** If you can't find the error directly (and unfortunately you usually won't), you can use 1-2-3's **/F**ile **X**tract **V**alues command to find the error.

First, recalculate and then save the current worksheet. Next, go to cell A1 and issue the /File Xtract Values command. Specify *half* the current worksheet for the range to be saved. For example, if the worksheet covers the range A1..Z100, select A1..Z50 as the range to be saved. Be sure to choose a name for this partial file that is different from the name of the entire file.

After the partial file is saved, reload it into the worksheet immediately with the /File Combine Copy Entire file command. Do not move the cursor before you reload the partial file. This command causes the partial file, which now contains only values, to be reloaded on top of itself in the worksheet.

Now recalculate the worksheet. If the circular reference was in the part of the worksheet that you just Xtracted and Combined, it will now be gone and the "CIRC" message will disappear. Why? When we saved the top portion of the file using the Values option and then Combined that partial file into the worksheet, we removed all the formulas from that part of the file. Because circular references are a kind of cancerous formula, when we removed the formulas, we also removed any circular references in the formulas.

If the "CIRC" message does disappear, you know that the circular reference is in the top half of the worksheet. If not, you know it is in the bottom half. Either way, you are now much closer to finding the error than before. You can repeat this process, Xtracting and Combining more and more of the worksheet, until you've pinned down the error.

5

"What If" and Sensitivity Analysis

Simple Sensitivity Analysis

Electronic spreadsheets like 1-2-3 make sensitivity analysis easy. When you build a model on an electronic spreadsheet like 1-2-3, you define all the mathematical relationships in the model. Until you decide to change them, every sum, product, division, subtraction, average, and net present value in the model remains the same. Each time you enter new assumptions into the model, all these mathematical relationships are calculated by the model with no effort on your part. And all the computations are correct because spreadsheets don't make math errors.

Even more important, electronic spreadsheets allow you to play "what if" with your model after it has been developed. *"What if" analysis*, also called *sensitivity analysis*, is the process of evaluating the changes to the results of your model caused by changes in the assumptions. Once a set of mathematical relationships has been built into the worksheet, the sheet can be recalculated for different sets of assumptions with amazing speed.

For example, suppose you build a financial projection for your business for the years 1984 through 1990. In building the forecast, you assume that your sales will grow at a rate of 10% per year. But what happens if sales grow at a rate of only 5%? What if your sales increase 15% each year? If you were using a pencil and a calculator to do this analysis, it would take you hours to compute each variation. With 1-2-3 all you need to do is change the growth-rate assumption in your worksheet and press the {Calc} key. The entire process takes just seconds.

93 **Tip:** When you're doing a sensitivity analysis, physically isolate the inputs you want to change so that it will be easy to vary them.

In the typical sensitivity analysis, you have one or several variables that you want to change so that you can note the effects on the model outputs for each set of inputs.

Figure 43 shows a sales projection model that has several varying inputs. The inputs are all located in the lower part of the worksheet. The "1984 Forecast" column is displayed in Text format so you can see the formulas. "GROWTH84" and "GRLA84" are range names assigned to

	A	B	C	D	E	F
301						
302						
303	SALES PROJECTIONS--ALL BRANCHES (3 YEARS)					
304						
305		1983	1984	1984	1985	1985
306	Branch	Sales	Forecast	% of Tot	Forecast	% of Tot
307	==					
308	Atl	$15,500	+B308+B308*$GROWTH84	5.05%	$21,390	4.71%
309	Chi	$103,000	+B309+B309*$GROWTH84	33.55%	$142,140	31.30%
310	LA	$156,000	+B310+B310*$GRLA84	57.45%	$273,780	60.30%
311	SF	$25	+B311+B311*$GROWTH84	0.01%	$35	0.01%
312	Minn	$999	+B312+B312*$GROWTH84	0.33%	$1,379	0.30%
313	Quebec	$11,111	+B313+B313*$GROWTH84	3.62%	$15,333	3.38%
314	TOTAL	$286,635	$353,030	100.00%	$454,056	100.00%
315						
316	Assumptions:	1. Current staffing level.				
317	***********	2. Ignores inflation.				
318		3. Growth factor may differ by year.				
319	Growth-General:	1984:	15.00%	1985:	20.00%	
320	Growth-LA:		30.00%		35.00%	

Figure 43

the growth factors in D319 and D320, respectively. The "1985 Forecast" uses different growth factors, stored in F319 and F320. Obviously, we have reason to believe that the L.A. branch will behave differently from the other cities, so we've set up special factors for L.A.

Placing the growth factors in a separate area makes it easy to change things in just one place and then immediately see the effects on the whole model. Figure 44 shows the results of changing the 1985 growth factors to 25% and 40%.

	A	B	C	D	E	F
301						
302						
303	SALES PROJECTIONS--ALL BRANCHES (2 YEARS)					
304						
305		1983	1984	1984	1985	1985
306	Branch	Sales	Forecast	% of Tot	Forecast	% of Tot
307	===					
308	Atl	$15,500	+B308+B308*$GROWTH84	5.05%	$22,281	4.72%
309	Chi	$103,000	+B309+B309*$GROWTH84	33.55%	$148,063	31.39%
310	LA	$156,000	+B310+B310*$GRLA84	57.45%	$283,920	60.19%
311	SF	$25	+B311+B311*$GROWTH84	0.01%	$36	0.01%
312	Minn	$999	+B312+B312*$GROWTH84	0.33%	$1,436	0.30%
313	Quebec	$11,111	+B313+B313*$GROWTH84	3.62%	$15,972	3.39%
314	TOTAL	$286,635	$353,030	100.00%	$471,708	100.00%
315						
316	Assumptions:		1. Current staffing level.			
317	***********		2. Ignores inflation.			
318			3. Growth factor may differ by year.			
319	Growth-General:		1984:	15.00%	1985:	25.00%
320	Growth-LA:			30.00%		40.00%

Figure 44

94   **Tip:** Record key assumptions in a prominent area of the worksheet.

This is a good idea both for your own benefit and for the benefit of others who interpret the results of your analyses. Because numbers can "lie" in so many ways, we should always be able to see the underlying assumptions of any analysis.

See the lower part of Figure 43 for an example of a special assumptions area of the worksheet.

Fancy Sensitivity Analysis

95 **Tip:** Use the **/D**ata **T**able command when you're making more than one or two sensitivity changes.

The /**D**ata **T**able command is one feature of 1-2-3 that sets it apart from other programs. Unfortunately, this command is not adequately documented in the 1-2-3 Manual, so the command's capabilities are not well known. As we will see later, you can use the /**D**ata **T**able command for many purposes, but its most obvious use is in sensitivity analysis.

Getting a /**D**ata **T**able to work requires advance preparation. If you want a good basic description of the /**D**ata **T**able command, see Chapter 11 of *Using 1-2-3*.

Refer to the example in Figure 43 that we used in the section on "Simple Sensitivity Analysis." Let's suppose that we want to vary the general 1984 growth factor over a range of values, from 10% to 20%, in steps of 5%. In this analysis we are interested only in Atlanta and Chicago. The /**D**ata **T**able **1** command allows us to see all the results at once so we can easily compare them.

Figure 45 shows a data table that presents what we want. It gives the 1984 sales forecasts for Atlanta, Chicago, and the totals for all branches for 10% growth, 15% growth, and 20% growth. To construct this table, we did the following:

1. Entered the three growth rates (.10, .15, and .20) that we wanted to test in the range A328..A330.

2. Entered formulas in the range B327..D327 that refer to the cells that compute total sales for Atlanta, Chicago, and the total for 1984.

3. Issued the /**D**ata **T**able **1** command.

4. Specified the range A327..D330 as the **T**able range.

5. Provided cell D319, named "GROWTH84," to the /**D**ata **T**able **1** command as the Input cell (the cell we want to vary). (See Figure 44.)

6. Pressed {Enter} to calculate the table.

```
        A       B       C       D       E       F       G
321
322 DATA TABLE SENSITIVITY ANALYSIS ON 1984 SALES PROJECTIONS
323 ============================================================
324
325 1984-Gen
326 Growth     Atl      Chi    Total
327          +C308    +C309   +C314
328     10%  $17,050 $113,300 $346,499
329     15%  $17,825 $118,450 $353,030
330     20%  $18,600 $123,600 $359,562
```

Figure 45

The table sequentially substitutes each value in the range A328..A330 into the Input cell, "GROWTH84." After each value is input, the worksheet is recalculated automatically so that the formulas in cells C308, C309, and C314 are recomputed. Cells B327, C327, and D327, which refer to C308, C309, and C314, respectively, are also recomputed. Because these formulas all depend on the value in "GROWTH84," the result of each formula is different for each input value. The different results are stored in the data table; each result is located under the equation and next to the input value that generated that number.

The outcome is the same as if we had constructed a table manually. For example, suppose we compute the value for the formula in cell B327 at the growth rate of 10% and enter that value in a table. Then suppose we recompute that formula at a growth rate of 15% and enter that value in the table. If we figure each formula using each rate, we duplicate the data table, but it will take minutes, as opposed to seconds with the /Data Table command.

We can use this same /Data Table definition with variations to do further analysis. For instance, suppose we use the /Data Table 1 command to change the Input Cell to "GROWTH85"; then change the formulas in B327..D327 to refer to cells E308, E309, and E310, which compute the "1985 Forecast" for the cities; and finally change the growth percentages in column A to 15%, 20%, and 25%.

To see the results, we press {Table}, which recalculates the data table. Figure 46 shows what we get. (Note that we have also changed the title in cell A325—a good practice.)

```
       A       B       C       D       E       F       G
321
322 DATA TABLE SENSITIVITY ANALYSIS ON 1985 SALES PROJECTIONS
323 =========================================================
324
325 1985-Gen
326 Growth     Atl     Chi    Total
327         +E308   +E309   +E314
328    15%  $20,499 $136,218 $456,685
329    20%  $21,390 $142,140 $464,196
330    25%  $22,281 $148,063 $471,708
```

Figure 46

Before we leave this example, let's look at a few related Tips.

96   **Tip:** It is good practice to format as Text the cells containing the formulas your data tables operate on.

The formulas on row 327 in Figures 45 and 46 are displayed in Text format. If you do not use the /**R**ange **F**ormat **T**ext command to format these cells as Text, they display the evaluated results of these formulas; seeing only the results is confusing and also deprives you of documentation.

97   **Tip:** The /**D**ata **F**ill command can frequently be used to enter the variables you wish to test in your data tables.

We employed the /**D**ata **F**ill command to fill in our series of growth percentages in the range A. For example, to fill the range A328..A330 in Figure 45, we issued the /**D**ata **F**ill command, specified A328..A330 as the Fill range, .10 as the Start value, .05 as the Step value, and .20 as the Stop value. 1-2-3 automatically entered the three values in cells A328..A330. This tip can be especially handy when you have a long list.

98   **Tip:** The formulas in a data table do not have to be simple direct references to cells outside the table.

In the data table in Figure 45, the formulas in cells B327, C327, and D327 are simple direct references to cells outside the data table— specifically, C308, C309, and C314. Data tables do not have to be constructed this way, however. The formulas in a data table can be as complex as you wish, and they can operate independently of any other computations in the worksheet. An example of a simple self-contained data table is shown in Figure 47.

	A	B	C
1		14. 95*A1	
2	.1	1. 495	
3	.2	2. 99	
4	.3	4. 485	
5	.4	5. 98	
6	.5	7. 475	
7	.6	8. 97	
8			

Figure 47

The Table range for this data table is A1..B7; the Input cell is A1. The numbers in cells B2 to B7 represent the products that result from multiplying 14.95 by each decimal fraction in the range A2..A7.

99 **Tip:** Use **/D**ata **T**able **2** instead of **/D**ata **T**able **1** when you want to vary two separate inputs and show the results of paired variables.

1-2-3 offers two different types of **/D**ata **T**ables. We saw in the previous Tip how **/D**ata **T**able **1** works. **/D**ata **T**able **2** performs a slightly different type of sensitivity analysis, the case where you want to vary two separate inputs at the same time and see the results of each pair of variable values.

Let's go back to the example we used in the previous Tip (see Figure 45). So far, we've ignored the Los Angeles branch, which has a set of growth factors different from the other cities'. Suppose we want to bring L.A. into the picture and see the effect on the 1984 total sales forecast of varying both the general growth factor and the L.A. growth factor at the same time. **/D**ata **T**able **2** is designed for just this type of situation.

Figure 48 shows the **D**ata **T**able **2** that does the job. The general growth factors we want to test are listed down column A, and the L.A. growth factors we want to test are across row 347. To construct this table, we did the following:

1.   Entered the three test values for the general growth rate (.10, .15, and .20) into the range A348..A350.

2. Entered the test values for the L.A. growth rate into the range B347..D347.

3. Entered a formula in cell A347 that points to the cell in which our output formula resides. The formula in cell A347 is +C314 because cell C314 contains the 1984 total sales forecast value.

4. Issued the /**Data Table Reset** command followed by the /**Data Table 2** command.

5. Specified the range A347..D350 as the Table range.

6. Provided cell D319, named "GROWTH84," to the /**Data Table 2** command as the **Input** cell 1 (the first cell we want to vary); we then provided cell D320, named "GRLA84," as **Input** cell 2 (the second cell we want to vary).

```
       A       B       C       D       E       F       G
342 DATA TABLE 2 SENSITIVITY ANALYSIS ON 1984 SALES PROJECTIONS
343 ===========================================================
344
345 1984-Gen
346 Growth       1984 Los Angeles Growth
347 +C314          15%     20%     25%
348      15% $329,630 $337,430 $345,230
349      20% $336,162 $343,962 $351,762
350      25% $342,694 $350,494 $358,294
351
```

Figure 48

At each intersection the table shows the overall 1984 total sales forecast resulting from that particular pair of growth factors. For instance, D349 shows the total sales forecast that corresponds to a general growth rate of 20% and an L.A. growth rate of 25%. As with /**Data Table 1**, we can change one or more elements and then immediately recalculate everything by pressing {Table}.

100 Tip: If you have several data tables in a model, use a macro to activate any one of them at any time.

Like /**Data Query** definitions (and unlike /**Graph** definitions), /**Data Table** definitions cannot be named and saved by a standard 1-2-3 command. Only one data table can be active at one time; so when you create a new table, you destroy the definition of any previous table. This means that if you want to try several data tables in turn and switch back and forth between them, you need to create each one from the keyboard every time you use it. Quite a bother!

This is just the kind of problem that macros solve perfectly. In Figure 184 in the chapter "Data Base," we show a macro that performs this function for the /**D**ata **Q**uery command. You can follow this general form and create a macro something like the one in Figure 49 for automating /**D**ata **T**ables.

	A	B	C	D	E	F	G
361	\T	/xmT_MENU~			Execute Data Table menu.		
362							
363	T_MENU	TABLE1	TABLE2		Data Table menu.		
364		Atl, Chi	LA vs Total				
365		/xgT1_MC~	/xgT2_MC~				
366							
367	T1_MC	/dt1DT1_RANGE~			Define Data Table 1 range.		
368		GROWTH84~			Define Input Cell 1.		
369		/gnuGRAPH1~			Set current graph.		
370							
371							
372							
373	T2_MC	/dt2DT2_RANGE~			Define Data Table 2 range.		
374		GROWTH84~			Define Input Cell 1.		
375		GRLA84~			Define Input Cell 2		
376		/gnuGRAPH2~			Set current graph.		

Figure 49

This macro contains a simple menu that offers two choices: Table 1 or Table 2. Each option causes the macro to issue a set of commands that define and compute a data table. (If you need more information on menu macros, see the Tips on macros.)

The last thing this macro code does for each **D**ata **T**able option is to activate a predefined graph that goes with the table. We describe using graphs in connection with data tables in the next Tip.

101 **Tip:** You will often find it useful to analyze your /**D**ata **T**able output graphically.

1-2-3 /**D**ata **T**ables are ideal input for 1-2-3 graphs. We saw in the previous tip that the last thing that the "Data Table Choice" macro does is activate a predefined graph associated with that data table. The

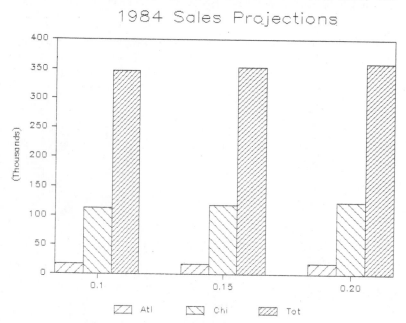

Figure 50

	A	B	C	D	E	F	G
381	\G	/gtb		Graph Type Bar.			
382		xA328.A330~		Put growth %s on as X axis labels			
383		aB328.B330~		Atl range.			
384		bC328.C330~		Chi range.			
385		cD328.D330~		Tot range.			
386		o		Start graph Options.			
387		laAtl~lbChi~lcTot~	Set Legends for each range.				
388		tf		{Set First Title.			
389		1984 Sales		{			
390		Projections~		{			
391		q		Quit Options.			
392		ncGRAPH1~		Name-Create the graph.			
393		q		Quit /Graph.			

Figure 51

graphs have all been named with the /Graph Name Create command. Figure 50 shows one of these graphs built from Figure 45, and Figure 51 presents the macro that creates its definition.

102 **Trap:** A two-variable /Data Table can take a long time to re-calculate.

Whenever you run a data table, either by issuing the /Data Table command or by pressing the {Table} key, 1-2-3 recalculates the worksheet as many times as needed to bring the data table up to date. With a large worksheet, a complex data table formula, and a large number of variables, the table can take *hours* to recalculate.

103 **Trick:** In some cases there are ways to get around the long recalculation time of a data table.

Sometimes the delays associated with big data tables can't be avoided, but at other times there are alternate ways of getting the same result without the use of a data table. Figure 52 shows a data table. (The data table range is J42..K45.) This data table was part of a large worksheet, and we found that it took several minutes of recalculation to bring the table up to date. However, in this case there's an alternative. The three values for which we wanted to compute @DCOUNT totals (the values 1, 2, and 3 in the lefthand column of the data table) can also be used as the "Bin" range for the /Data Distribution command. If we also specify the correct column of the data base as a "Values" range, we have what we want. (The source data for both the /Data Table and the /Data Distribution commands is in a data base that is off the screen.)

	I	J	K	L
41				
42	TOTAL=>>>>		@DCOUNT(GE50..HA90,1,T131..T132)	
43	BOX #1	1		28
44	BOX #2	2		10
45	BOX #3	3		6
46				
47				

Figure 52

Figure 53 shows the /Data Distribution table that gives the same result as the /Data Table in Figure 52. We produced this table with the /Data

Distribution command in a few seconds, as opposed to the few minutes
that we had to wait for the /Data Table command to accomplish the
same task.

	I	J	K	L
41				
42			44	= TOTAL
43		1	28	= BOX #1
44		2	10	= BOX #2
45		3	6	= BOX #3
46				
47				

Figure 53

6
Printing

104 **Tip:** You can use macros for immediate recall of previous print definitions.

You cannot name and save a print definition directly the way you can a graph definition. However, you can get the same effect by writing a print macro. The macro in Figure 54 first cancels whatever print definition previously existed and then sets up a new definition. To activate these print parameters, all you need to do is press {Alt} P.

	AA	AB	AC	AD	AE
1	\P	/PPCA	Clears all print parameters		
2		R{?}~	Defines Range		
3		OOU~	Options Other Unformatted		
4		ML0~	Left margin 0		
5		Q	Quit from Options Menu		
6		AGQ	Align, Go, Quit		
7					

Figure 54

Printer Adjustments

105 **Trap:** You can get the wrong spacing on printouts if you use the form-feed and line-feed controls on your printer to adjust your paper.

Once your printer is at the top of a page and you select the **A**lign option of the /**P**rint command, 1-2-3 is synchronized with the position of the paper. You can maintain this synchronization by using 1-2-3's **P**age and **L**ine commands to adjust your paper instead of using the controls on your printer. If you use the printer controls, 1-2-3 may get out of sync with the printer. To restore synchronization, position the paper at the top of form and issue the **A**lign command again.

106 **Trap:** Make sure the number of lines per page on your printer and in 1-2-3 match.

Nearly every printer available for microcomputers assumes that each printed page contains 66 lines of text. 1-2-3's /**P**rint command also assumes 66 lines in its default condition. However, the **L**ines option in the 1-2-3 /**P**rint **P**rinter **O**ptions menu allows you to tell 1-2-3 how many lines should appear on each page. Many printers also have controls for lines per page. If you change the number of lines per page, be sure that 1-2-3 and your printer agree on the number of lines that should be on each printed page. Otherwise, you'll get strange results when you print.

107 **Trap:** When printing in **F**ormatted option, you may get more lines at the top and bottom of the page than you expect.

When you want automatic page breaks at the end of a page, choose **O**ptions **O**ther **F**ormatted (this is the default setting). This setting assumes that you have headers and footers, so 1-2-3 allocates lines for headers and footers and for spacing before and after them whether you select them or not. This is why you get more blank lines at top and bottom than you specified in your top and bottom margin settings. If you want complete control over spacing, use the **U**nformatted command and issue your own **P**age and **L**ine commands.

If you want automatic page breaks without the lines for headers and footers, send a control code to your printer, telling it to skip at the perforations. (See the /**P**rint **P**rinter **O**ptions Setup Tip below.)

108   Trap: When you are using footers, you will lose the last one unless you issue the **Page** command before quitting the **/P**rint command.

1-2-3 does not print the footer on a page until the print head actually gets to the end of the page. This characteristic is useful when you want to issue several separate range commands to fill out a page, but it's a bother when you forget to issue that last **Page** command and therefore lose your last footer. If you're using print macros and have footers, be sure to put a **Page** command in the macro.

109   Tip: You can stop the printer if you want to cancel printing in the middle.

To cancel printing in the middle of a job, press {Ctrl} {Break} to stop 1-2-3 and then turn the off printer to stop the printer itself. You can then turn the printer on again. Be sure to realign the paper in the printer to the proper top of form and issue the **Align** command from within 1-2-3 to get the program and the printer in sync again.

110   Trap: If you issue a **/P**rint **P**rinter **G**o with the printer turned off, you may get unpredictable results when you turn the printer on again.

When 1-2-3 tries to print to an off-line or turned-off printer, nothing will be printed. However, even though nothing appears on the printer, 1-2-3 *thinks* that it is printing. Suppose you start to print a 1-2-3 worksheet and then realize that the printer is turned off. You press {Ctrl} {Break} to stop 1-2-3, turn on the printer, and restart the print. However, while the printer was off-line, 1-2-3 "printed" a few lines of the worksheet, even though the printer did not move. Thus, because 1-2-3 and the printer now disagree on the alignment of the paper in the printer, you may have the wrong page breaks in your document.

To overcome this problem, be sure to issue the **Align** command before restarting the print job. This will bring 1-2-3 and the printer back into agreement.

Long Reports

111 Tip: When it prints, 1-2-3 can automatically divide reports that are wider and/or longer than a single page.

Figures 55 and 56 show two views of a large worksheet. The actual dimensions of the area to print are A1..Z200, an area far too large to fit on a single page. Fortunately, you don't have to worry about creating several smaller print ranges to fit on single pages and then doing enough prints to create the complete report. 1-2-3 automatically prints the report in single-page sections. The first page shows the upper-left section of the worksheet, from row 1 to row 56 and from column A to about column H (assuming that you use the default column width and lines per page). Page 2 includes the area of the worksheet directly below the first, or roughly A57..H113. 1-2-3 continues to print the contents of columns A to H, 56 rows at a time, until it reaches the bottom of the print range. At that point, the program loops back to the top of the worksheet and begins printing columns I through P. Once the entire contents of this range have been printed, the program will print columns Q through X, 56 lines at a time, and finally, columns Y and Z.

Borders

112 Tip: You can have both column and row borders appear on each page of a multipage report.

One problem with 1-2-3's approach to breaking a large report into page-sized chunks for printing is that frequently the top rows and the far-left columns, which appear on only a few of the final printed pages, contain important headers that you want on every page. For example, in Figure 55, you might want the row descriptions in columns A and B and the report header in rows 1 through 5 to appear on every page.

Fortunately, 1-2-3 offers a way to accomplish this task, the **/P**rint **P**rinter **O**ptions **B**orders command. This command has two options: Rows and Columns. You can use either one or both together to force certain rows or columns to appear on every page of a multipage report.

```
        A        B        C        D        E        F        G        H
1  ============================================================================
2  AN INDEPENDENT LABORATORY
3  ============================================================================
4                      Question Question Question Question Question Question
5  Date    Respondent     1        2        3        4        5        6
6  01-Jan       1         A        B        D        B        A        B
7  02-Jan       2         B        C        E        A        B        C
8  03-Jan       3         A        C        A        A        A        C
9  04-Jan       4         C        A        C        C        C        A
10 05-Jan       5         A        B        C        A        A        B
11 05-Jan       6         A        C        A        B        A        C
12 06-Jan       7         D        A        B        A        D        A
13 07-Jan       8         C        B        E        C        C        B
14 08-Jan       9         A        B        A        A        A        B
15 09-Jan      10         A        B        D        B        A        B
16 10-Jan      11         B        C        E        A        B        C
17 11-Jan      12         A        C        A        A        A        C
18 12-Jan      13         C        A        C        C        C        A
19 12-Jan      14         A        B        C        A        A        B
20 12-Jan      15         A        C        A        B        A        C
```

Figure 55

In our example, we want columns A and B and rows 1 to 5 to appear on every page. To accomplish this, we issue the command /**P**rint **P**rinter **O**ptions **B**orders, select the **C**olumns option, and provide the range A1..B1. Next, we select the **R**ows option and provide the range A1..A5. Finally, we modify the print range to be C6..Z200. That's all there is to it. Figures 57, 58, 59, and 60 show several pages from the finished report.

113 **Trap:** When using /**P**rint **O**ptions **B**orders, make sure that neither Borders range overlaps with the other (if it exists) or with the print range.

Did you wonder why, in the previous Tip, when we added Borders to the print specifications we changed the Range as well? Figure 61 shows the first page of our report printed with Borders and the print Range A1..Z200. Notice that the Borders and the regular Range overlap and cause the printer to double-print rows 1 through 5 and columns A and

	S	T	U	V	W	X	Y	Z
181	A	B	C	A	A	B	C	A
182	A	C	A	B	A	C	A	B
183	D	A	B	A	D	A	B	A
184	C	B	E	C	C	B	E	C
185	A	B	A	A	A	B	A	A
186	A	B	D	B	A	B	D	B
187	B	C	E	A	B	C	E	A
188	A	C	A	A	A	C	A	A
189	C	A	C	C	C	A	C	C
190	A	B	C	A	A	B	C	A
191	A	C	A	B	A	C	A	B
192	D	A	B	A	D	A	B	A
193	C	B	E	C	C	B	E	C
194	A	B	A	A	A	B	A	A
195	A	B	D	B	A	B	D	B
196	B	C	E	A	B	C	E	A
197	A	C	A	A	A	C	A	A
198	C	A	C	C	C	A	C	C
199	A	B	C	A	A	B	C	A
200	A	B	C	A	A	B	C	A

Figure 56

B. Changing the print range so that there is no overlap avoids this problem.

114 **Trap:** When you examine the current **B**orders settings, use {Esc} to exit.

If you think there are no Borders defined in the current worksheet but want to check, use the **/Print O**ptions **B**orders (**C**olumn or **R**ow) command to look at the settings. However, after you've verified the current settings, you must press {Esc} and not {Enter} to get out of the **B**orders menu. Otherwise, you'll set a spurious border consisting of either column A or row 1 and mess up your printed report.

```
=======================================================================
AN INDEPENDENT LABORATORY
=======================================================================
                 Question Question Question Question Question Question
Date   Respondent   1        2        3        4        5        6
01-Jan     1        A        B        D        B        A        B
02-Jan     2        B        C        E        A        B        C
03-Jan     3        A        C        A        A        A        C
04-Jan     4        C        A        C        C        C        A
05-Jan     5        A        B        C        A        A        B
05-Jan     6        A        C        A        B        A        C
06-Jan     7        D        A        B        A        D        A
07-Jan     8        C        B        E        C        C        B
08-Jan     9        A        B        A        A        A        B
09-Jan    10        A        B        D        B        A        B
10-Jan    11        B        C        E        A        B        C
11-Jan    12        A        C        A        A        A        C
12-Jan    13        C        A        C        C        C        A
12-Jan    14        A        B        C        A        A        B
12-Jan    15        A        C        A        B        A        C
13-Jan    16        D        A        B        A        D        A
14-Jan    17        C        B        E        C        C        B
15-Jan    18        A        B        A        A        A        B
16-Jan    19        A        B        D        B        A        B
16-Jan    20        B        C        E        A        B        C
17-Jan    21        A        C        A        A        A        C
18-Jan    22        C        A        C        C        C        A
19-Jan    23        A        B        C        A        A        B
19-Jan    24        A        C        A        B        A        C
20-Jan    25        D        A        B        A        D        A
20-Jan    26        C        B        E        C        C        B
20-Jan    27        A        B        A        A        A        B
20-Jan    28        A        B        D        B        A        B
21-Jan    29        B        C        E        A        B        C
22-Jan    30        A        C        A        A        A        C
23-Jan    31        C        A        C        C        C        A
24-Jan    32        A        B        C        A        A        B
25-Jan    33        A        C        A        B        A        C
26-Jan    34        D        A        B        A        D        A
27-Jan    35        C        B        E        C        C        B
27-Jan    36        A        B        A        A        A        B
28-Jan    37        A        B        D        B        A        B
29-Jan    38        B        C        E        A        B        C
30-Jan    39        A        C        A        A        A        C
31-Jan    40        C        A        C        C        C        A
31-Jan    41        A        B        C        A        A        B
01-Feb    42        A        C        A        B        A        C
02-Feb    43        D        A        B        A        D        A
03-Feb    44        C        B        E        C        C        B
04-Feb    45        A        B        A        A        A        B
05-Feb    46        A        B        D        B        A        B
06-Feb    47        B        C        E        A        B        C
06-Feb    48        A        C        A        A        A        C
07-Feb    49        C        A        C        C        C        A
08-Feb    50        A        B        C        A        A        B
09-Feb    51        A        C        A        B        A        C
```

Figure 57

```
=====================================================================
AN INDEPENDENT LABORATORY
=====================================================================
                Question Question Question Question Question Question
Date    Respondent  7       8        9       10       11       12
01-Jan      1       D       B        A        B        D        B
02-Jan      2       E       A        B        C        E        A
03-Jan      3       A       A        A        C        A        A
04-Jan      4       C       C        C        A        C        C
05-Jan      5       C       A        A        B        C        A
05-Jan      6       A       B        A        C        A        B
06-Jan      7       B       A        D        A        B        A
07-Jan      8       E       C        C        B        E        C
08-Jan      9       A       A        A        B        A        A
09-Jan     10       D       B        A        B        D        B
10-Jan     11       E       A        B        C        E        A
11-Jan     12       A       A        A        C        A        A
12-Jan     13       C       C        C        A        C        C
12-Jan     14       C       A        A        B        C        A
12-Jan     15       A       B        A        C        A        B
13-Jan     16       B       A        D        A        B        A
14-Jan     17       E       C        C        B        E        C
15-Jan     18       A       A        A        B        A        A
16-Jan     19       D       B        A        B        D        B
16-Jan     20       E       A        B        C        E        A
17-Jan     21       A       A        A        C        A        A
18-Jan     22       C       C        C        A        C        C
19-Jan     23       C       A        A        B        C        A
19-Jan     24       A       B        A        C        A        B
20-Jan     25       B       A        D        A        B        A
20-Jan     26       E       C        C        B        E        C
20-Jan     27       A       A        A        B        A        A
20-Jan     28       D       B        A        B        D        B
21-Jan     29       E       A        B        C        E        A
22-Jan     30       A       A        A        C        A        A
23-Jan     31       C       C        C        A        C        C
24-Jan     32       C       A        A        B        C        A
25-Jan     33       A       B        A        C        A        B
26-Jan     34       B       A        D        A        B        A
27-Jan     35       E       C        C        B        E        C
27-Jan     36       A       A        A        B        A        A
28-Jan     37       D       B        A        B        D        B
29-Jan     38       E       A        B        C        E        A
30-Jan     39       A       A        A        C        A        A
31-Jan     40       C       C        C        A        C        C
31-Jan     41       C       A        A        B        C        A
01-Feb     42       A       B        A        C        A        B
02-Feb     43       B       A        D        A        B        A
03-Feb     44       E       C        C        B        E        C
04-Feb     45       A       A        A        B        A        A
05-Feb     46       D       B        A        B        D        B
06-Feb     47       E       A        B        C        E        A
06-Feb     48       A       A        A        C        A        A
07-Feb     49       C       C        C        A        C        C
08-Feb     50       C       A        A        B        C        A
09-Feb     51       A       B        A        C        A        B
```

Figure 58

```
===========================================================================
AN INDEPENDENT LABORATORY
===========================================================================
            Question Question Question Question Question Question
Date   Respondent  13      14      15      16      17      18
15-Apr    154       A       B       D       B       A       B
16-Apr    155       B       C       E       A       B       C
17-Apr    156       A       C       A       A       A       C
18-Apr    157       C       A       C       C       C       A
18-Apr    158       A       B       C       A       A       B
19-Apr    159       A       C       A       B       A       C
19-Apr    160       D       A       B       A       D       A
20-Apr    161       C       B       E       C       C       B
20-Apr    162       A       B       A       A       A       B
21-Apr    163       A       B       D       B       A       B
21-Apr    164       B       C       E       A       B       C
21-Apr    165       A       C       A       A       A       C
22-Apr    166       C       A       C       C       C       A
23-Apr    167       A       B       C       A       A       B
23-Apr    168       A       C       A       B       A       C
23-Apr    169       D       A       B       A       D       A
23-Apr    170       C       B       E       C       C       B
24-Apr    171       A       B       A       A       A       B
25-Apr    172       A       B       D       B       A       B
26-Apr    173       B       C       E       A       B       C
26-Apr    174       A       C       A       A       A       C
26-Apr    175       C       A       C       C       C       A
26-Apr    176       A       B       C       A       A       B
27-Apr    177       A       C       A       B       A       C
28-Apr    178       D       A       B       A       D       A
29-Apr    179       C       B       E       C       C       B
30-Apr    180       A       B       A       A       A       B
01-May    181       A       B       D       B       A       B
01-May    182       B       C       E       A       B       C
02-May    183       A       C       A       A       A       C
02-May    184       C       A       C       C       C       A
02-May    185       A       B       C       A       A       B
02-May    186       A       C       A       B       A       C
03-May    187       D       A       B       A       D       A
03-May    188       C       B       E       C       C       B
04-May    199       A       B       A       A       A       B
05-May    190       A       B       D       B       A       B
06-May    191       B       C       E       A       B       C
07-May    192       A       C       A       A       A       C
08-May    193       C       A       C       C       C       A
08-May    194       A       B       C       A       A       B
08-May    195       A       B       C       A       A       B
```

Figure 59

```
=======================================================================
AN INDEPENDENT LABORATORY
=======================================================================
                 Question Question Question Question Question Question
Date   Respondent    19       20       21       22       23       24
15-Mar    103         C        C        C        A        C        C
15-Mar    104         C        A        A        B        C        A
15-Mar    105         A        B        A        C        A        B
16-Mar    106         B        A        D        A        B        A
17-Mar    107         E        C        C        B        E        C
18-Mar    108         A        A        A        B        A        A
18-Mar    109         D        B        A        B        D        B
18-Mar    110         E        A        B        C        E        A
18-Mar    111         A        A        A        C        A        A
18-Mar    112         C        C        A        C        C        C
18-Mar    113         C        A        A        B        C        A
19-Mar    114         A        B        A        C        A        B
20-Mar    115         B        A        D        A        B        A
21-Mar    116         E        C        C        B        E        C
22-Mar    117         A        A        A        B        A        A
23-Mar    118         D        B        A        B        D        B
23-Mar    119         E        A        B        C        E        A
23-Mar    120         A        A        A        C        A        A
23-Mar    121         C        C        C        A        C        C
24-Mar    122         C        A        A        B        C        A
24-Mar    123         A        B        A        C        A        B
25-Mar    124         B        A        D        A        B        A
26-Mar    125         E        C        C        B        E        C
26-Mar    126         A        A        A        B        A        A
26-Mar    127         D        B        A        B        D        B
27-Mar    128         E        A        B        C        E        A
27-Mar    129         A        A        A        C        A        A
27-Mar    130         C        C        C        A        C        C
28-Mar    131         C        A        A        B        C        A
28-Mar    132         A        B        A        C        A        B
28-Mar    133         B        A        D        A        B        A
29-Mar    134         E        C        C        B        E        C
30-Mar    135         A        A        A        B        A        A
31-Mar    136         D        B        A        B        D        B
31-Mar    137         E        A        B        C        E        A
01-Apr    138         A        A        A        C        A        A
02-Apr    139         C        C        C        A        C        C
03-Apr    140         C        A        A        B        C        A
04-Apr    141         A        B        A        C        A        B
05-Apr    142         B        A        D        A        B        A
06-Apr    143         E        C        C        B        E        C
07-Apr    144         A        A        A        B        A        A
08-Apr    145         D        B        A        B        D        B
09-Apr    146         E        A        B        C        E        A
10-Apr    147         A        A        A        C        A        A
10-Apr    148         C        C        C        A        C        C
11-Apr    149         C        A        A        B        C        A
11-Apr    150         A        B        A        C        A        B
12-Apr    151         B        A        D        A        B        A
13-Apr    152         E        C        C        B        E        C
14-Apr    153         A        A        A        B        A        A
```

Figure 60

```
==========================================================================
AN INDEPENDENT LABAN INDEPENDENT LABORATORY
==========================================================================
                              Question Question Question Question
Date    RespondentDate    Respondent    1        2        3        4
==========================================================================
AN INDEPENDENT LABAN INDEPENDENT LABORATORY
==========================================================================
                              Question Question Question Question
Date    RespondentDate    Respondent    1        2        3        4
01-Jan       1  01-Jan       1        A        B        D        B
02-Jan       2  02-Jan       2        B        C        E        A
03-Jan       3  03-Jan       3        A        C        A        A
04-Jan       4  04-Jan       4        C        A        C        C
05-Jan       5  05-Jan       5        A        B        C        A
05-Jan       6  05-Jan       6        A        C        A        B
06-Jan       7  06-Jan       7        D        A        B        A
07-Jan       8  07-Jan       8        C        B        E        C
08-Jan       9  08-Jan       9        A        B        A        A
09-Jan      10  09-Jan      10        A        B        D        B
10-Jan      11  10-Jan      11        B        C        E        A
11-Jan      12  11-Jan      12        A        C        A        A
12-Jan      13  12-Jan      13        C        A        C        C
12-Jan      14  12-Jan      14        A        B        C        A
12-Jan      15  12-Jan      15        A        C        A        B
13-Jan      16  13-Jan      16        D        A        B        A
14-Jan      17  14-Jan      17        C        B        E        C
15-Jan      18  15-Jan      18        A        B        A        A
16-Jan      19  16-Jan      19        A        B        D        B
16-Jan      20  16-Jan      20        B        C        E        A
17-Jan      21  17-Jan      21        A        C        A        A
18-Jan      22  18-Jan      22        C        A        C        C
19-Jan      23  19-Jan      23        A        B        C        A
19-Jan      24  19-Jan      24        A        C        A        B
20-Jan      25  20-Jan      25        D        A        B        A
20-Jan      26  20-Jan      26        C        B        E        C
20-Jan      27  20-Jan      27        A        B        A        A
20-Jan      28  20-Jan      28        A        B        D        B
21-Jan      29  21-Jan      29        B        C        E        A
22-Jan      30  22-Jan      30        A        C        A        A
23-Jan      31  23-Jan      31        C        A        C        C
24-Jan      32  24-Jan      32        A        B        C        A
25-Jan      33  25-Jan      33        A        C        A        B
26-Jan      34  26-Jan      34        D        A        E        A
27-Jan      35  27-Jan      35        C        B        E        C
27-Jan      36  27-Jan      36        A        B        A        A
28-Jan      37  28-Jan      37        A        B        D        B
29-Jan      38  29-Jan      38        B        C        E        A
30-Jan      39  30-Jan      39        A        C        A        A
31-Jan      40  31-Jan      40        C        A        C        C
31-Jan      41  31-Jan      41        A        B        C        A
01-Feb      42  01-Feb      42        A        C        A        B
02-Feb      43  02-Feb      43        D        A        B        A
03-Feb      44  03-Feb      44        C        B        E        C
04-Feb      45  04-Feb      45        A        B        A        A
05-Feb      46  05-Feb      46        A        B        D        B
```

Figure 61

Options

115 Trick: You can use **/P**rint **O**ptions **S**etup to make your printer do all sorts of fancy tricks.

The **S**etup option allows you to send control codes to instruct your printer to do such things as print in compressed characters, print with a double strike, change the line spacing, etc. We produced the compressed print in Figures 57 through 60 by supplying a **S**etup code of \015, which sends a control code of decimal 15 to the Epson printer. To the Epson a decimal 15 represents "Shift In," or the compressed-character code. (Appendix B of the Epson MX Printer Manual shows all the necessary control codes. If you have a different printer, your printer manual should also have a table of control codes.)

Any printer state that you set with a setup code will remain on during the current session unless you turn it off. You can turn off compressed print and return to normal on the Epson by sending a **S**etup code of \018.

Figure 62 shows a sentence that we first printed in the normal single-strike manner; it then shows the same sentence printed in double-strike,which looks more like "letter quality." A \027 (the code for the {Esc} key) followed immediately by a \071 produces double-strike printing. To switch back to single strike, we send the **S**etup string \027\072.

```
Figure 62 shows a sentence that we first printed in normal strike and
then in double strike mode. The second version looks more like letter
quality.


Figure 62 shows a sentence that we first printed in normal strike and
then in double strike mode. The second version looks more like letter
quality.
```

Figure 62

116 Trap: If you're doing a series of prints with different parameters, you may get surprising results because of the way 1-2-3 remembers parameters.

1-2-3 remembers the last set of print parameters supplied. It's easy to forget, but 1-2-3 assumes that the last set of parameters remain the same unless you give different instructions. The safest thing is to execute a /Print Printer Clear All before you supply the new set of parameters; then you know you're starting from the standard default parameters.

117   Trap: If you're in Manual Recalculation mode, don't forget to recalculate before printing.

If you're in Manual Recalculation mode and forget to use the {Calc} key before printing, you may end up with a printout that is not properly recalculated. Learn to look for the "CALC" indicator on the screen whenever you're in MANUAL mode and you've made changes without recalculating. If you're printing from a macro, put a {Calc} in the macro before the /Print command to make certain that your printed reports are up to date.

118   Tip: You can write a macro that substitutes other headings for the data base field names before printing and replaces the data base field names after printing.

When you define a data base, 1-2-3 requires that the row immediately above the first row of data contain field names for the respective fields in the data base. Only by providing this row of field names can you use the /Data Query command on the data base. Unfortunately, when you print a report from this data base, you may want something different in the row immediately above your data.

One thing you can do is write a macro to copy in a special header line just for printing and then copy back the data base field names when you're finished. Let's suppose we have the data base shown in Figure 63. We've placed two work areas above it: The first, called "DASHES," is what we want to copy in over the field names for printing. The second, called "NAMES," contains the field names we have to copy back after we're done.

Figure 64 shows the macro that does this; it makes a call to another macro that does the printing, and then the first macro returns to copy back the field names. Figure 65 shows what the printout looks like.

119   Tip: You can use the period key (.) to allow you to view all the edges of a print range while you are defining the range.

Suppose you're trying to verify the dimensions of a print range that covers a large number of cells, like the range A1..Z200 that we have been working with. Imagine that you've added a few more rows to the model;

```
         I         J        K       L         M
21   DATE      NAME              AMOUNT    I<=NAMES
22
23
24
25   -------------------------------------I<=DASHES
26
28   Date of   Customer          Amount
29   Receipt   Name              Due
30   DATE      NAME              AMOUNT
31     11-Nov  Murphy, J.        $23.45
32     13-Nov  Feinberg, R.      $12.12
33     15-Nov  Peebles, P.      $145.00
34     17-Nov  Flint, F          $18.54
35     19-Nov  Grover, G.       $235.67
36     21-Nov  Cleveland, C.     $18.18
37     23-Nov  Alexander, A.     $10.00
38
```

Figure 63

```
         N         O        P        Q        R
21   \P            /cDASHES~FIELD1~      Copy dashes into line XX
22                 /xcPRINT_DB_MACRO~    Call print macro
23                 /cNAMES~FIELD1~       Copy back data base headers
24
25
```

Figure 64

```
Date of   Customer          Amount
Receipt   Name              Due
----------------------------------
11-Nov  Murphy, J.        $23.45
13-Nov  Feinberg, R.      $12.12
15-Nov  Peebles, P.      $145.00
17-Nov  Flint, F          $18.54
19-Nov  Grover, G.       $235.67
21-Nov  Cleveland, C.     $18.18
23-Nov  Alexander, A.     $10.00
```

Figure 65

you don't know exactly which row is the last; and these new rows fill only columns A through G and so are blank in columns X, Y, and Z.

To change the range, issue the command /**Print Printer R**ange. The cursor immediately expands to cover the range A1..Z200, the previous print range. You now want to modify this range to include the extra cells. However, because the new rows are blank in the columns near column Z, you cannot tell which rows to include in the new print range just by looking at the screen.

To overcome this problem, simply press the period (.) key. The screen changes so that you are looking at the lower-left corner of the print range instead of the lower-right corner. The cursor is in cell A200. Because the new rows contain information in columns A through G, you can easily see which rows should be added to the print range. To add these rows, simply point with the ↓ key.

If that is the only change you need to make, press {Enter} to lock in the new range. If, however, you want to view the upper-left corner of the range, press the period key again. The cursor moves to cell A1. Pressing period again allows you to view the upper-right corner of the range, and a fourth press moves the cursor back to the lower-right corner.

This same Tip can be used with any of 1-2-3's command ranges.

120 **Tip:** To obtain a listing of all the contents of every cell in the worksheet, use the /**Print Printer Options Other Cell-Formulas** command.

This command causes the contents of the specified print range to be printed, not as a rectangular worksheet, but as a series of cell definitions, one cell to a line. Listings created with /**Print Printer Options Other Cell-Formula** are handy for documenting your worksheets. Remember, though, that a worksheet of 26 columns and 200 rows contains 5,000 cells and so requires 5,000 lines to print.

121 **Tip:** You can create a version of your worksheet that can be edited with a word processor and included in text documents using the /**Print File** command.

Have you ever wished that you could transmit a table or other information from 1-2-3 directly into your word processor? You can, with the /**Print File** command. /**Print File** creates a printed report identical to those created with /**Print Printer**, but on disk instead of on paper. The disk version of the report is a standard ASCII text file that can be read into almost any word processor.

For more on the /**P**rint **F**ile command, see the Tips on sharing data with other programs.

122   Tip: You can include dates and page numbers in headers and footers and vary the alignment of the headers and footers with certain 1-2-3 options.

The /**P**rint **P**rinter **O**ptions command allows you a great deal of flexibility in formatting your printed reports. The **H**eader and **F**ooter choices can be used to create standard header and footer lines that appear at the top of all of your printed reports. 1-2-3 even offers the ability to put the current date and a page number in a header or footer. The date is entered by including the symbol "@" in the header or footer text. The page number is entered by using the symbol "#". You can also specify whether portions of a header or footer should be left-justified, right-justified, or centered by separating sections of the string with vertical bars (|).

For example, if you issue the /**P**rint **P**rinter **O**ptions **H**eader command and enter the string

> **Report Date: @ | Sales Forecast | Company Confidential**

You create a header that looks like this:

Report Date: 12-Mar-84   Sales Forecast   Company Confidential

If you select the **F**ooter option and enter the string

> | -#-

the result is a page number set off by hyphens and centered at the bottom of every page.

7
Functions

The @SUM Function

123 **Tip:** When possible, include an extra row or column in your @SUM ranges.

Consider the example shown in Figure 66. You've created a simple worksheet that summarizes the total performance for your three salespersons for the month of January.

```
         A        B        C        D
1                Jan
2 John       $132,833
3 Jenny      $156,289
4 James       $92,130
5             --------
6            $381,252
7
```

Figure 66

Cell B6 contains the @SUM formula

    B6: @SUM(B2..B4)

Suppose you add a new salesperson and want to add a row to the summary worksheet. You position the cursor on row 5, issue the /**W**orksheet **I**nsert **R**ow command, and add the new salesperson's name and amount in the new row. But there's a problem with this new worksheet—the formula in cell B7 is still

    B7: @SUM(B2..B4)

It does not include the new data. You need to edit this cell to change it to the new correct formula

    B7: @SUM(B2..B5)

Editing this one formula is no problem, but imagine how much time could be involved if the worksheet included hundreds of functions to be changed.

Fortunately, there is a better way. If the original formula in B6 had been

    B6: @SUM(B2..B5)

then the formula would have been automatically adjusted to

    B7: @SUM(B2..B6)

when the new row was added. Because the original cell B5 contains a label—a set of hyphens—which 1-2-3 gives a value of 0, including this cell in the range will not affect the value of the function. But including this cell provides a way to add a new row at the bottom of the column without forcing you to edit the @SUM function.

The @AVG Function

124   **Trap:** A blank cell and a cell containing a zero are not the same to 1-2-3's @AVG function.

The @AVG function computes the average, or mean, of the values in a range of cells. For example, the function

    @AVG(A1..A4)

returns the value 5 from the worksheet shown in Figure 67.

	A	B	C
1	2		
2	4		
3	6		
4	8		
5			

Figure 67

If we change the function to

@AVG(A1..A5)

the result is still 5. In making the calculation, the @AVG function ignored cell A5, which is blank. But if we fill cell A5 with the value 0, the function will return the value 4. Be alert for this difference when you use @AVG.

125   Trap: If you use the @COUNT function on a one-cell range, you may get surprising results.

The result of using @COUNT on a one-cell range is always 1. The value 1 is returned even if the cell being @COUNTed is blank. This is odd because @COUNT is supposed to tell you the number of nonblank cells in a range. Fortunately, the number of situations in which you can get in trouble with @COUNT is probably small. This problem is more likely to cause trouble when you are using the function in a macro. The chapter on Macros shows a Trick that solves the problem.

The @ROUND Function

126   Trap: The @ROUND function and **/R**ange Format Fixed command do not accomplish the same thing.

It is easy to get confused about the difference between 1-2-3's @ROUND function and the /**R**ange Format Fixed command. Both cause numbers to appear in the worksheet with a specific number of decimal places. For example, the function

@ROUND(1234.4444444,2)

results in the value 1234.44. If we format a cell containing the value 1234.44444 with the /**R**ange Format Fixed command, the cell contents also display as 1234.44. Although these numbers look alike, they are, in fact, different. The @ROUND function actually rounds the number off to two decimal places; all digits following the number specified are dropped. The /**R**ange Format command, on the other hand, simply causes the value to be displayed with two decimal places; all the other digits are retained, even though you don't see them.

As an example, consider the cases in Figure 68. The first column shows the values stored in two cells; an @SUM function totals those values. Column 2 shows the same addition, but this time the two values have been formatted to display in fixed format with two decimal places. Although the values seem to be rounded off to two places, the actual values are still accurate to three places. The sum appears to be incorrect; that is, 123.03+123.03 does not equal 246.05. In the third case, the values have been modified with the function @ROUND(123.025,2). In this case the total agrees with the numbers being added.

Values Stored	Values Displayed as /**R**ange Format Fixed **2**	Values Rounded to 2 Places
123.025	123.03	123.03
123.025	123.03	123.03
-------	------	------
246.050	246.05	246.06

Figure 68

127   Tip: The @ROUND function can accept a negative number as its second argument.

If you want to round the value 123.025 off to the hundreds place, you can do so with the function

@ROUND(123.025,-2)

The result of this function will be 100.

128   Trap: The @INT (value) function and the @ROUND(Value,0) functions are not the same.

The @INT function truncates all digits to the right of the decimal. The @ROUND function rounds a number, taking into account the fraction portion of the number before it is rounded. For example, @INT (1234.56) returns the value 1234, while the function @ROUND (1234.56,0) returns the value 1235.

The @PV and @NPV Functions

129 Trap: The @PV and @NPV functions are different.

The @PV function is a specialized case of the @NPV function. @PV computes the present value of a stream of equal payments. @NPV computes the net present value of any stream of payments even if the amounts of the payments are different.

130 Tip: When you use the @NPV function, make sure your periods are correct.

The @NPV function assumes that the first value in the range being discounted represents a flow that occurs at the *end* of the first period. For example, if cell A1 contains the value 110 and B2 contains the value 0, the function

    @NPV(.1,A1..B2)

returns the value 100. (B2 is included only to meet the requirement that the @NPV function operate on at least a two-cell range. Because B2 contains a zero, it has no impact on the calculation.) Notice that the @NPV function has discounted the value in A1; that is, the function assumes that the value in A1 is a flow that occurs at the end of the first period.

131 Trick: If you work with problems where the flows do not occur exactly one year (or month), two years, and so forth from the current date, you'll need to manipulate the @NPV function to achieve the correct answer.

Assume that you want to make an investment that will pay three payments of $100. The first will occur in 6 months, the second in 18 months, and the last in 30 months. This set of flows is shown in Figure 69.

	A	B	C	D
1	100	100	100	
2				
3				

Figure 69

If you want to use a discount rate of 10% per year, the following function

$$(@NPV(.10,B1..C1)+A1)/1.05$$

computes the correct NPV. The first part of the equation computes the net present value of the second and third payments up to a date 6 months from the present. This net present value is added to the payment that will occur in 6 months, and the total is divided by 1.05 to discount it to the present. Dividing by 1.05 is the same as computing the present value at 10% per year of the amount you'll have in 6 months.

If this formula is confusing to you, don't worry. Net present value analysis is not simple; it is frequently confusing to people who are not experienced with it. For a more detailed explanation of the @NPV function, see page 157 in *Using 1-2-3*.

132   Tip: If you forget the exact form of a 1-2-3 function, use the {Help} key to review the form quickly.

Sometimes even experienced 1-2-3 users forget the exact form of a 1-2-3 function. For instance, do you remember the proper order of the principal, interest rate, and term factors in the @PV function? If you forget the function, however, don't forget that {Help} is always one key away in 1-2-3. Pressing {Help} and following the Help menus lets you quickly verify the proper form of a function.

The @HLOOKUP and @VLOOKUP Functions

133   Tip: @HLOOKUP and @VLOOKUP can be used to create mini-data-bases.

The @HLOOKUP and @VLOOKUP functions can be used to create minidata-bases that can be accessed without the use of the /**Data Query** commands. These functions can look up information stored in a preconfigured table in the worksheet. Figure 70 shows a simple vertical lookup table.

	A	B	C	D
1	1	12		
2	3	16		
3	7	200		
4	10	15		
5	15	134		
6	100	17		

Figure 70

There are several things to notice about this table. First, the values in column A are in ascending numeric order. These are the key numbers that will be looked up by the @VLOOKUP function. Second, for each value in column A there is a value in column B. The values in column B will be returned by the function.

Third, the @VLOOKUP function has the form

@VLOOKUP(key,table range,offset)

The *key* is the value you want to look up. The *table range* defines the location and size of the table, and the *offset* describes the location in the table of the value that should be returned by the function. (The form of @HLOOKUP is identical except for the function name. @HLOOKUP works on a table that is arranged horizontally instead of vertically.) A function that will look up information from the table shown Figure 70 is

@VLOOKUP(3,A1..B6,1)

This function looks up the value 3 in the table and returns the value next to 3 in column B—16.

There are many rules for setting up and using @HLOOKUP and @VLOOKUP functions. If you want to know more about these basic rules, see Chapter 6 of *Using 1-2-3* or consult your Lotus 1-2-3 Manual.

134 Trap: The offset used in the @HLOOKUP and @VLOOKUP functions can be confusing.

The last term of every @HLOOKUP or @VLOOKUP function is the offset. This term tells the function which column or row of the table contains the data that should be returned. For example, in the function

@VLOOKUP(12,A1..B6,1)

the offset 1 tells the table to look for the data to be returned in the column with an offset of 1.

The problem is that the column with an offset of 1 is the second column in the table—B. Column A is considered to have an offset of 0. In all lookup tables the first row or column is assigned an offset of 0; the next row or column an offset of 1; and so on. If you are not familiar with the @LOOKUP functions, this rule can be confusing.

135 **Trap:** If your @HLOOKUP or @VLOOKUP function returns an @ERR, check to see whether the offset and the table range are compatible.

Consider the following function:

@HLOOKUP(10,A1..E5,5)

Can you tell at a glance what the error in this function is? Notice that this horizontal table, as defined by the term A1..E5, is 5 rows deep, but that the offset term is 5. The maximum offset possible with a five-row lookup table is 4 (0,1,2,3,4), so the offset of 5 causes an error.

We've found this error many times while modifying our own lookup tables. If your function returns an ERR value, you might want to check to see whether you've made this mistake.

136 **Trap:** The @HLOOKUP and @VLOOKUP functions can be used to look up only values from a table.

One of the limitations of the @LOOKUP functions is that they cannot be used to look up text from a table. For example, if we had the table shown in Figure 71, the function

@VLOOKUP(2,A1..B4,1)

would return the value 0 instead of the label "Sam" because "Sam" is impossible to look up.

	A	B	C	D
1	1 David			
2	2 Sam			
3	3 Steve			
4	4 Jenny			
5				

Figure 71

137   **Trick:** You can simulate a "label lookup" by using the **/D**ata **Q**uery command in a macro.

Releases 1 and 1A of 1-2-3 do not allow us to use a label either as the argument of the @VLOOKUP or @HLOOKUP functions or as an element in the lookup table. This limitation is fairly serious because we often want to translate a numeric code into a descriptive label. Figure 72 shows such a situation. We want to print a report on "Median Income by County" in California. However, the actual county names are in another table. We really want to do a "label lookup," but we can't with Release 1A.

	I	J	K	L	M
83					
84	MEDIAN INCOME BY COUNTY				
85	=======================				
86					
87	County Code	County Name		Income	
88	02			$15,000	
89	05			$18,000	
90	03			$22,000	
91	01			$10,000	
92	04			$12,000	
93					

Figure 72

First, we set up our "COUNTY NAME TABLE" (Figure 73), define it as a /**D**ata **Q**uery **I**nput range, and set up corresponding **C**riterion and **O**utput ranges (Figure 73). We use /**R**ange **N**ame **C**reate to give the name "CODE" to the "CODE" field in the criterion range and the name "NAME" to the "NAME" field in the output range. We then construct the macro shown in Figure 74. This macro assumes that we start with the cursor resting on the first "COUNTY CODE" in the report area (I88). The first part of the macro counts the number of rows in the report. (See the section about Macros for a detailed discussion of this technique.)

	R	S	T	U
81		COUNTY NAME TABLE		
82		=================		
83		Code	Name	
84		01	Yolo	
85		02	Merced	
86		03	Marin	
87		04	Kern	
88		05	Alameda	
89				
90		CRITERION RANGE		
91		===============		
92		Code	Name	
93		04		
94				
95		OUTPUT RANGE		
96		============		
97		Code	Name	
98		04	Kern	
99				

Figure 73

The second part of the macro is a loop that we go through once for each row in the report area. Each time through, we copy the "COUNTY CODE" for that row to the "CODE" field of the criterion range in Figure 73 and execute a /Data Query. (This code assumes that the last type of query we executed was of the Extract type.) As a result of this query, the corresponding "COUNTY NAME" from the table will be extracted to the "NAME" field at T98 in the output range. The macro then copies this name into the "COUNTY NAME" column in the report and continues to the next row. We go out of the loop and end the macro when we get to the last row of the report area.

Figure 75 shows what the report looks like after the macro has been executed.

```
         I        J         K        L        M        N        O
101 \L           /rncHERE~{end}{down}~        Count cells
102              /dfNCELLS~                     in column
103              @COUNT(HERE)~~~
104              /rndHERE~                     Delete range
105              /dfCOUNT~0~~~
106 LOOP         /c~CODE~                      Copy County code to
107              {query}                        Criterion range & Query
108              /cNAME~{right}~               Co. Name to Income Report
109              /dfCOUNT~                     Increment Loop
110              COUNT+1~~~                     Counter
111              {down}                        Down to next row
112              /xi(COUNT<NCELLS)~/xgLOOP~    Loop test
113
114
115 NCELLS
116 COUNT
```

Figure 74

```
         I        J         K        L        M
83
84 MEDIAN INCOME BY COUNTY
85 =======================
86
87 County Code  County Name      Income
88 02           Merced           $15,000
89 05           Alameda          $18,000
90 03           Marin            $22,000
91 01           Yolo             $10,000
92 04           Kern             $12,000
93
```

Figure 75

The @CHOOSE Function

138 Tip: The @CHOOSE function is an even more compact way to store a data base.

The @CHOOSE function allows you to create a minidata-base in only one cell. The @CHOOSE function looks like this

@CHOOSE(key,value0,value1,value2,value3,...,valuen)

The key is the value used to look up one of the values from the "CHOOSE" list. A key of 0 will cause "value0" to be returned. A key of 2 will cause "value2" to be returned. (Notice that the same rules of numbering the offset we saw in the @LOOKUP functions are used in the @CHOOSE function.)

For example, the function

@CHOOSE(3,100,200,300,400,500)

will return the value 400. The function

@CHOOSE(0,100,200,300,400,500)

will return the value 100.

Most of the time the key in your @CHOOSE functions will be a cell reference. By varying the value in the key cell, you can easily vary the results of your @CHOOSE function.

139   Trick: By combining the @CHOOSE function and a lookup table, you can create dynamic lookup tables.

Consider the lookup table shown in Figure 76.

	A	B	C
1			
2			
3			
4	1	@CHOOSE(A1, 2, 3, 4, 5)	
5	2	@CHOOSE(A1, 3, 7, 3, 8)	
6	3	@CHOOSE(A1, 4, 5, 2, 9)	
7	4	@CHOOSE(A1, 10, 3, 6, 1)	
8	5	@CHOOSE(A1, 12, 66, 2, 1)	

Figure 76

The range B4..B8 has been formatted with the /**R**ange Format Text command. If we change the format back to General and enter a 1 in cell A1, the lookup table will look like Figure 77. If we enter a 3 in cell A1, the table will look like Figure 78.

	A	B	C	D
1	1			
2				
3				
4	1	3		
5	2	7		
6	3	5		
7	4	3		
8	5	66		

Figure 77

	A	B	C	D
1	3			
2				
3				
4	1	5		
5	2	8		
6	3	9		
7	4	1		
8	5	1		

Figure 78

The table changes as we enter different values in cell A1. Obviously, the @LOOKUP function operating on this table returns a different value for each different value in A1. Instead of needing four lookup tables, we can get by with only one and thus save memory and setup time. This technique can be used effectively to create dynamic tax tables and depreciation tables.

The @RAND Function

140 Tip: Don't forget the @RAND function.

@RAND can be very useful. We frequently use it, for example, to fill a worksheet with information that can be used to test a new technique. We simply enter the function @RAND in a cell and then /Copy that value into the entire range we want to test. The range is instantly filled with values, each one different.

The @RAND also has more serious uses in applications like Monte Carlo Simulation and other forms of risk analysis. Although you'll probably use @RAND less than you do other functions, don't forget that it is available.

The @MOD Function

141 Tip: The @MOD function can be extremely useful.

Consider the following problem. You have 1,457 Cabbage Patch dolls that you want to distribute evenly among your 7 toy stores. If you send the same number of dolls to each store, how many dolls will be left?

1-2-3 can answer this question easily with the @MOD function. @MOD computes the remainder of the division of two numbers. The function @MOD(1457,7) gives the correct remainder—1—instantly.

@MOD function can also be used in date arithmetic. In another Tip we show a technique using the @MOD function that can help you compute the sum of two dates.

The @IF Function

142 Tip: 1-2-3's @IF function can help you set up "variable" cells.

Suppose you are the sales manager at a small wholesale company. You want to build a 1-2-3 worksheet that computes the weekly commissions due your salespeople, but the problem is that your salespeople work on an escalating commission plan. Each salesperson gets a 2% commission for sales under $10,000 per week; 4% for sales between $10,000 and $20,000; 6% for sales between $20,000 and $30,000; and 8% for more than $30,000. How can you create a formula in 1-2-3 that can compute the correct commissions with the variable rates?

You can do it with the @IF function. The formula

@IF(SALES>30000, 1200+.08*(SALES-30000),@IF(SALES>20000, 600+.06*(SALES-20000),@IF(SALES>10000, 200+0.04*(SALES-10000), 0.02*SALES)))

does the trick. This formula includes three nested @IF functions. 1-2-3 places almost no limit on nesting @IF functions this way.

Combinations

143   Trap: If you combine many functions in one long formula, you may confuse yourself or others.

Because you can use a function wherever you can use a number, you can nest functions within other functions. You can take this a long way before 1-2-3 gives you a "formula too long" message. For example, the following is a valid formula:

@IF(F13>@MAX(A5..A10),10,@HLOOKUP(@ABS(A27), B5..B7,1))

Unfortunately, it's also obscure! It is better to put the lookup function in a separate cell, to which you give the name "LOOKUP." Then enter the following instead of the original long formula:

@IF(F13>@MAX(A5..A10),10,LOOKUP)

144   Tip: You can use @ERR to force entry of certain data items in the worksheet.

Suppose we want to make sure that someone makes an entry in every cell of the table in Figure 79. The fact that we've "preloaded" the table with @ERR in every cell means that if the data entry person forgets an entry, the total at the bottom will show as ERR, thus making it obvious that something has been omitted. (There's an @SUM formula in the total cell.)

145   Tip: To check quickly for an @ERR cell anywhere in a large worksheet, create a range that covers the whole worksheet and then use @ISERR to check an @SUM on that range.

Figure 80 shows a sample worksheet in which we have a cell that shows ERR (K149). If this were a large worksheet, it might not be so obvious.

```
     A         B         C
1 Item      Amount
2 --------- --------
3 Salt                ERR |
4 Cereal              ERR |<=ITEMS
5 Bread               ERR |
6 Oranges             ERR |
7 --------- --------
8 Total               ERR
```

Figure 79

What we've done here is to give the entire range J144..M153 the name "ALL." We then placed the function

> @SUM($ALL)

in cell K156. When any cell in the range "ALL" evaluates as ERR, this function also evaluates as ERR, telling us immediately that something's amiss. Note that K156 indeed evaluates as ERR.

```
         I       J       K       L       M       N
141
142
143
144              1       6       11      16
145              1       6       11      16
146              1       6       11      16
147              1       6       11      16
148              1       6       11      16
149              1       ERR     11      16
150              1       6       11      16
151              1       6       11      16
152              1       6       11      16
153              1       6       11      16
154
155
156                      ERR
157
```

Figure 80

If you have macro control, you can go one step further. You can place a /XI@ISERR statement in the macro to check for an ERR in cell K156. If there is an ERR, you can have the macro take appropriate action. This is one way to have a macro stop itself if certain kinds of error conditions occur.

146   Tip: If a formula evaluates as @ERR as soon as you enter it, you may be dividing by 0.

Sometimes when building a worksheet, you'll enter a division formula in which the denominator (the bottom part of the fraction) includes a reference to an empty cell. If so, the formula will evaluate as ERR at first. Don't be dismayed. Things should straighten themselves out as soon as you enter a nonzero number into the cell to which the formula refers. In giving the ERR message, 1-2-3 is simply being mathematically reasonable. Dividing by 0 gives a result that is mathematically undefined, so 1-2-3 considers it to be an error and displays @ERR.

147   Tip: @ISERR and @NA can be used to remove unnecessary ERR and NA messages from the worksheet.

If you think that a cell may have an ERR value for any reason, but you don't want that ERR message to display on the worksheet, you can use the @ISERR function to hide the message. For example, the formula

@IF(@ISERR(A1/A2),0,A1/A2)

will trap an error that could result from dividing A1 by A2. Such an ERR could arise because of a zero or a blank in cell A2.

Date Arithmetic

Manipulating the Date Function

148 **Tip:** 1-2-3's Date functions are among the program's most valuable features.

1-2-3 allows you to enter a date into a cell by using either the @TODAY function for the current date or the @DATE function for any date. Although you enter the dates in a reasonably familiar form, 1-2-3 stores each date as a pure number equal to the number of days elapsed since December 31, 1899. For instance, January 1, 1984, is entered as @DATE(84,1,1) but is stored as the number 30687.

To display the date in a more understandable form, you can use any of the three Date formats: DD-MMM-YY, DD-MMM, or MMM-YY. Each of these formats is useful at different times. However, even when the date is displayed in one of these formats, it is still stored as 30687.

Because dates are just another kind of number, you can perform arithmetic functions on them, compare them to each other in logical tests in criterion ranges, and do other kinds of things that you normally do with numbers. For example, Figure 81 shows a table used to plan the tasks involved in building a house. Both the "DAYS" and "SLACK" columns contain formulas (shown in Text format) that refer to the dates in the "START" and "END" columns. Figure 82 shows the same table in General format. You can see that the dates evaluate in formulas just like other numbers. The "DAYS" columns shows the number of days between "START" and "END" for each task. The "SLACK" column shows the number of slack days between the end of one task and the start of another that is dependent on the first task. We have entries in the "SLACK" column only where such a dependency exists.

```
         I        J         K        L       M       N
161 PROJECT:BUILDING A HOUSE
162 =========================
163
164 TASK #    DESCRIPTION START      DAYS      END      SLACK
165 -------------------------------------------------------------
166       1 GET PERMIT   19-Oct +M166-K166  25-Oct
167       2 DIG FOOTINGS 25-Oct +M167-K167  26-Oct +K167-M166
168       3 ORDER CEMENT 24-Oct +M168-K168  26-Oct
169       4 POUR CEMENT  28-Oct +M169-K169  30-Oct +K169-M168
170
```

Figure 81

```
         I        J         K        L       M       N
161 PROJECT:BUILDING A HOUSE
162 =========================
163
164 TASK #    DESCRIPTION START      DAYS      END      SLACK
165 -------------------------------------------------------------
166       1 GET PERMIT   19-Oct +M166-K166  25-Oct
167       2 DIG FOOTINGS 25-Oct +M167-K167  26-Oct         0
168       3 ORDER CEMENT 24-Oct +M168-K168  26-Oct
169       4 POUR CEMENT  28-Oct +M169-K169  30-Oct         2
170
```

Figure 82

149 Trap: A Date Value and a Date Format are two different things.

1-2-3 users sometimes are confused by the two-step method of creating a date in 1-2-3. Don't let dates confuse you. Remember that to create a 1-2-3 date, you must first use the @DATE or @TODAY function to enter the date, and then you must **F**ormat the cell containing the date to display it in a conventional form.

150 **Trap:** A date displayed in the DD-MMM-YY format cannot be displayed in a standard-width column.

One unavoidable problem with 1-2-3's date formats is that the **Date 1** format, DD-MMM-YY, is too wide to fit in a standard nine-character column. To overcome this problem, either widen the column containing the date to ten or more characters with the /**W**orksheet **C**olumn **S**et command or the /**W**orksheet **G**lobal **C**olumn command (which changes the default column width), or choose a different format.

151 **Tip:** To create a date that falls after December 31, 1999, use a year number over 100.

The year term of the @DATE function accepts only the last two digits of the year number. For example, 1984 is entered as 84 and 1999 as 99. The only exception is dates in the years 2000 through 2099. For these dates enter the year as a three-digit number; for example, enter the date March 3, 2002, as @DATE(102,3,3).

152 **Tip:** Like all functions, the terms of a Date function can be cell references instead of simple numbers.

All 1-2-3 functions allow the use of cell references instead of numbers in any argument. For example, the function

A5: @CHOOSE(A1,A4,A5,A6,A7,A8)

is just as acceptable as

A5: @CHOOSE(1,4,5,1,8,9)

Date functions are just like other functions in this regard. For example, the function

A5: (D1) @DATE(A1,A2,A3)

is just as meaningful to 1-2-3 as the function

A5: (D1) @DATE(84,1,1)

as long as one condition is met: the values in cells A1, A2, and A3 must fall within 1-2-3's acceptable limits.

153 **Trap:** The @DATE function will not accept entries for the month, day, or year that are not "correct" values.

1-2-3 expects the year portion of a date to have a value between 1 and 199, the month portion to fall between 1 and 12, and the day term to be between 1 and 31 (or 30 or 28, depending on the month number). If one term falls outside these limits, the @DATE function will return an ERR message.

You may think that this is a rather obvious trap; everyone knows, for instance, that there is no thirteenth month, so why would anyone create a date like @DATE(84,13,2)? But consider the case shown in Figure 83.

	A	B	C	D	E
1		Start	Duration	End	
2	Year	84	0	84	
3	Month	12	1	13	
4	Day	2	0	2	
5					
6	ERR				

Figure 83

This worksheet is a simple project-planning template. The numbers in column B represent the starting date for the project. Column C shows the duration of the project. Since this project will take one month to complete, we've entered a 1 in cell C3. The cells in column D compute the completion date by adding the start date and the duration; for example, cell D3 contains the formula

    D3: +B3+C3

Because we want to display this date as a single number, we've created a date function in cell A6

    A6: (D1) @DATE(D2,D3,D4)

The 13 in cell D3, however, causes this function to evaluate as ERR. This is a "real world" case where we would want 1-2-3 automatically to carry over a year (12 months) from the months column to the years column so that the date is legal. But the program can't do it.

154 Tip: You can use the @DAY, @MONTH, or @YEAR commands to extract the day, month, or year portion of a date to another cell.

1-2-3 includes three functions—@DAY, @MONTH, and @YEAR—that can be used to isolate the day, month, and year portions of dates. For example, the function @DAY(@DATE(84,1,1)) returns the number 1; the function @MONTH(@DATE(84,1,1)) returns the month term, 1; and the function @YEAR(@DATE(84,1,1)) returns 84, the year portion.

The arguments for the @DAY, @MONTH, and @YEAR functions do not have to be @DATE functions. As always, these functions can have cell references as their arguments. For example, if cell A1 contains the function @DATE(84,3,21), and cell A2 the function @DAY(A1), A2 still returns the value 21.

155 Tip: You can use @YEAR, @MONTH, and @DAY within @DATE.

Suppose you want to create a column of dates that refer to the first day of a series of succeeding months. You can use the @MONTH function as an argument of @DATE to accomplish this. Here's how. Suppose that our first date is 01-Feb and we've placed it as @DATE(84,2,1) in A10. We now put the following formula in A11:

@DATE(@YEAR(A10),@MONTH(A10)+1,@DAY(A10))

This gives us 01-Mar in A11. We can then copy this same formula all the way down the column. Of course, this formula runs into problems when we get past December, since the @DATE function will not accept a month greater than 12. You could handle this with a more complex formula. Try to create one as an exercise.

156 Trick: To convert the result of any @YEAR function into a four-digit year number, just add 1900.

In the previous Tip the function @YEAR(@DATE(84,1,1)) returned the value 84. Although this is an understandable representation for the year 1984, there are times when you'd like to see the *19* as well as the *84*. To make this conversion, just add 1900 to the @YEAR function. For example, the following formula equals 1984:

@YEAR(@DATE(84,1,1))+1900

This Trick works just as well if the date in question falls after December 31, 1999. For example, the function

@YEAR(@DATE(100,1,1))

returns the number 100. Adding 1900 to this number creates the year number 2000, the correct result.

Using Date Arithmetic

157 **Tip:** You can use date arithmetic in a macro as a "tickler" to tell you when a certain date condition has been reached.

Suppose you have the project-management application in Tip 148 controlled by a macro, and you want the macro to let you know when the date to order the cement arrives. First, make this an automatic startup macro.

An automatic startup macro is one named \0. Beginning with Release 1A, during /**F**ile **R**etrieve 1-2-3 checks for the existence of a \0 macro in the worksheet being retrieved. If 1-2-3 finds the \0 macro, it is executed automatically.

Figure 84 shows the macro, which assumes that you've used /**R**ange **N**ame **C**reate to name K168 "CEMENT_DATE" and K172 "MES-SAGE." Therefore, when the current date equals "CEMENT_DATE," you get the message shown in Figure 85.

	AA	AB	AC	AD	AE	AF
1	\Ø	/xi(CEMENT_DATE=@TODAY)~/xgTICKLE~				Cement order date?
2		/xq				No--quit.
3	TICKLE	{goto}MESSAGE~				Yes--message!
4		{edit}ORDER CEMENT!~				
5						
6						

Figure 84

158 **Trap:** The @TODAY function will work correctly only if you supplied the correct System Date to the operating system when you booted up.

If you fail to supply the correct date to DOS when you boot your system, your date arithmetic in 1-2-3 will be incorrect. There are also

```
          I        J        K        L        M        N
161 PROJECT:BUILDING A HOUSE
162 =========================
163
164 TASK #    DESCRIPTION START     DAYS      END      SLACK
165 -------------------------------------------------------------
166       1 GET PERMIT   19-Oct +M166-K166  25-Oct
167       2 DIG FOOTINGS 25-Oct +M167-K167  26-Oct       0
168       3 ORDER CEMENT 24-Oct +M168-K168  26-Oct
169       4 POUR CEMENT  28-Oct +M169-K169  30-Oct       2
170
171
172
173       MESSAGE=>  ORDER CEMENT!
174
```

Figure 85

other good reasons to make sure you supply the correct System Date and Time every time you boot up. For instance, supplying the date ensures that your disk directories show the correct date and time for each file.

159   **Tip:** If you have a habit of skipping through the Time and Date commands in DOS, get a system clock for your PC.

The safest way to get the correct date is to have a battery-backed clock in your computer. You can get such a clock on many memory expansion boards available for the IBM PC. Then you can set up an AUTO-EXEC.BAT file to query the clock and set the date and time automatically when you boot up.

160   **Tip:** To enter a large number of consecutive dates, use the **/D**ata **F**ill function.

The /**D**ata **F**ill command is used to enter series of numbers into the 1-2-3 worksheet. Because 1-2-3 treats functions exactly like numbers (in every case that we can think of), the /**D**ata **F**ill command can be used to enter a series of dates. See Chapter 2 for more on the /**D**ata **F**ill command.

9
Files

Loading and Saving

161 Trap: The **/F**ile **R**etrieve command destroys the worksheet in memory.

/File **R**etrieve is the primary command used to load a file into the 1-2-3 worksheet. However, this command erases the current worksheet before it loads the new file. If the worksheet is empty or contains information you don't care about, it doesn't matter that /File **R**etrieve erases the worksheet. But if the worksheet contains important data that hasn't been saved, issuing the /File **R**etrieve command will lose the data forever.

162 Trap: Do not remove your data disk after a **/F**ile **S**ave command until the red light goes off on your disk drive.

There's a possible problem here because 1-2-3 flashes "READY" in the upper-right corner of the screen just before 1-2-3 has actually completed writing the file to the disk. What's even more misleading is that the red light on the drive may go off momentarily and then come back on again before the drive has entirely finished. If you try to remove your disk as soon as you see the "READY," you may damage the disk, and the disk drive will just sit there and "whirr" at you with the red light on until you either reboot or put a disk back in the drive. Putting a disk back in the drive can also damage the disk, so you may be forced to reboot without having saved the current version of your worksheet. Wait a few seconds after the "READY" before you remove your disk.

163 Tip: You can have 1-2-3 load a particular worksheet automatically whenever the program is loaded.

With Release 1A, when 1-2-3 loads, it always looks for a file called AUTO123.WKS on the default disk. If such a file exists, 1-2-3 will automatically **/F**ile **R**etrieve that file into memory.

This feature can be particularly useful when you've created a model for someone else to run, and you want the model run with a minimum of effort and chance for error.

On the IBM PC, you can further automate by creating on your Lotus disk an AUTOEXEC.BAT file that contains the single command "Lotus."

This file causes the operating system to prompt for the date and time and then automatically load the Lotus Access System menu when the system is booted. At this point the user simply presses {Enter} to load 1-2-3. As 1-2-3 loads, it will check disk B: (or other default disk) for the file AUTO123.WKS. If the file is found, it will automatically be loaded into the worksheet.

164 Tip: You can have 1-2-3 execute a particular macro automatically after a **/F**ile **R**etrieve command.

With Release 1A, whenever 1-2-3 executes a **/F**ile **R**etrieve command, the program searches the worksheet being loaded for a macro named \0. If a \0 macro exists, it will be executed automatically immediately after the worksheet is loaded.

You can use this feature together with AUTO123.WKS to create a 1-2-3 model that is fully automated from the beginning. Figure 86 shows a \0 macro that presents a menu of options. (The menu shown activates a series of macros, which we assume are present elsewhere in the worksheet.)

```
        I        J         K          L           M          N          O
1
2  \0       /xmMENU1~
3
4  MENU1  Load      Backup      Update       Graph       Print      Quit
5         Load File Backup File Make Changes Create Graph Print File End Session
6         /xgL_MAC~ /xgB_MAC~   /xgU_MAC~    /xgG_MAC~   /xgP_MAC~  /xgQ_MAC~
7
```

Figure 86

165 **Tip:** Create a macro that will force you to back up key worksheets automatically.

It's a good practice to keep a second disk with current backup copies of all important worksheets. Floppy disks (and even hard disks) can get damaged, so you may one day be dismayed to find that an important worksheet file is unreadable.

Because it's easy to forget to back up your files, create a macro to do it for you. Figure 87 shows a Backup macro. Because this macro has been named \0, it will run automatically when the worksheet is retrieved. This macro prompts you to change disks; then the macro uses the /File Save command to create the backup copy.

```
         I        J          K          L           M          N          O
41
42  \0       /xmBKUP?~
43
44  BKUP?    Backup
45           Insert disk to back up current worksheet; then press Enter.
46           /xgBK_MAC~
47
48  BK_MAC   /fsSALESB~              SAVE BACKUP OF CURRENT WORKSHEET
49           r                       REPLACE OLD COPY
```

Figure 87

If you want to stop the macro before it creates the backup file, just press {Ctrl} {Break}. As always, {Ctrl} {Break} will stop the macro in its tracks.

166 **Tip:** If your files are taking too long to load, consider purchasing a hard disk.

One of the few drawbacks of 1-2-3 is that it creates worksheet files that are much larger than those of most other spreadsheet programs. (This is due in part to the extra information 1-2-3 must store in a worksheet in order to make possible "Natural" order of recalculation.) As a result, it can take quite a while to read and write 1-2-3 worksheet files on floppy disks. A hard disk makes loading much faster. Beginning with Release 1A, 1-2-3 can be installed on a hard disk.

167 **Tip:** The **/File Directory** command can be used to change the default disk drive.

The standard default drive for 1-2-3 is B:; that is, drive B is the active disk for storing and retrieving files. Sometimes, however, you'll want to use a different drive as the default. You can do this with the /File Directory command. For example, to change the default drive to A:, issue the command /File Directory A:. Until you specifically re-designate the default directory, 1-2-3 will use drive A: as the default.

If you want to load only one file from a nondefault drive, you don't need to go through the whole /File Directory command. To load a single file, simply issue the /File Retrieve command and preface the name of the file you are loading with the letter name of the correct drive. For example, if you want to load file BUDGET.WKS from drive A:, issue the command /File Retrieve **A:Budget**.

168 **Tip:** To change the default directory permanently, use the **/Work**sheet **Global Default Directory** command.

The /File Directory command changes the default drive only for the duration of the current 1-2-3 session. When 1-2-3 is reloaded into memory the next time, the default will revert to standard. To change the default directory permanently, use the /Worksheet Global Default Directory command to specify the new directory and the /Worksheet Global Default Update command to store the change to the 1-2-3 configuration file.

This command is especially important for 1-2-3 users with a fixed disk and DOS 2.0. Under these circumstances, it is unlikely that you will want the default drive to be B:. Instead, the default will probably be something like C:\Plan\123\Files. This directory can be specified as the default with the /File Directory command.

169 Trap: Beware of wild-card characters in file names you supply to /File Erase.

The /File Erase command will accept wild-card characters (* and ?) in response to its file name prompt. If you decide to use a wild-card character, be careful. You may delete more files than you really want to. You should also be aware that if you supply nothing but an asterisk in response to the file name prompt, you will delete all files on the disk of the type selected from the Erase menu.

170 Trap: It is possible to create a worksheet file that is too large to fit on a single diskette.

Disks formatted under DOS 1.1 have a capacity of about 320K, but DOS 2.0 and DOS 2.1 format disks with a capacity of about 360K. If your computer has more than 400K of memory, you can create a worksheet that is too large to save on a single disk.

The chances of this happening are small; few worksheets ever reach a size that cannot be saved on a floppy disk. If you do run into this problem, though, you have two choices: get a hard disk (any hard disk has the capacity for any worksheet) or use the technique explained in the next Tip to divide the worksheet before saving it.

171 Tip: Use /File Xtract Formulas to break up a file into smaller files for storage on several disks.

If you do create a file that is too large to fit on a single diskette, use the /File Xtract command to save the worksheet in several parts. For example, suppose you create a worksheet that is 1,000 rows deep and 100 columns wide. Such a sheet may be too big to save on one diskette. You can, however, save the worksheet by the following procedure:

1. Issue the /File Xtract Formulas command and specify the range to be saved as A1..AX500. Choose file names for the partial worksheets that will remind you of their contents.

2. After the first portion of the worksheet is saved, replace the disk in the default drive with a blank disk.

3. Issue the /File Xtract Formulas command again, this time saving the bottom half of the worksheet, A501..AX1000.

When you want to retrieve this worksheet into memory, use the following sequence of commands:

1. **/F**ile **R**etrieve the first half of the worksheet from the first diskette.

2. Move the cursor to cell A501.

3. Replace the disk in the default drive with the disk containing the second half of the worksheet.

4. Issue the /File **C**ombine **C**opy **E**ntire command and specify the name of the file containing the second half of the worksheet.

This method of saving large files is far from perfect, however; for one thing, any range names in the second half of the worksheet will be lost when that file is Combined with the first half of the worksheet. In addition, you must be very careful when saving and loading the worksheet to position the cursor properly and specify the range names correctly.

Extracting

172 **Tip:** To save only values (not formulas) into a file, use the **/F**ile **X**tract **V**alues command.

Some spreadsheet programs have a **V**alues option on the **C**opy command that allows you to make a copy of a range that turns all formulas into their current pure values. This feature is useful for certain types of accumulation and consolidation. Unfortunately, Releases 1 and 1A of 1-2-3 do not have such an option.

To convert a series of formulas into pure values in 1-2-3, use the /File **X**tract **V**alues command. This command saves the range specified by the user and translates all formulas and functions in this range into their current values. However, a file saved with the /File **X**tract **V**alues command cannot be used for "what if" analysis. Because all the formulas in the worksheet have been converted to values, the formulas cannot adapt to changes made to the worksheet.

An alternative way to convert a cell from a formula into its pure value is to use the {Edit} and {Calc} keys together. This method converts the cells from formulas to values one cell at a time.

173 **Tip:** The **/**File **X**tract **V**alues command can be used to "freeze" the current status of a worksheet.

Sometimes you'll want to create a "snapshot" of a worksheet that retains all the current values in the sheet permanently, perhaps when you want to share the results but not the formulas of a worksheet with another person. Because the /File Extract Values command saves only the values in a file and not the formulas, it is perfect for "freezing" a worksheet.

174 **Tip:** The **/**File **X**tract **F**ormulas command can be used to save portions of a worksheet.

Occasionally, you'll want to save a portion of a worksheet into a separate file, perhaps to reuse the portion in other worksheets. To save a part of the current worksheet, issue the /File Xtract Formulas command and specify the range of cells that you wish to save. The range can be as small as a single cell or as large as the entire worksheet.

The file that results from a /File Xtract Formulas command contains all the formulas, range names, and graph names found in the range saved.

Combining

175 **Tip:** Use the **/**File **C**ombine command to load one worksheet, or part of a worksheet, on top of another.

If you want to "cut and paste" one worksheet onto the worksheet already in memory, use the /File Combine Copy command with the cursor resting on the cell where you want the second worksheet to load; you will then have a file combining the two worksheets.

Do not confuse the /File Retrieve command with the /File Combine command. Remember that /File Retrieve erases the contents of the worksheet before loading the new file, but /File Combine preserves the contents of the first worksheet and loads a new file on top of the old.

176 **Trap:** If you don't use **/**File **C**ombine carefully, you can wipe out part of your existing worksheet.

The /File Combine command begins loading at the current cursor position. You, therefore, must be sure that you've positioned the cursor exactly where you want the Combined file before you execute /File Combine. Otherwise, the file being Combined can overwrite and erase important parts of the worksheet in memory.

To help avoid this problem, you should know the precise location of everything on the worksheet already in memory and the exact size of the worksheet (or range) that you're Combining. This is one good reason to keep up-to-date "maps" of each worksheet file.

177   Trap: When a file or range is Combined into the current worksheet, the new file does not bring any range names with it.

If you're wondering why some macros that you brought into the current worksheet with /File Combine aren't working, this may be the reason. Any range names in the file being Combined (including the names of macros in that file) are not Combined into the worksheet in memory.

One way to compensate is to place all the labels used as range names in your macros in a column just to the left of the macros (and menus and work fields) themselves. Then you can quickly rename all necessary ranges with one /Range Name Labels Right command. For example, you could do this with the labels in Figure 87 by executing a /Range Name Labels Right command on the range I42..I48.

178   Trap: Even protected cells can be wiped out by /File Combine.

This is a subtle Trap because you would think that, with protection enabled, a protected cell would stay protected under just about any condition. This is not the case, however. The /File Combine command erases even protected cells in the worksheet in memory.

This Trap underlines the fact that you must be very careful with /File Combine to avoid wiping out an area of the current worksheet that you wanted to keep.

179   Trap: You can get puzzling results if you try to Combine with Add or Subtract over cells containing formulas.

When you use /File Combine Add or Subtract, numeric cells in the file being Combined are ignored if they overlap label or formula cells in the worksheet in memory. This feature protects your formulas from being changed but can sometimes create puzzling results. Figure 88 shows a worksheet used to estimate a small plumbing job. Column L contains formulas that are displayed in Text format. Suppose you want to combine the results of another estimate (shown in Figure 89) with this one. You've already created through the /File Xtract Values command a file that contains only the values in column L of the worksheet in Figure 89.

```
       I         J       K        L
21
22           ESTIMATE 1
23           ==========
24
25 ITEM      QUANTITY PRICE    EXTENSION
26 1/2"PIPE      10    $2.00 +J26*K26
27 1/4"PIPE      20    $1.50 +J27*K27
28 BRACKET       15    $2.75 +J28*K28
29 A-BOLT         3    $1.33 +J29*K29
30 1"COPPER      50    $1.00 +J30*K30
31
```

Figure 88

```
       I         J       K        L
21
22           ESTIMATE 2
23           ==========
24
25 ITEM      QUANTITY PRICE    EXTENSION
26 1/2"PIPE      15    $2.00     $30.00
27 1/4"PIPE      12    $1.50     $18.00
28 BRACKET       15    $2.75     $41.25
29 A-BOLT         3    $1.33      $3.99
30 1"COPPER      50    $1.00     $50.00
31
```

Figure 89

You next want to use the /File Combine Add Entire command to combine this second file into column L of Figure 88. If you try it, however, the command will have no effect. Because the *values* in the file being Combined are loaded on top of the *formulas* in column L of the worksheet in memory, the values will not be combined into the worksheet.

To make the Combine work, first turn the formulas in column L into pure values by performing an {Edit}{Calc} on each cell in the column (a good job for a macro if the column is a long one).

180 Tip: You can use **/F**ile **C**ombine **C**opy to produce a "simple" consolidation.

The consolidation of a number of similar tables is a common function in budgeting and certain other applications. The typical case is one in which you have budgets for several departments, and you want to consolidate the budgets into a division or company budget.

This is a relatively simple tip with 1-2-3, provided that all the detail budgets have exactly the same form. Figure 90 shows two divisional sales forecasts that have exactly the same form. Assume that both budgets are already on the disk with file names of BUDG1.WKS and BUDG2.WKS, respectively.

```
        A           B           C           D
  1 Division 1
  2
  3 Sales
  4   Widgets              $10,000
  5   Gadgets              $52,000
  6   Wombats              $32,000
  7
```

```
        A           B           C           D
  1 Division 2
  2
  3 Sales
  4   Widgets              $17,000
  5   Gadgets              $14,000
  6   Wombats              $73,000
  7
```

Figure 90

To consolidate these files, first /File **R**etrieve BUDG1.WKS and change the label in cell A1 to "Consolidated." With the cursor on A1, issue the command /File Combine Add Entire, specifying BUDG2.WKS as the file to be combined. The results of this command are shown in Figure 91.

	A	B	C	D
1	Consolidated			
2				
3	Sales			
4	Widgets		$27,000	
5	Gadgets		$66,000	
6	Wombats		$105,000	
7				

Figure 91

If one department had an additional line (say for Didgets), or if one department had the same lines but in a different order, or if one department had multiple lines for Widgets, we would not get the correct result if we combined these files with /File Combine. The next Trick shows a different technique that can handle these kinds of complications.

181   Trick: To produce a complex consolidation, concatenate all the input tables into one, and then use a **/D**ata Table with @DSUM formulas.

The method we use here overcomes the limitations of the method of "simple" consolidation described in the previous Tip. It permits both the following complications:

1.   The detail lines can be in any order in all the input tables.

2.   Any table can have either zero or multiple lines for any possible detail item.

Figure 92 shows two departmental budgets that have the types of complications the "simple" method cannot deal with.

This Trick is rather complex, so let's go through it one step at a time. The first step is to /Copy the contents of both budgets into another part of the worksheet. We /Copy the range I46..J49 into I65 and the range L46..M48 into I69. Next, we create the following range names: "INPUT," I64..J71; "CRITERION," O64..O65; and "OUTPUT," I74..I81. Figure 93 shows the worksheet after this step.

	I	J	K	L	M	N	O	P
43						CONSOLIDATED		
44	DEPARTMENT 1		DEPARTMENT 2			ITEM	QTR1	
45	ITEM	QTR1	ITEM	QTR1			@DSUM(INPUT,1,CRITERION)	
46	FIDGETS	10000	WIDGETS	15000	XXXXX			0
47	DIDGETS	2000	GIDGETS	3000	XXXXX			0
48	WIDGETS	12000	FIDGETS	12000	XXXXX			0
49	FIDGETS	12000			XXXXX			0
50					XXXXX			0
51					XXXXX			0
52					XXXXX			0
53					XXXXX			0
54					XXXXX			0
55					XXXXX			0
56								

Figure 92

	I	J	K	L	M	N	O	P
63								
64	ITEM	QTR1	|<=INPUT		ITEM	|<=CRITERION	
65	FIDGETS	10000						
66	DIDGETS	2000						
67	WIDGETS	12000						
68	FIDGETS	12000						
69	WIDGETS	15000						
70	GIDGETS	3000						
71	FIDGETS	12000						
72								
73								
74	ITEM		<=OUTPUT					
75								
76								
77								
78								
79								
80								
81								

Figure 93

Notice that these range names correspond to the ranges used by the
/Data Query command. In fact, we're setting up the worksheet to do a
/Data Query Unique. This command will give us one—and only one—
copy in "OUTPUT" of each label in "INPUT." To accomplish this,

issue the /Data Query command. The Input range is "INPUT," the Criterion range is "CRITERION," and the Output range is "OUT-PUT." Issuing the Unique command then creates the list shown in Figure 94.

	I	J	K	L	M	N	O	P
63								
64	ITEM	QTR1		I<=INPUT			ITEM	I<=CRITERION
65	FIDGETS	10000	I					I
66	DIDGETS	2000	I					
67	WIDGETS	12000	I					
68	FIDGETS	12000	I					
69	WIDGETS	15000	I					
70	GIDGETS	3000	I					
71	FIDGETS	12000	I					
72			I					
73								
74	ITEM		I<=OUTPUT					
75	FIDGETS	I						
76	DIDGETS	I						
77	WIDGETS	I						
78	GIDGETS	I						
79		I						
80		I						
81		I						

Figure 94

We now have a list in "OUTPUT" of each unique Item name in the two departmental budgets. Our next step is to /Copy this list to O46 in our consolidation area. Then we set things up for the /Data Table. To define the table, issue the /Data Table command, specifying O45..P55 as the Table range and cell O65 as the Input cell. As the /Data Table runs, it substitutes each unique Item name in turn into the predefined Input Cell (O65). This substitution causes the @DSUM formula in P45 to be recalculated for each Item name grouping and gives us the consolidation totals we want in the cells of the Data Table in column P.

We can get a grand total by making a simple change and recalculating the Data Table. Before we press the {Table} key, we erase cell O55, the last cell in the left-hand column of the data table. When this empty cell is substituted in the Item criterion cell in "CRITERION," all records are evaluated for the @DSUM calculation; and cell P55 displays a grand total of all items.

	I	J	K	L	M	N	O	P
43							CONSOLIDATED	
44	DEPARTMENT 1		DEPARTMENT 2			ITEM	QTR1	
45	ITEM	QTR1	ITEM	QTR1			@DSUM(INPUT,1,CRITERION)	
46	FIDGETS	10000	WIDGETS	15000		FIDGETS		34000
47	DIDGETS	2000	GIDGETS	3000		DIDGETS		2000
48	WIDGETS	12000	FIDGETS	12000		WIDGETS		27000
49	FIDGETS	12000				GIDGETS		3000
50						XXXXX		0
51						XXXXX		0
52						XXXXX		0
53						XXXXX		0
54						XXXXX		0
55								66000
56								

Figure 95

Figure 95 shows the result, after the final step of pressing the {Table} key. There's a lot going on here, so you should go over the steps carefully to make sure you have followed everything. Because it is easy to make mistakes setting all this up, this process is a good candidate for a macro.

There are several possible traps in this whole procedure. To avoid them,

1. Make sure your **Input, Output,** and **Data Table 1** ranges are large enough; otherwise, you'll end up with incomplete and incorrect results.

2. Make sure that you don't get a second empty line into your Criterion range, or you'll retrieve everything in the data base for each cell in the Data Table.

3. Make sure that you don't include any extra fields in the **O**utput range, or you'll retrieve duplicate Item names instead of a unique list. (Note that "ITEM" is the only field in the Criterion range in Figure 93.)

10

Sharing Data with Other Programs

Sharing Data with dBASE II

182 Tip: To convert a dBASE II data base directly to a 1-2-3 worksheet file, use the Lotus Translate utility.

Beginning with Release 1A of 1-2-3, the Translate utility (on the separate utility disk), will convert a dBASE II data base (a file with a .DBF extension) into a 1-2-3 worksheet file (with a .WKS extension). Figure 96 shows the main menu of the Translate utility with the cursor resting over the "DBF to WKS" option.

```
LOTUS File Translation System V.1A (C) 1983 LOTUS Development Corp  MENU
------------------------------------------------------------------------
VC to WKS   DIF to WKS   WKS to DIF   DBF to WKS   WKS to DBF   Quit
Translate .DBF data file to 1-2-3 worksheet file
========================================================================
```

Figure 96

Suppose we want to convert the dBASE data base shown in Figures 97 and 98 to a 1-2-3 worksheet. Figure 97 shows the structure of the data base, and Figure 98 shows the contents.

133

```
.  DISPLAY STRUCTURE
STRUCTURE FOR FILE:  B:SALES.DBF
NUMBER OF RECORDS:   00007
DATE OF LAST UPDATE: 12/26/83
PRIMARY USE DATABASE
FLD     NAME      TYPE  WIDTH   DEC
001     CITY       C     009
002     SALESMAN   C     009
003     OCTDEC     N     009
004     JANMAR     N     009
005     APRJUN     N     009
006     JULSEP     N     009
007     QUOTA?     L     001
** TOTAL **              00056
```

Figure 97

```
CITY-----   SALESMAN- OCTDEC--- JANMAR--- APRJUN--- JULSEP--- Q
ATL         JONES       65500     40100     55600     65000 T
BOS         JONES       87900     83900     77050     94300 F
CHI         SMITH       12660     22590     44100     47900 Y
CHI         OOPS           10         5         4         3 N
DEN         ROCKY       33000     19800     32700     38600
STL         MOSES       10000    100000     12000    150000
QUE         FRENCHY     40000     40000     40000     40000
```

Figure 98

To perform the conversion, insert the Utility disk in drive A, type
LOTUS to load the Lotus Access System, and choose "Translate" from
the Lotus Access System menu and then "DBF to WKS" from the main
Translate menu. The Translate program will lead you quickly through a
chain of simple menus to complete the conversion.

Translate gives the new 1-2-3 worksheet file the same file name as the
source dBASE data base, except the extension becomes .WKS. In our
example we created a worksheet file called SALES.WKS. The first row
of the new worksheet contains the field names, which are taken from the
field names of the source dBASE data base.

The resulting worksheet is shown in Figure 99. Note that the "QUOTA?"
field on the far right displays asterisks in rows 2 and 3. In the dBASE data
base this field was a logical field, a type of field that always has a length

of one character. Because the Translate utility uses the widths of the fields in the dBASE II data base to determine the widths of the columns in the 1-2-3 worksheet, the column headed "QUOTA?" is only one character wide. This is not wide enough to display the contents of the field, so 1-2-3 displays asterisks in the field.

	A	B	C	D	E	F	G	H
1	CITY	SALESMAN	OCTDEC	JANMAR	APRJUN	JULSEP	QUOTA?	
2	ATL	JONES	65500	40100	55600	65000	*	
3	BOS	JONES	87900	83900	77050	94300	*	
4	CHI	SMITH	12660	22590	44100	47900		
5	CHI	OOPS	10	5	4	3		
6	DEN	ROCKY	33000	19800	32700	38600		
7	STL	MOSES	10000	100000	12000	150000		
8	QUE	FRENCHY	40000	40000	40000	40000		
9								

Figure 99

This problem illustrates the fact that you'll often have to use /Work-sheet Column-Width Set to make adjustments after you've loaded your translated worksheet. Figure 100 shows the same worksheet with column H widened.

	A	B	C	D	E	F	G	H
1	CITY	SALESMAN	OCTDEC	JANMAR	APRJUN	JULSEP	QUOTA?	
2	ATL	JONES	65500	40100	55600	65000	1	
3	BOS	JONES	87900	83900	77050	94300	0	
4	CHI	SMITH	12660	22590	44100	47900		
5	CHI	OOPS	10	5	4	3		
6	DEN	ROCKY	33000	19800	32700	38600		
7	STL	MOSES	10000	100000	12000	150000		
8	QUE	FRENCHY	40000	40000	40000	40000		
9								

Figure 100

Why would you want to go to all this bother to transfer data from dBASE II to 1-2-3? The reason is that dBASE II is good for storing fairly large data bases, but it is not as good as 1-2-3 for "what if" and graphical analyses; nor is dBASE II as flexible as 1-2-3. There are, therefore, situations where you may want to store your primary data base in dBASE II and move selected portions of the data base to 1-2-3 for various types of analysis and experimentation. (The Translate utility, however, will convert only complete dBASE data bases to 1-2-3 worksheet files; if you want to transfer only part of a dBASE data base, you'll have to use the dBASE COPY command, or something similar, to create a subset data base especially for transfer.)

183 Trap: If a 1-2-3 worksheet on the target disk has the same name as the one that the Translate utility creates, the 1-2-3 worksheet will be destroyed.

The Translate utility does not check to see whether a file already exists with the same name as the file that is created. If such a file exists, it will be overwritten by the utility. Be sure that you do not let this happen to you.

184 Trap: If the dBASE data base has more than 2,047 records, the Translate utility will not translate the data base correctly.

Because the 1-2-3 worksheet has only 2,048 rows, the largest data base 1-2-3 can hold is 2,047 records. If your dBASE file has more than 2,047 records, the Translate utility will not produce a worksheet that can be loaded into 1-2-3.

A partial solution to this problem is to use the dBASE II COPY command to break the large data base into two or more smaller files, each with fewer than 2,047 records. These smaller files can then be translated into 1-2-3, with each file becoming a separate 1-2-3 work-sheet. However, because the data base is now in several different worksheets, it is impossible to perform extracts or finds, or to compute statistics on the entire data base at once.

Another solution is to eliminate any unneeded records before the translation is made. For example, suppose you have an order-entry data base of 5,000 records, and you want to use 1-2-3 to analyze only the orders receved during the past week. By using dBASE II's COPY command, you can create a smaller file that contains just the records you wish to analyze in 1-2-3. If this file contains fewer than 2,047 records, it can be translated directly into 1-2-3.

185 Trap: There are problems in the transfer of logical fields from dBASE to 1-2-3.

For dBASE, a logical "true" is either a T or a Y, and a logical "false" is either an F, an N, or an empty field. The Translate utility recognizes only the T (which it translates as @TRUE = 1) and the F (which it translates as @FALSE = 0). It ignores all other logical values. Compare column G in Figure 98 (the dBASE file) with column G in Figure 100 (the 1-2-3 worksheet) for an illustration of this problem. Notice that the values in the field "QUOTA?" have been translated for the first two records but are blank for records 3 to 7.

186   **Tip:** To convert a 1-2-3 data base directly into a dBASE II data base, use the Lotus Translate utility.

You may want to make a conversion in this direction if your application has gone beyond either 1-2-3's data storage capabilities or its programming capabilities. You may also be working with projections or budgets in 1-2-3 that at some point become "official." When they become official, you may want to move the data over to a dBASE data base where your historical data resides.

The same Translate utility that performed the conversion in the other direction will also do the job here. Figure 101 shows the Translate main menu with the cursor resting over the "WKS to DBF" option. If we make this choice, the utility will present us with another menu (Figure 102) that will ask us whether we wish to translate an entire worksheet or a named range. To use the "Range" option, we need to have named the part of the worksheet we want to translate.

```
LOTUS File Translation System V.1A (C) 1983 LOTUS Development Corp  MENU
-----------------------------------------------------------------------
VC to WKS   DIF to WKS   WKS to DIF   DBF to WKS   WKS to DBF   Quit
Translate 1-2-3 worksheet to .DBF data file
=======================================================================
```

Figure 101

```
Translate entire worksheet or a named range in the worksheet      .WKS to .DBF
-----------------------------------------------------------------------
Worksheet   Range
Translate a named range in the worksheet
=======================================================================
```

Figure 102

Let's use the worksheet in Figure 103 as an example. Here we have a small sales projection data base. We've used /**R**ange Name Create to assign the name DATABASE to the range A15..E18. Note that we included the field names row of the data base in this definition, just as we would in defining a data base for 1-2-3's own purposes. The field names row must be part of the range because Translate uses these names in assigning names to the fields in the dBASE data base it creates. Assuming that we choose the "Range" option, we then supply "DATABASE" when the prompt asks us which range we wish to translate.

```
         A          B         C          D          E
 9   SALES PROJECTIONS
10   ==================
11
12   ASSUMPTIONS
13                        GROWTH=          10.00%
14
15   CITY        SALES:83  SALES:84   SALES:85   SALES:86
16   ATL         $65,500.00 $72,050.00  $79,255.00  $87,180.50
17   BOS         $87,900.00 $96,690.00 $106,359.00 $116,994.90
18   CHI
19
```

Figure 103

Figure 104 shows the resulting structure and contents of the dBASE data base that Translate creates.

```
***  dBASE II/86   Ver 2.3D  29 Nov 82
. SET DEFAULT TO B:
. USE SALES123
. LIST STRUCTURE
STRUCTURE FOR FILE:   SALES123.DBF
NUMBER OF RECORDS:    00003
DATE OF LAST UPDATE:  12/26/83
PRIMARY USE DATABASE
FLD      NAME    TYPE  WIDTH   DEC
001     CITY      C     009
002     SALES:83  N     011    002
003     SALES:84  N     011    002
004     SALES:85  N     012    002
005     SALES:86  N     012    002
** TOTAL **            00056

. LIST ALL
00001  ATL     65500.00    72050.00     79255.00     87180.50
00002  BOS     87900.00    96690.00    106359.00    116994.90
00003  CHI         0.00        0.00         0.00         0.00
```

Figure 104

There are a number of things that can go wrong in transferring files from 1-2-3 to dBASE. The various ins and outs of the process could probably be the subject of a small book. The following Traps point out some of the more troublesome problems that can arise.

187   Trap: If you're not careful, you'll end up with dBASE fields with the wrong number of decimal places.

The Translate utility decides how many decimal places to assign to a dBASE field it creates. The decision is based on the format assigned to the first cell in the corresponding field in the source 1-2-3 data base. In our example this row was formatted **F**ixed with two decimal places, so that's how Translate created the dBASE fields.

If the first cell had been formatted to **G**eneral (the default format), the resulting dBASE field would have the same number of decimals as the first cell in the 1-2-3 field. For example, if the 1-2-3 worksheet looked like this

	A	B	C
1	Name	Number	
2	AAA	100	
3	BBB	100.34	
4	CCC	100.112	
5			

the number field in the dBASE data base would have no decimal places.

188   Trap: The field names in the field names row of the source 1-2-3 data base must be valid dBASE names, or you'll end up with a damaged dBASE data base.

In dBASE, field names can be from 1 to 10 characters long, must start with a letter, and may contain only letters, digits, and an embedded colon. If the Translate utility is to work correctly, the field names in your 1-2-3 data base must meet these requirements.

189   Trap: dBASE II is limited to 32 fields in a data base, so your source 1-2-3 data base can have no more than 32 fields.

190   Trap: If you're not careful, you can end up with some fields truncated after translation.

The Translate utility decides how large to make the target dBASE fields based on the column widths of the source 1-2-3 fields. If a 1-2-3 cell contains more characters than the width of the column can display, the extra characters are lost in the translation.

191   Trap: If a dBASE data base already exists with the same name as the one that the translation will create, that existing data base will be destroyed.

Like the other Translate utilities, the WKS to DBF utility does not check for conflicting file names before it begins to translate. Overwriting a dBASE data base can be costly, so always check your directory before you begin to translate.

192   Trap: Dates created with the @DATE function will be translated as numeric values in dBASE II.

The 1-2-3 @DATE function is a simple way to create dates in the 1-2-3 worksheet. The result of the @DATE function is always a number that represents the number of days between December 31, 1899, and the date in the @DATE function. The /**R**ange **F**ormat command is used to display that number in a more conventional date form.

When the Translate utility operates on an @DATE function, the utility ignores the format and translates the value only. Thus, the function @DATE(83,1,1) is translated as 30317.

To avoid this problem, convert all dates to labels of the form DD/MM/YY before you use the Translate utility.

Translating VisiCalc Files

193   Tip: If you have an old VisiCalc file, you can convert it to a 1-2-3 worksheet file with the Translate utility.

The Translate utility can convert a file in VisiCalc format into a 1-2-3 worksheet file that you can then load directly into 1-2-3.

If you are like many other 1-2-3 users, you started your spreadsheeting career with VisiCalc. Having a utility that can translate your VisiCalc files into 1-2-3 files is a real advantage.

194   Trap: 1-2-3 cannot translate VisiCalc's @NOT, @AND, and @OR functions properly.

Because in 1-2-3 the @NOT, @AND, and @OR functions are handled by the phrases #NOT#, #AND#, and #OR#, which use a completely different syntax from the VisiCalc @ functions, these VisiCalc functions cannot be translated by the utility. Cells containing these functions will trigger an error message and will be converted to labels by the utility. You can correct the problem by editing the cells containing these functions after the translation is completed.

195 Trap: All cells formatted with VisiCalc's **$** format will automatically be translated into 1-2-3's **C**urrency **2** format.

1-2-3 assumes that any cell formatted with VisiCalc's /Format **$** command should be translated into 1-2-3's **C**urrency **2** format. Experienced VisiCalc users know that because of VisiCalc's limited number of formats, the **$** format is used for several purposes other than currency. Some **$** formats would be best translated into 1-2-3's **P**ercentage format; others should be translated into **F**ixed **2** format. You'll probably need to reformat some of your worksheet after the translation is completed.

196 Trap: 1-2-3 balks at translating VisiCalc cells that are formatted but blank.

Frequently VisiCalc files (and 1-2-3 files, for that matter) contain cells that are formatted but do not contain a value, a label, or a formula. When the Translate utility runs across one of those cells, the utility presents a message like

    Formula error at J38

This error message seems to be just a protest, however, because 1-2-3 can translate a worksheet containing this kind of cell without any problem.

Sharing Information with Word-Processing Programs

197   **Tip:** To pass data from 1-2-3 to a word-processing program, use the **/P**rint **F**ile command to create an ASCII text file.

The /**P**rint **F**ile command creates an ASCII text file with a .PRN extension. Such a file can be read by any common word-processing program, including WordStar, Volkswriter, and others.

To avoid including extra lines and spaces in the file you create, make sure you use the following print options whenever you use the /**P**rint **F**ile command.

1.   Choose /**P**rint **F**ile **O**ptions **O**ther Unformatted to cut out headers, footers, and associated spacing.

2.   Set left, top, and bottom margins to 0.

3.   Set the right margin small enough so that the word processor you plan to use can read the lines you create. Some word processors cannot read lines greater than a certain length.

198   **Tip:** To pass data from a word-processing program to 1-2-3, use **/F**ile **I**mport **T**ext to load the word-processing file.

You can load any ASCII text file into your worksheet with /**F**ile **I**mport **T**ext, provided you have given that file a .PRN extension. First, position the cursor in the cell where you want the upper-left corner of the imported file. 1-2-3 will load each line from the text file into a cell in the column that contains the cursor. The first line will go into the cell containing the cursor, the second line into the cell immediately beneath the first cell, and so on. Figure 105 shows a WordStar file that we loaded into 1-2-3 this way.

If your word-processing file contains control characters, you may have to delete them once you've loaded the file into a 1-2-3 worksheet.

Sometimes the /**F**ile **I**mport **T**ext command duplicates in subsequent columns some of the information in the first column. So be sure to examine the results carefully when you use this command.

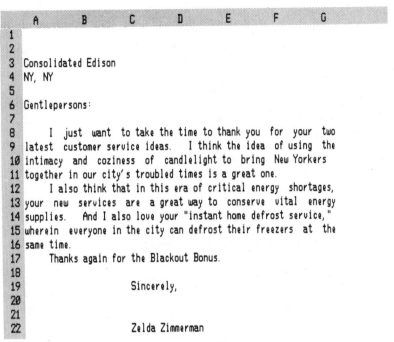

Figure 105

199 Tip: If you want 1-2-3 to read a file produced by a BASIC program, write it with the BASIC WRITE# command and load it into 1-2-3 using **/F**ile Import **N**umbers.

The BASIC WRITE# command creates a comma-delimited file, which has all fields separated by commas, and nonnumeric text fields bounded by double quotes. You can load such a file directly into a 1-2-3 worksheet with **/F**ile Import **N**umbers; the file will load where you have the cursor positioned when you issue the command. The file must have a file extension of .PRN for this command to work.

Figure 106 shows a comma-delimited file. Figure 107 shows what the file looks like after it has been loaded into 1-2-3 by /File Import Numbers.

With a variation of the COPY command, dBASE II can also create a comma-delimited file. A dBASE comma-delimited file can be read directly into the 1-2-3 worksheet with the /File Import Numbers command.

```
A>TYPE B:SALESDEL.PRN
"ATL    ",   65500.00,   72050.00,    79255.00,   87180.50
"BOS    ",   87900.00,   96690.00,   106359.00,  116994.90
"CHI    ",            ,            ,            ,
```

Figure 106

```
         A        B       C        D       E
1 ATL      65500    72050    79255   87180.5
2 BOS      87900    96690   106359  116994.9
3 CHI
4
5
```

Other Data Sharing Possibilities

200 **Tip:** To share data with programs that read and/or write DIF format
files, use the Translate utility.

Many spreadsheet and graphics programs can read and/or write files in
Data Interchange Format (DIF). This format was developed by
Software Arts, the original creators of the electronic spreadsheet
VisiCalc. A program reading a DIF file can distinguish field from field
in the input data and can also tell which fields are numeric and which are
nonnumeric text. The DIF format has become something of a standard
among spreadsheet programs.

The Lotus Translate utility can translate a DIF file directly into a 1-2-3
worksheet file and also convert in the other direction. Figure 108 shows
a portion of a DIF file, and Figure 109 shows the same DIF file after the
Translate utility converted the file and we loaded it into 1-2-3 with a
/File Retrieve.

201 **Tip:** If other methods fail, use dBASE II as an intermediary.

If none of the methods discussed fits your data-sharing situation, you
may be able to solve your problem by using dBASE II as an
intermediary.

For example, if you want 1-2-3 to read a file containing numeric
information from program X, but X cannot create either a DIF file or a
comma-delimited file, the chances are good that program X can create a

standard ASCII text file. You can load an ASCII file into a dBASE data base using the **SDF** (**S**ystem **D**ata **F**ormat) option of the dBASE

```
TABLE
0,1
""

VECTORS
0,5
""

TUPLES
0,25
""

DATA
0,0
""

.

.

.
""
-1,0
BOT
1,0
"CITY"
1,0
"SALES:83"
1,0
"SALES:84"
1,0
"SALES:85"
1,0
"SALES:86"
-1,0
BOT
1,0
"ATL"
0,6.5500000000000000E+04
V
0,7.2050000000000000E+04
V
0,7.9255000000000000E+04
V
0,8.7180500000000000E+04
V

.

.

.
```

Figure 108

```
     A        B        C        D        E
 8  SALES PROJECTIONS
 9  =================
10
11  ASSUMPTIONS
12                            GROWTH=      0.1
13
14  CITY SALES:83 SALES:84 SALES:85 SALES:86
15  ATL     65500    72050    79255  87180.5
16  BOS     87900    96690   106359 116994.9
17  CHI
18
```

Figure 109

APPEND command. You can then use the Translate program to convert this file into a 1-2-3 worksheet file. (You can't just load the ASCII text file into 1-2-3 using /File Import Text and have 1-2-3 distinguish fields from each other and recognize numeric fields as numeric.)

Similarly, if you want 1-2-3 to write a file for program X to read but X can't read a DIF file, you can solve the problem if X can read a comma-delimited file. 1-2-3 can't write a comma-delimited file directly, so you need to use dBASE as an intermediary. First, use Translate to convert your 1-2-3 worksheet file into a dBASE II data base. Then use the "DELIMITED WITH" option of the dBASE COPY command to create a comma-delimited file.

11
Keyboard Macros

Ways to Make Macros Easy to Use

202 **Tip:** When possible, store your macros in the same area on all your worksheets.

If your worksheet contains several macros, you may find it convenient to store all the macros in one part of the sheet. Storing all the macros together makes it easier to find a macro when you need to edit it and also prevents accidental overwriting of a macro that is stored in an active part of the worksheet.

One common location is columns AA and AB. These columns are outside the normally used part of the worksheet, so it is unlikely that your model will conflict with your macros. Other users like to store their macros under the last rows of their model in columns A and B. These cells also have the advantage of being out of the way. Macros stored in the latter location also waste less memory.

203 **Tip:** Keep your macros as short and simple as possible.

The 1-2-3 macro language is versatile enough to create complex chains of macros that produce large menu-driven systems. In some cases these chains are appropriate, but there's also a danger here: if you get too complex and too cute, you'll stretch 1-2-3 beyond where it was intended to go. Despite its power, the macro language is not a full-fledged programming language; and when you try to do too much, the macro may get so complicated that you might as well have used a more traditional programming tool in the first place.

It's best to start with short, simple macros that do limited, well-defined jobs. The macros we've looked at in earlier sections of this book are that type.

204   Trap: If the macro notation is obscure, you'll have trouble under-standing it later unless you space it out and comment on it liberally.

Here's an example of a macro that works well:

AA	AB	AC	AD
1 /gtpak9. N9~xK5. N5~otfJanuary Grain Sales~gv~			

When we write the macro this way, however, it's difficult to distinguish the various commands and tell what the macro is doing. If we write the macro like this, however,

AA	AB	AC
1 /gtp		select graph type
2 aK9. N9~		define A range
3 xK5. N5~		define X range
4 otfJanuary Grain Sales~g		define first title
5 v~		view graph

the macro is much more understandable. Notice that we've placed separate pieces of macro code on different lines and have put comments to the right of each line. We recommend that you write all your macros this way.

205   Tip: Use descriptive names for macros where possible.

You must give each macro a name with the **/R**ange Name Create command or the **/R**ange Name Labels command. The named range must have the first cell of the macro as its upper-left corner.

What we call a *startup* macro must have a two-character name in which the first character is a backslash (\) and the second character is any letter of the alphabet, for example, \A, \F, etc. Activate a startup macro by holding down the {Alt} key together with the letter of the macro, such as {Alt} A or {Alt} F.

A startup macro can chain to other macros in three different ways: through a menu that executes a macro for each menu choice, through a call using the /XC command, or through a direct transfer of control by the /XG command. You may give the macros farther down in the chain any name composed of up to a maximum of 15 characters.

The best practice is to give your second-tier macros descriptive names. For example, you might name a macro that updates a data base "UPDATEMACRO." A descriptive name makes it easier to understand the macro code. Startup macros are harder to name, but you can probably find single-letter names that suggest the function of the macro, such as \P for a print macro, \C for a copy macro, and so on.

206 Tip: With complex macro-driven applications, use a *structured top-down* approach in writing the macro.

Structured top-down is programmer terminology for a simple concept: create a separate macro for each specific task and call all the macros in sequence from one high-level macro. Figure 110 shows an example. This *mainline* macro is nothing but a series of calls to macros that perform the specific tasks described by their names and the comments.

	I	J	K	L	M	N	O
7	MGT_MC	/xcINIT_MC~			Call Initialization macro.		
8		/xcDATE_MC~			Call Date selection macro.		
9		/xcDATA_T1_MC~			Call Data Table 1 macro.		
10		/xcDATA_DIS_MC~			Call Data Distribution macro.		
11		/xcQUIT_MC~			Call Quit & cleanup macro.		
12		/xmMGT_MENU~			Go back to main menu.		
13							

Figure 110

This approach has definite advantages. First, you can look at the mainline macro for a quick idea of the overall logic of the system. Second, because each function is in a separate routine, it is relatively easy to isolate problems, make changes, and test out the macro logic.

207 Tip: Combine widely applicable macros into a *macro library* worksheet and use this worksheet as the base for all your 1-2-3
applications.

You will find that you use certain macros frequently with few or no
changes. If you create one worksheet containing all your favorite
macros, you can include them in any 1-2-3 application without retyping.
The worksheet becomes your macro library and should be given a name
like LIBRARY.WKS.

Using the macro library is very simple. Once the library worksheet has
been created, use it as the base for all your new 1-2-3 worksheets. Load
the library worksheet into memory and start creating your new
application. When you save the new worksheet for the first time, be sure
to give it a name other than LIBRARY.WKS. Once saved, the macros
are an integral part of the new worksheet.

Figure 111 shows part of a macro library. Notice that we've placed the
name of each macro in a column to the left of the macro. This makes the
macros easier to name (Use the /**R**ange **N**ame **L**abels **R**ight command.)
and helps you remember the names assigned to the macros. As your
library grows, you'll really appreciate this Tip.

208 Tip: You can generalize your macros by prompting the user for
variable information with the {?} command.

The generalized macro is written so that it prompts the user for all
variable information. Figure 112 shows a simple print macro that
prompts for the range to be printed. The {?}~ in the macro code is the
prompt command; it causes the macro to stop, accept user input, and
start again when you press {Enter}.

In a print macro like this one, the {?} makes it possible to point out the
range to be printed. This same technique can be used to designate the
range for the /**C**opy, /**R**ange Format, /**G**raph, and /**D**ata commands
from within macros.

The {?} can also be used for entering numbers or labels into the
worksheet. However, the /XN and /XL commands are better for
entering data.

	AA	AB	AC	AD	AE	AF	AG
1	Numeric Keypad Macro						
2							
3	\K	{?}	Accepts numeric entry.				
4		{right}	Moves cursor to the next cell on the right.				
5		/xg\K~	Loops back to beginning to accept new entry.				
6							
7	Date Entry Macro						
8							
9							
10	\D	@DATE(	Enter the constant beginning part of date function.				
11		{?}	Accept year, month, day and Return.				
12		)~	Fill in end of function and Enter.				
13		{down}	Jump down to next cell in column.				
14		/xg\D~	Loop back and start entering next date.				
14							
15	Label to Number Macro						
16							
17	\N	/rncHERE~~			Name current cell.		
18		/xi@isna(HERE)~/xgEND~			@NA loop ender present?		
19		{edit}{home}{del}~			Change to number.		
20		/rndHERE~~			Delete range name.		
21		{right}			To next cell in row.		
22		/xg\N~			Loop back to check next cell.		
23	END	/rndHERE~~			Delete range name before quitting.		
24		/xq~			Quit.		
25							

Figure 111

	I	J	K	L	M	N
231	\P	/pp		Print to printer.		
232		r{?}~		Get range from user.		
233		gq		Go print & quit.		
234						

Figure 112

Menu Macros

209 **Tip:** You can use the /XM macro command to create your own
menus.

The /XM macro command allows you to create your own customized
menus, which function substantially the same as 1-2-3's own command
menus. Like regular 1-2-3 menus, macro menus, when activated, appear
in the control panel at the top of the screen. Macro menus present
one-word options followed by explanatory lines. A choice can be made
from a macro menu by either pointing to the desired function or typing
the first letter of the name of that choice. With menu macros you can
lead yourself, or someone else, through a complex process rather
simply.

Figure 113 shows an example of a user-defined menu and the macro
that activates it. The first line of a menu macro is composed of from one
to eight choices; these choices appear on the top line of the screen when
the menu is activated. In this case, there are four choices: Menu 1.1,
Menu 1.2, Menu 1.3, and Quit. The second line of the menu definition is
composed of longer descriptions that explain the menu options. You
can't read the second line in this example because the descriptions in the
cells overlap. The cell under Menu 1.1 actually reads, "Access Menu
1.1."

```
          AA         AB         AC         AD         AE
 1 \X         /xmMenu 1~
 2
 3 Menu 1      Menu 1.1   Menu 1.2   Menu 1.3   Quit
 4             Access Menu Access Menu Access Menu Exit from the macro
 5             /xmMenu 1.1~/xmMenu 1.2~/xmMenu 1.3~/xq~
 6
 7 Menu 1.1    Enter      Delete     Quit
 8             Make a new EDelete an EnReturn to previous menu
 9             /xnEnter a Nu(?)       /xmMenu 1~
```

Figure 113

The third line of the menu definition contains the instructions that will
be executed if that menu option is selected. When you choose a menu
option by pointing the cursor at it and pressing {Enter}, the 1-2-3 macro
processor executes the command from the third line in the column

under that menu choice. In Figure 113 each macro on the third line of the menu definition is a one-line macro consisting only of a /XM command. The /XM command causes 1-2-3 to transfer control to another menu macro located elsewhere in the worksheet. If we choose the first option on this menu, 1-2-3 will execute the Menu 1.1 macro.

It's wise to give each menu definition a range name. The range must cover at least one cell and begin in the upper-left corner of the menu definition. We have named the main menu in Figure 113 MENU1 and have placed that name just to the left of the menu definition itself. This location allows us to use the /**R**ange Name **L**abels **R**ight command to name the menu and any other macros and menus that begin in the same column.

Once you have defined and named a menu, you can activate the menu from a macro by issuing the /XM command. The \X macro in Figure 113 issues this command for Menu 1. This example shows how a macro can chain to a menu, which in turn chains to other macros, which in turn can chain to other menus, etc. (Figure 114 shows what this menu looks like when displayed.)

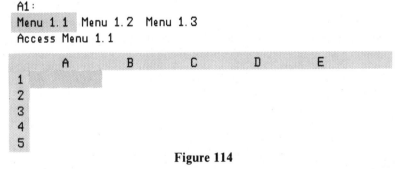

Figure 114

210   **Tip:** You can chain menus to each other to produce a hierarchy of
         menus.

You can produce your own hierarchy of menus at different levels just like 1-2-3 does with its commands. Let's look again at the menu example in Figure 113. When we first pressed {Alt} X, Menu 1 appeared in the control panel. If we had chosen the first option from that menu, we would have chained to the Menu 1.1 macro, shown in rows 7, 8, and 9 of Figure 113. This macro offers some simple choices about entering and deleting worksheet entries.

211 Trap: One of the most important differences between menu macros and regular 1-2-3 menus is that, in most cases, the {Esc} key does not cause the menu macros to "back up" one level.

With regular 1-2-3 menus, pressing {Esc} always moves you back up one level of menus. For example, if you are in the /**P**rint **P**rinter **O**ptions menu, pressing {Esc} will back you up to the /**P**rint **P**rinter menu. Pressing {Esc} again will move you up to the /**P**rint menu, and pressing {Esc} a third time will return you to the Ready mode.

This technique usually does not work with macro menus, however. Because macro menus are supposed to emulate regular menus, this discrepancy is a bit irritating. For novice 1-2-3 users, this difference can be confusing and lead to serious problems.

212 Trick: If you concatenate /XM commands, you can use {Esc} to move back up the menu hierarchy.

You can simulate the action of the {Esc} key in menu macros through careful programming. If you follow each /XM command in your macros with a string of /XM commands that lead you backwards up the menu hierarchy to the top, the {Esc} key will work as expected.

Let's expand the first choice in the Menu 1 menu shown in Figure 113 so that we can see all the information hidden by overlapping cells. This expanded version is shown in Figure 115.

	AA	AB	AC	AD	AE
1	\X	/xmMenu 1~			
2					
3	Menu 1	Menu 1.1			
4		Access Menu 1.1			
5		/xmMenu 1.1~/xmMenu 1~			
6					
7	Menu 1.1	Enter	Delete	Quit	
8		Make a new EDelete an EnReturn to previous menu			
9		/xnEnter a Nu{?}		/xmMenu 1~	

Figure 115

Notice that there are two /XM commands in cell AB5. (Only the first was visible in the Figure 115 because the length of the command caused the second part to be hidden by the contents of cell AC5.) The first /XM command, /XMMenu 1.1~, moves the macro to Menu 1.1. The second,

/XMMenu 1~, causes the macro to "back up" one step to the main menu (Menu 1) if you press {Esc} after selecting this option.

This technique works because of 1-2-3's reaction to the {Esc} key. When the 1-2-3 macro processor senses an {Esc} in response to a menu, 1-2-3 resumes processing in the cell from which the /XM command for that menu was issued. If that cell contains other /XM commands that direct the macro back up the menu tree, the {Esc} key appears to work perfectly. For example, if {Esc} is pressed in response to Menu 1.1, the macro resumes processing in cell AA5 with the command /XMMenu 1~, which returns control of the macro to Menu 1.

This Trick can make macro menus work just like regular 1-2-3 menus. We suggest that you use it in all your macro menus.

213 **Tip:** It's a good idea to put an explicit Quit option in each menu.

Menu 1.1 in Figure 115 has an explicit Quit option. The command that lies under this selection is /XMMenu 1~, which should be very familiar by now. When the user selects the Quit option from this menu, control of the macro is returned to Menu 1, the next higher menu. The Quit option in this menu is similar to the Quit option in the standard 1-2-3 /Graph Options menu.

Notice that Quit serves the same purpose as the Trick shown above. Including Quit options in your menus allows you to move back through the menu tree even if you've forgotten to put in the chain of /XM commands described under the previous Tip.

214 **Tip:** Menu macros can be used for unusual purposes.

In Chapter 2 we presented a simple macro that can be used to enter a series of numbers with the numeric keypad. "Keyboard Macros" in the book *Using 1-2-3*, published by Que Corporation, contains a more sophisticated version of this macro (repeated in Figure 116).

After each entry the macro in *Using 1-2-3* lets you choose the direction you want the cursor to jump. This clever macro may sometimes be useful.

The version shown in Figure 116 uses a slightly different method of prompting for input; this method uses the /XN macro command, which allows you to enter only numeric data. After the number is entered, control is given to the menu named "Menu," which begins at cell AB4.

```
         AA        AB        AC        AD        AE
 1 \K       /xnEnter a number in the current cell :~~
 2          /xmMenu~
 3
 4 Menu             8         6         2         4
 5          Use the cursor keys to move the cursor
 6          {up}      {right}   {down}    {left}
 7          /xg\K~    /xg\K~    /xg\K~    /xg\K~
 8
```

Figure 116

The menu choices—8, 6, 2, and 4—may seem confusing at first; but notice that the 8, 6, 2, and 4, respectively, are the shifted versions of the ↑, →, ↓, and ← cursor keys. This menu makes the numbers behave like their shifted counterparts, the cursor-movement keys.

To move the cursor with this macro, simply press the key you would normally press to move the cursor in the direction you choose. For example, pressing 8 moves the cursor up; striking 4 moves the cursor right. Unlike most menus, you cannot point to the menu choices because the cursor keys are disabled by the {Num Lock} key. However, this is just what we want.

215   Tip: You can use menus just to give the user messages of various types.

Sometimes you want to send messages to the user from within a macro. They may be warnings, confirmations, instructions, reminders, etc. You can use menus to do this without having to take up any space on the screen.

Figure 117 shows a series of menus and macros that allow you to delete a line. Because deletion is so dangerous, we've included a series of message menus as both warnings and confirmations. First is a macro (\D) that simply activates the menu DELIM; this menu gives you the chance to cancel the delete action. If selected, the CANCEL option activates the instructional message menu CANIM, which says that the line has not been deleted and returns to the main menu (not shown).

If DELETE is selected from the DELIM menu, the menu chains to the macro DELMC, which performs the actual delete at the current line.

```
           I        J        K        L        M        N
401  \D       /xmDEL_IM~            Activate warning message menu.
402
403
404  DEL_IM   CANCEL      DELETE
405                                Cancel delete--leave existing line intact.
406           /xmCAN_IM~ /xgDEL_MC~
407
408  CAN_IM   INSTRUCTION
409                                Line NOT deleted.  Please hit RETURN.
410           /xmUPD_MN~/xmMAIN_MN~
411
412  DEL_MC   /wgpd/wdr{?}~         Disable protection & delete line.
413           /wgpe                 Enable protection again.
414           /xmDEL_DEL_IM~        Activate delete confirmation menu.
415
416  DEL_DEL_IM INSTRUCTION
417                                Line deleted.  Please hit RETURN.
418           /xmUPD_MN~/xmMAIN_MN~
419
```

Figure 117

The macro then activates the menu DELDELIM, which confirms the delete and returns to the main menu.

216   Trap: Don't confuse the {GoTo} command with the /XG command.

The {GoTo} macro command merely moves the cursor to the cell address or range name that follows, as in

{GoTo}A16~

The /XG command transfers control of macro execution to the destination cell. In effect, /XG says: Macro, continue processing with the instructions in the cell address that follows.

217   Trap: When you use the /XC command to cause one macro to call another, don't forget the /XR statement at the end of the called macro.

The /XC command is similar to the /XG command. Both commands instruct the macro to get its next instruction from a specific cell address. However, in the /XC macro, when the called macro is finished executing, the sequence of execution returns to the calling macro at the point immediately after the call.

Figure 110 shows a macro that includes several /XC commands. After the first called macro (called a subroutine in programming jargon) has executed, control returns to the main macro. The second /XC statement then passes control to the subroutine at the range named "DATE_MC." This second subroutine again returns control to the calling macro when the subroutine is finished.

Remember, though, that the called macro will not return to the calling macro unless you place a /XR return statement at the end of the called macro. For example, if the /XR were left out of the "DATA_T1_MC" macro in Figure 118, the macro execution would stop after the third line, and 1-2-3 would return to READY mode.

```
     AA            AB          AC
1   DATA_T1_MC   /dt1
2                MGT_DT1~
3                DBASE_CR_DTRCD~
4                /xr~
```

Figure 118

Looping Macros

218   **Tip:** You can create an infinitely looping macro by putting a /XG statement at the end of the macro that loops back to the beginning.

Figure 119 shows a simple macro that allows you to turn on the {Num Lock} key on the IBM PC and then use the numeric keypad to enter a column of numbers without having to turn off {Num Lock} to use the l cursor key. The cursor moves down automatically after each {Enter} because of the {DOWN} command included in the macro. Because we don't know how long the column will be, we've made this macro loop infinitely. The /XG\N~ statement creates the loop. This statement causes the macro to continue processing at the cell named \N. Because \N is the name of the first cell in the macro, this command sends control back to the beginning of the macro and allows entry into another cell in the column.

	AA	AB	AC	AD	AE	AF	AG
1	\N	{?}	Prompt for user input				
2		{down}	On Enter move cursor down one cell.				
3		/xg\N~	Loop for input to new cell. (Ctrl Break ends.)				

Figure 119

We've put no counter or break in the macro, so it will continue to loop until we deliberately stop it. To stop this or any other macro, press the {Ctrl} and {Break} keys simultaneously.

219 Tip: When you have a continuous sequence of cells to loop through, you can use @COUNT to control your loop.

Figure 120 shows an accumulation macro. The left part of Figure 120 shows the columns of numbers on which the macro operates. We assume that when the macro begins, the cursor rests in cell L426. This code causes any new entry in this column to be automatically accumulated into the corresponding cell in column K.

	J	K	L	M	N	O
425	SALESMAN	YR-TO-DT	CURRENT	\A	/re~{?}~	Erase old, get new
426	Aardvark	$27,000	$10,000		{left}{edit}+	To yr-to-dt
427	Peebles	$20,000	$10,000		{up}	To point mode
428	McNose	$55,000	$10,000		{right}{down}	Point to current
429					~	End yr-to-dt form
430					{edit}{calc}~	Formula=>Number
431					{right}{down}	Next current cell
432					/rncT~{up}~	T=2 cell test range
433					/xi(@COUNT(T)=2)~/rndT~/xg\A~	
434					/rndT~	Test for col end &
435						delete range T
436						
437						

Figure 120

We want this macro to loop until it gets to the bottom of column L and then end automatically. The trick we use involves the @COUNT function. Look at the eighth line of code, which reads

        /rncT~{up}~

This line creates a range name, T, that covers two cells: the one where the cursor currently rests and the one above it. Therefore, the {UP} command includes the cell above the current cell in the range. The next line is a /XI statement that checks to see how many nonblank cells are in range T. As long as there are two nonblank cells in this range, we know that the current cell has an entry in it, and we have not completed the column. (Recall that the @COUNT function counts the number of nonblank cells in a range.) After the /XI statement deletes the range name we created, the remainder of the line uses /XG to loop back to the beginning of the macro for another entry.

If @COUNT evaluates as not equal to 2, we know that we've reached a blank cell and have passed the bottom of the column. In that case, we execute the line immediately following the /XI statement, which deletes our range name T and terminates the macro.

We delete the range name T every time we use it because redefining a range name without first deleting it can sometimes cause trouble. We'll treat this problem in a subsequent Tip.

Don't forget that this particular loop-control technique depends on there being no blank cells in the middle of the column or row you're stepping through. See the next Tip for a method you can use if there are blank cells mixed with nonblank cells.

Figure 121 shows our accumulation table after the macro has finished executing. We entered 10,000 in each cell in column L, and the macro updated column K accordingly.

	J	K	L
425	SALESMAN	YR-TO-DT	CURRENT
426	Aardvark	$37,000	$10,000
427	Peebles	$30,000	$10,000
428	McNose	$65,000	$10,000
429			

Figure 121

220 **Trap:** The @COUNT function always returns a value of one when it operates on a one-cell range.

We created a two-celled test range rather than just one in the previous Tip because @COUNT always evaluates as one for a one-celled range, whether that cell is blank or not. For this reason all macro counters that rely on the @COUNT function to see if a cell is empty must operate on a two-cell range.

221 Trick: When you want to loop an indeterminate number of times and you don't want to press {Ctrl}{Break}, you can stop a loop with a special "stopper" entry.

Figure 122 shows a data entry area where we're entering three items that we'll later copy into a data base. Figure 123 shows a data entry macro that prompts for this data, makes sure it's valid, and then copies it to the end of the data base.

```
      A        B        C
1 ENTRY_AREA:
2 REFNO_E  DATE_E   AMT_E
3     10    8311.11  10000
4
```

Figure 122

```
      I                    J                           K
1 \E    /xlEnter reference number (1 to 100): ~REFNO_E~  Prompt for REFNO.
2       /xnEnter date (YYMM.DD form): ~DATE_E~           Prompt for DATE.
3       /xi@ISNA(DATE_E)=1~'/xq~                         Quit if stopper entered.
4       /xnEnter amount (0 to 100,000): ~AMT_E~          Prompt for AMT.
5       /cENTRY_RECORD~                                  Copy record to data base.
6       NEXT_DB_RECORD~
7       /xcNEXT_MC~                                      Set next empty data base record.
8       /xg\E~                                           Loop back to beginning.
9
```

Figure 123

When we finish entering records, we enter the function @NA in the date field. The /XI@ISNA statement in the macro tests this field for a value of @NA. When the macro finds @NA, the /XQ statement is executed, and the macro terminates.

As long as the macro does not find an @NA, the macro continues to loop back to the beginning, expecting you to enter another record. Figure 124 shows what the data entry area looks like after we've entered the stopper.

```
      A        B        C
1 ENTRY_AREA:
2 REFNO_E  DATE_E   AMT_E
3     10     NA      10000
4
```

Figure 124

This stopper Trick can also be used when you have a column or row of
entries to cycle through and some cells are blank. If you enter @NA as a
stopper at the end of the column or row, the macro can terminate when
it finds the stopper. Figure 125 shows a macro that uses this technique to
change a row of labels into numbers. We assume that the user has placed
@NA at the end of the row.

	I	J	K	L	M
1	\N	/rncHERE~~		Name current cell.	
2		/xi@isna(HERE)~/xgEND~		@NA loop ender present?	
3		{edit}{home}{del}~		Change to number.	
4		/rndHERE~~		Delete range name.	
5		{right}		To next cell in row.	
6		/xg\N~		Loop back to check next cell.	
7	END	/rndHERE~~		Delete range name before quitting.	
8		/xq~		Quit.	
9					

Figure 125

222 Trick: When you know how many times you want to loop, you can
set up a counter, increment it, and test it each time through
the loop.

Figure 126 shows a simple budget consolidation macro. (The data it
operates on is shown in Figure 127.) In this case there are two budgets to
consolidate, so we can use the counter technique.

	A	B	C	E	F	G	H	I
1	\C	/dfDEPT_CT~			Increment department			
2		DEPT_CT+1~~~			count			
3		/cDEPT_CT~DEPT_NO~			Copy DEPT_CT into DEPT_NO			
4		{goto}DEPT_NO~			Turn DEPT_NO into			
5		{edit}{home}'~			a label			
6		{goto}CONS_AREA~			Position cursor for combine			
7		/fcaeBUDG			Combine next			
8	DEPT_NO				budget file			
9		~						
10		/xi(DEPT_CT<2)~/xg\C~			Loop till done			
11								
12	DEPT_CT	0						
13								

Figure 126

	A	B	C		E	F	G	H	I
14	DEPARTMENT 1				DEPARTMENT 2			CONSOLIDATED	
15	ITEM	QTR1			ITEM	QTR1		ITEM	QTR1
15	WIDGETS	10000			WIDGETS	15000		WIDGETS	
16	GIDGETS	2000			GIDGETS	3000		GIDGETS	
17	FIDGETS	12000			FIDGETS	12000		FIDGETS	
18									

Figure 127

The counter is a named range called "DEPT_CT"; we have set it up right after the macro itself, in cell B12, with an initial value of 0. The first two lines in the macro code use the /**D**ata **F**ill command to increment "DEPT_CT" by 1 every time through the loop. The last statement in the macro checks to see if "DEPT_CT" has reached 2 yet. If not, the macro loops back to the beginning with a /XG\C~. If the count has reached 2, we terminate the macro because we're done.

Figure 128 shows both the consolidation area and the macro after it has finished executing.

	A	B	C		E	F	G	H	I
1	\C	/dfDEPT_CT~			Increment department				
2		DEPT_CT+1~~~			count				
3		/cDEPT_CT~DEPT_NO~			Copy DEPT_CT into DEPT_NO				
4		{goto}DEPT_NO~			Turn DEPT_NO into				
5		{edit}{home}'~			a label				
6		{goto}CONS_AREA~			Position cursor for combine				
7		/fcaeBUDG			Combine next				
8	DEPT_NO	2			budget file				
9		~							
10		/xi(DEPT_CT<2)~/xg\C~			Loop till done				
11									
12	DEPT_CT		2						
13									
14	DEPARTMENT 1				DEPARTMENT 2			CONSOLIDATED	
15	ITEM	QTR1			ITEM	QTR1		ITEM	QTR1
16	WIDGETS	10000			WIDGETS	15000		WIDGETS	25000
17	GIDGETS	2000			GIDGETS	3000		GIDGETS	5000
18	FIDGETS	12000			FIDGETS	12000		FIDGETS	24000
19									

Figure 128

You may have noticed that this macro does an unusual thing: it uses a /Copy statement to modify its own code while it is executing. We'll cover this Trick next.

223 **Trick:** You can introduce variability into macros by having them modify themselves.

You can accomplish this *dynamic self-modification* of macros by including /Copy statements that copy in new code as needed. We used this technique in the macro discussed in the previous Trick. We wanted to consolidate several departmental budgets that were stored on the disk separately in files named BUDGn (*n* was 1 or 2). To have the macro perform a /File Combine Add Entire file operation on each file, we have to find a way to allow the macro to address each file separately in turn.

We can do this with the dynamic self-modification technique. Recall that the first two lines of this macro use the /Data Fill command to increment the "DEPT_CT" counter. The third line then copies the current value of that counter to the empty cell after the "DEPT_NO" label (Figure 126). So the first time through the loop, we get 1 in that cell. When the /File Combine Add Entire file on line 7 is executed, the macro will bring in the file called BUDG1. The second time through, the /Copy statement will copy in a 2, and the file called BUDG2 will be combined into our worksheet.

This Trick depends on the fact that the 1-2-3 macro processor generally does not care whether you continue entering keystrokes in the same cell or in the cell directly below. Note that to accomplish this Trick, we had to put in one cell the /FCAEBUDG, in another cell the "DEPT_NO" cell we're modifying, and in a third cell the ~ that supplies the carriage return to finish off the file name. If we had not done this, our /Copy would have overlaid code that we wanted to keep. Luckily, we have complete freedom here to split up the code into different cells.

We mentioned that in general the 1-2-3 macro processor does not care whether you continue in the same cell or go to the one below it. There is one exception to this rule: After a /XI statement (an IF statement), as in the one at the end of the macro we're considering, 1-2-3 expects the code for the "True" case to follow the IF statement on the same line.

Accuracy and Protection in Macros

224 Tip: Use the protection feature to keep from destroying unintentionally macro code or other vital information.

After you have created a complex macro or set of macros, you will usually want to protect the code so that the user does not inadvertently destroy or confuse it. An ill-advised /Copy, /Move, /Worksheet Insert, or /Worksheet Delete can create havoc on a worksheet that depends on a complicated macro. If you use /Range Protect to protect those cells you want to keep safe and execute /Worksheet Global Protection Enable, you can prevent most problems.

However, there are circumstances when you want the user to be able to do an Insert or a Delete, but you must control the actions closely. One reason for allowing Inserts and Deletes is that 1-2-3 automatically adjusts range names that are affected by Inserts and Deletes so that the macro keeps up with changes to the worksheet.

To allow selective use of /Worksheet Insert or Delete under macro control, disable protection, perform the Insert or Delete, and then enable protection again. The delete macro shown in Figure 117 uses this technique.

225 Tip: By executing a /Range Input command, you can restrict what the user can do without using the protection feature.

While the /Range Input command is in effect, 1-2-3 limits the movement of the cursor to only the unprotected cells in the range specified. The user is also restricted in the following ways:

1. The cursor keys will not move the cursor outside the range specified.

2. Only the {Help}, {Edit}, and {Calc} function keys are active. All other function keys and all 1-2-3 commands are inactive. (You can use {Esc} and the {Back Space} key in EDIT mode.)

It is not necessary to use /Worksheet Global Protection Enable to enable protection prior to issuing the /Range Input command. This command enables protection while it is in effect. However, there must be at least one unprotected cell in the specified range.

You will often use /**R**ange **I**nput to receive input during macro execution. You can also use the command to display information, restrict what the user can do during the display, and then return the cursor to where it was before the /**R**ange **I**nput command began. Figure 129 shows a help macro that uses this command to display the help screen in Figure 130. After you have read the help message, press {Enter}; the /**R**ange **I**nput command terminates, and you return to wherever you were before you pressed {Alt} H. We have, of course, used /**R**ange **U**nprotect to unprotect cell I211 on this screen; otherwise, the command would not work.

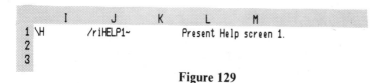

	I	J	K	L	M
1	\H	/riHELP1~		Present Help screen 1.	
2					
3					

Figure 129

	I	J	K	L	M	N
211	1. THE \S MACRO INITIALLY CONTAINS THE "UNFREEZE" VERTICAL TITLES CODE.					
212						
213	2. THE FIRST TIME YOU HIT ALT S, THEREFORE, THE "UNFREEZE" CODE WILL					
214	BE EXECUTED. HOWEVER, THE LAST THING THIS CODE DOES IS TO COPY					
215	THE ENTIRE "FREEZE" MACRO TO \S.					
216						
217	3. THEREFORE, THE NEXT TIME YOU HIT ALT S, THE "FREEZE" CODE WILL BE					
218	EXECUTED. AND THE LAST THING THAT CODE DOES IS TO COPY THE "UN-					
219	FREEZE" CODE BACK TO \S, SO WE'RE RIGHT BACK WHERE WE STARTED!					
220						
221	4. THE RESULT IS TO MAKE ALT S A TOGGLE SWITCH THAT TURNS ON AND					
222	OFF VERTICAL TITLES AND ALWAYS RETURNS YOU TO WHERE YOU STARTED.					
223						
224	5. THE PURPOSE OF ALL THIS IS TO ALLOW THE USER TO FREEZE VERTICAL					
225	TITLES FOR DISPLAY PURPOSES, BUT TO UNFREEZE WHEN THE USER ACTUALLY					
226	WANTS TO MODIFY THOSE TITLES.					
227						
228						
229						
230						

Figure 130

226 Tip: The /XN and /XL commands can be used instead of **/R**ange Input to force the user to enter information in certain cells.

1-2-3 offers two input commands that are alternatives to **/R**ange **I**nput: /XL and /XN. These commands are identical except that /XL accepts only label entries, and /XN accepts only numeric entries. The forms of the two commands are the same:

/xnMESSAGE~LOCATION~

/xlMESSAGE~LOCATION~

The MESSAGE is a prompt that instructs the user about the type of input required. The LOCATION is an instruction to 1-2-3; the entry made in response to the command will be stored in that location.

For example, the command

/xlEnter first name: ~A15~

causes the message

Enter first name:

to appear in the control panel. The user then types a label entry and presses {Enter}. The label is automatically entered in cell A15. If the user enters a formula or value in response to this prompt, 1-2-3 interprets the entry as a numeric label. For example, if the user enters the number 1234 in response to the prompt, the label '1234 is stored in cell A15.

If, on the other hand, the user enters a label in response to the command

/xlEnter subscriber number: ~A15~

1-2-3 rejects the entry with the message

Illegal number input

When the user presses any key, 1-2-3 offers another chance to make an acceptable entry.

227 Tip: If you put a colon and a space between the last character in the MESSAGE and the tilde, the command line will be easier to understand when the macro runs.

If you enter the word *Johnson* in response to the macro command

/xlEnter a label~A15~

the message in the control panel is

> Enter a labelJohnson

If, on the other hand, the macro command is

> /xlEnter a label: ~A15~

the control panel reads

> Enter a label: Johnson

The second version has a cleaner appearance and is far easier to read than the first.

228 Trick: If you don't supply a LOCATION to the /XN or /XL commands, the input will be made in the current cell.

Suppose you create the command

> /xnEnter a number: ~~

When this macro is run, the prompt

> Enter a number

appears in the control panel. You make a numeric entry, and 1-2-3 stores that entry in the current cell—the cell in which the cursor currently resides.

229 Trick: If you enter a function in response to the /XN command, 1-2-3 stores only the current value of the function and not the function itself.

Suppose you enter the function @TODAY in response to the command

> /xnEnter today's date: ~A15~

If today were March 23, 1984, the number 30764—the 1-2-3 equivalent of March 23, 1984—would be entered in cell A15.

230 Tip: You can use the **/XL** command to enter numeric labels.

The **/XL** command can be used to enter a numeric label in your worksheet. Just enter a number in response to the **/XL** command, and 1-2-3 stores that number as a label.

231 Tip: Construct a special macro when you need input validation beyond checking for numeric.

The /XN macro command forces you to enter numeric data where required. However, there are times when you want different kinds of validation, such as checking that a number is within a particular range, or a code is in a table. Figure 131 shows a macro that performs this type of special validation.

	AA	AB	AC	AD
1	\V	/xnEnter a number :~TEST~		
2		/xiTEST<100~/xgAB5		
3		/xgMAIN~		
4				
5		/RETEST~/xg\V~		
6				

Figure 131

This simple macro fragment uses the /XN command to get a numeric input, which is stored in a cell named "TEST." The second line of the macro uses the /XI command to test the value of the entry. If the value is less than 100, the entry is unacceptable; and the macro transfers control to cell AB5, which erases "TEST" and loops back for a new input. If the entry is acceptable, the macro transfers control to a new cell location called "MAIN" (not shown in this fragment).

232 Tip: Control the updating of critical information with a macro that requires the user to supply a valid password before updating the data base.

A limitation of most microcomputer software is that it provides little in the way of security. Yet some small companies are using spreadsheet programs for tasks as sensitive as running a payroll. For some applications minimum security measures may be worth building into your macro.

Here is one way of doing it with 1-2-3: First, set up a table of valid passwords for gaining access to the data base Update macro. (See the "OK_PASSWORD" data base and its accompanying criterion range in Figure 132.) Next, write a macro that prompts for a password and then checks its validity against the table. The macro in Figure 133 performs these tasks. This macro assumes that you have defined the password table as a data base (including the assignment of a range name to the "OK_PASSWORD" field) and that you have defined the associated criterion range. The macro checks the results of an @DCOUNT on the password data base. If the password is valid, the macro executes the update macro. If not, it gives you three attempts at a valid password before the password macro kicks you out of 1-2-3.

```
        J      K      L          M       N
30                        OK_PASSWORD        |
31                        marsh              |
32                        marshmallow        |<PASSWORDS
33                        martian            |
34                        marcia             |
35
36                        OK_PASSWORD        |<CRITERION
37 CRIT_PASSWORD>                            |
38
```

Figure 132

```
        J      K          L                    M       N
21  \P      /dfCOUNTER~COUNTER+1~~~         Increment attempt counter.
22          /xiCOUNTER>3~/qy                After 3 attempts, exit 1-2-3.
23          /riINPUT_SCREEN~                Go into Range Input.
24          /cPASSWORD_IN~CRIT_PASSWORD     Copy input to criterion cell.
25          /xi@dcount(PASSWORDS,0,CRITERION)=1~/xgUPDATE_MACRO~
26          /xg\P~                          Above goes to update if pswd ok.
27          /xq~                            Else loop for another attempt.
28
29  COUNTER          0
30
```

Figure 133

Figure 134 shows the /**R**ange Input screen on which you enter the password.

Of course, anyone who understands how 1-2-3 macros work can easily defeat this scheme merely by pressing {Esc} or {Ctrl}{Break}. We could make the macro considerably more obscure, but, even in this form, it will discourage the average unauthorized user.

233 Tip: You can use the dynamic self-modification technique to create a toggle switch.

Sometimes the same action on the same switch can accomplish opposite tasks. For example, pressing the {Num Lock} key on the IBM PC keyboard causes the keypad to shift for numeric entry. Pressing that same key again causes the keypad to shift back for cursor movement.

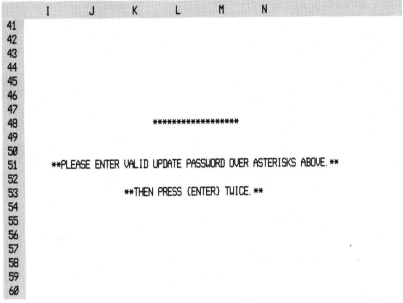

Figure 134

This kind of switch is called a toggle switch. With macros it is possible to create a toggle in the 1-2-3 worksheet.

Figure 135 shows the toggle macro described by the help screen in Figure 130. This macro is designed to turn worksheet titles on and off. We'll ignore the many details it takes to accomplish this, however. The important thing is that the \S macro becomes a toggle switch because \S alternately copies one of two macros ("FRZ" or "UNFRZ") back onto itself. When "FRZ" is finished, the macro copies "UNFRZ" to \S; and when "UNFRZ" is done, the macro copies "FRZ" to \S. (Of course, we've defined the ranges "FRZ" and "UNFRZ" to include the whole macros, not just the first cells.)

As a result, the first time you push {Alt} S, the macro will lock the titles on the screen using the /**W**orksheet **T**itles command. The next time you press {Alt} S, the macro will clear those titles.

Toggle macros can be very useful.

	I	J	K	L	M	N	O
1	UNFRZ	/wgpd/rndCUR_CELL~/rncCUR_CELL~~				{"UNFREEZE" TITLES	
2		/wtc{goto}REPORT~				{PROT OFF+MARK POS	
3		{goto}LINE0~{down}{down}/wth				{CLR TITLES+TO RPT	
4		{goto}CUR_CELL~				{SET HORIZ TITLE	
5		/cFRZ~\S~				{ TO ORIG POS	
6		/wgpe				{COPY FREEZE MACRO	
7						{ TO S MACRO AREA	
8	FRZ	/wgpd{right}{right}/rndCUR_CELL~				"FREEZE" TITLES,	
9		/rncCUR_CELL~~				PROT OFF+MARK POS	
10		/wtc{right}{right}{right}{right}				CLR TITLES	
11		{right}{goto}REPORT~				TO REPORT AREA	
12		{goto}LINE0~{DOWN}{DOWN}{RIGHT}				SET BOTH TITLES	
13		/wtb{goto}CUR_CELL~				TO ORIG POS	
14		/cUNFRZ~\S~				COPY UNFREEZE MACRO	
15		/wgpe				TO S MACRO AREA	
16							
17	\S	/wgpd/rndCUR_CELL~/rncCUR_CELL~~					
18		/wtc{goto}REPORT~					
19		{goto}LINE0~{down}{down}/wth					
20		{goto}CUR_CELL~					
21		/cFRZ~\S~					
22		/wgpe					

Figure 135

Ways to Test Macros

234 Tip: You can use Step mode to test macros.

Beginning with Release 1A of 1-2-3, you can press {Alt} F1 to put the macro processor in Step mode. In this mode the macro moves one keystroke at a time. After each keystroke the macro pauses and waits for the user to type any key on the keyboard. (The space bar is usually easiest.) With this feature you can step through your macro keystroke by keystroke to find any bugs.

Sometimes Step mode is too slow. An alternate way to stop a macro at any predefined point is to insert temporarily a blank cell in the macro at that point. This blank cell causes the macro processor to stop, and you can see whether the macro has executed correctly so far. To restart the macro at any point, assign a temporary name to the cell at which you want to begin and then use the {Alt} key and the letter assigned to start up again.

235 Trap: If you don't test your macros carefully, you're in for trouble.

You can use the suggestions under the previous Tip to test your macros. Carefully test every possible condition you can think of before you release the macro into production, especially if others are going to use it. It can also be helpful to have someone else look at your code and suggest things that could go wrong.

236 Tip: Use /Worksheet Window in testing macros.

If you put your macro code in one window and the area that the macro affects in another window, you can view both the code and the action in the worksheet as the macro runs. This is usually practical only if you execute your macro in Step mode; otherwise, things will probably happen too fast for you to see what's really going on.

237 Tip: You can create a "Next" macro, which you keep modifying in situations where you want to give up macro control and then pick it up again.

Sometimes you want to move into READY mode, outside of macro control, so that you can move around the worksheet and make updates freely and then pick up macro control when you are finished with READY mode. But how do you know which macro to start up next?

Solve this problem with the rule: Whenever you want to start up a macro again, press {Alt} N (N for "Next"). Then make sure that before your last macro gives up control, it copies the proper code into the range named \N.

Here's an example. Suppose you're finishing up a macro and want to move into READY mode; you know that when you are ready to go back under macro control, you want to present MENU_2. Make sure that your current macro finishes with code something like this:

    {GoTo}\N~/re~'/xmMENU_ 2~

This statement places the code /xmMENU_ 2 in \N.

Remember that the cell immediately below \N must contain a single tilde (~). Notice that the command copied into \N does not contain any tildes. It is impossible to enter a tilde in a cell from within a macro because the tilde always terminates the cell entry. However, the /XM command must end with a tilde. Placing a single tilde in the cell below \N overcomes this problem.

The next time you press {Alt} N, 1-2-3 will automatically display MENU_ 2. Suppose that after MENU_ 2 runs, you want to return control to the user again. After this second free stage, you want to run another macro named MENU_ 3. The last line of the macro called by MENU_ 2 should read

   {GoTo}\N~/re~'/xmMENU_3~

Repeat this process as often as you wish to toggle back and forth between the READY and COMMAND modes.

238 Trap: If you forget the tilde (~) at the end of some macro commands, you'll get puzzling results.

Most macro commands require a ~ at the end. (/XQ and /XR are exceptions.) Don't forget this tilde!

Names

239 Trap: If you don't delete a range name before redefining it, you can get into trouble.

Often in macros we want to redefine a range name continually so that it refers first to one cell and then to another. 1-2-3 allows you to use /**R**ange Name **C**reate to redefine a range name without having first used /**R**ange Name **D**elete to delete the first range name. The correct practice, however, is to use /**R**ange Name **D**elete first. (See Figure 125.)

The Trap is this: Suppose you give cell A7 the range name HERE. As soon as you do that, 1-2-3 changes any formulas that refer to A7 so that they refer to "HERE." For instance, if C7 contained the formula

   C7:+A7*B7

it now contains the formula

   C7:+HERE*B7

So far so good. But what happens if we use /**R**ange Name **C**reate to redefine "HERE" to refer to A8? The formula in C7 still reads

C7: +HERE*B7

The problem is that the definition of "HERE" has changed so that it now refers to A8. Therefore, HERE*B7 is equivalent to A8*B7 instead of the original A7*B7. Not what we want!

However, if we first use the /**R**ange **N**ame **D**elete command to destroy the range name before we reassign it to cell A8, there is no problem. When the range name is **D**eleted, the formula in cell C7 reverts to

C7: +A7*B7

When we then reassign the name "HERE" to cell A8, the formula in C7 is not affected.

Because this problem can cause you no end of grief, follow this strict rule: Always do a /**R**ange **N**ame **D**elete before you redefine a range name.

240   Trick: You can give a macro more than one name.

One handy use of this Trick occurs when you have a \0 autoexec macro in your worksheet that you would also like to be able to execute from the keyboard. Since the \0 macro cannot be executed from the keyboard, you need to give the macro another name—for example, \A—and use that name whenever you want to execute the macro from the keyboard.

241   Tip: The /XI command can be used to enter text in a cell in response to a conditional test.

One of 1-2-3's main limitations is the program's inability to handle a function like

A1: @IF(A2>=55,'Sell,'Hold)

This function might be used in a stock portfolio application to flag a stock that has reached a predetermined sell price. If the stock price is greater than or equal to $55 per share, you want to sell, and the label "Sell" should appear in cell A1. Otherwise, the label "Hold" should appear in that cell. Unfortunately, 1-2-3 cannot interpret this kind of function.

One way around this problem is to use the /XI command in a macro like the one shown in Figure 136.

	AA	AB	AC	AD
1	\T	/xiA2)=55~/xgAB4~		
2		{GoTo}A1~' Hold~		
3				
4		{GoTo}A1~' Sell~		
5				

Figure 136

This macro uses the /XI command to compare the value in cell A2 with the predetermined sell price. If the current stock price in A2 is greater than the sell price of $50, the /XG command transfers control to cell AB4, which enters the label "Sell" into cell A2. If the current price is less than the sell price, line 2 of the macro enters the label "Hold" in cell A2.

This is a simple example of the way that the /XI command can be substituted for the @IF function. This same technique can be used in many other ways to enter labels into cells in response to a logical test.

12
Graphics

Defining Graphs

242 **Tip:** Use /Graph View frequently as you define a graph.

Defining the type of graph you want is an iterative process, especially until the /Graph options have become second nature to you. You can sit for a long time wondering whether you've chosen the right options; don't do it. The best approach is to choose a few options, then use /Graph View to see what you have. If something is not right, go back and experiment with a different choice of options and select View again. Keep experimenting until you have what you want.

If you have trouble getting going with graphs, Chapter 9 in *Using 1-2-3*, "Creating and Displaying Graphs," may be helpful to you.

243 **Tip:** When you try a new type of graph for the first time, write down the options you've chosen.

Record the options you've chosen when you create a new type of graph. You'll have a reliable guide when you produce the same type of graph a second time and so avoid scratching your head at all the same places you did the first time.

177

If you know you're going to repeat graphs frequently with slight variations in different worksheets, you may want to create a macro that defines, for instance, a generic XY graph. You can then save that macro into a file with /File Xtract and Combine it into many different worksheets, modifying the graph as needed each time you use it.

Figure 137 shows data on grain sales from which we want to create a pie graph. We know we'll be creating similar graphs in the future, so we write a macro (Figure 138) to save the keystrokes. The resulting graph is shown in Figure 139.

This macro can be included in a worksheet by the /File Combine command. Remember, however, that a Combined worksheet does not bring range names with it. After the Combine you must rename the macro before you can execute it. In this case we rename the macro \P and execute it by holding down {Alt} P.

```
         I        J       K       L        M        N
1
2                   January Grain Sales
3                   ====================
4
5                   Cotton   Corn    Oats    Barley
6                   --------  --------  --------  --------
7   Unit Price       $12.32   $5.50   $18.21   $15.47
8   Unit Sales       12,100   5,000   22,438   25,018
9   Total Sales    $149,072  $27,500 $408,596 $387,028
10
```

Figure 137

```
         I        J       K       L        M        N
21
22  \P      /gtp               Graph type: Pie
23          aK9.N9~             Set data range
24          xK5.N5~             Set pie slice lables
25          otfJanuary Grain Sales~   Options, Title, First
26          q                  Quit Options
27          v                  View
28
```

Figure 138

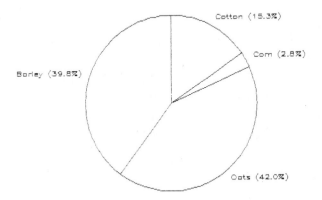

January Grain Sales

Cotton (15.3%)

Corn (2.8%)

Barley (39.8%)

Oats (42.0%)

Figure 139

244 Trap: When you **/File** **C**ombine a worksheet, the graph definitions in the worksheet being combined do not become a part of the final combined worksheet.

You might think you could use the same graph definition in several worksheets simply by saving the file containing the graph definitions with the /File Save or Xtract commands and then Combining that file into a new worksheet. Unfortunately, this procedure won't work because the graph definitions don't come along when you Combine.

245 Tip: Use 1-2-3's memory to create new graphs from old ones that are similar.

Because 1-2-3 remembers all the parameters of a graph until you issue the /Graph Reset command, you can use the existing parameters as a guide when you create a new graph. In some cases you may have to change only a few settings to create your new definition. When you're finished and a View has satisfied you that you have what you want, save the new graph under a new name using /Graph Name Create. Be careful. If you use the name of the first graph, you'll replace that graph definition instead of adding a new one.

246 **Tip:** If you have both monochrome and graphics displays, you can view the spreadsheet on the monochrome and a graph on the graphics display simultaneously.

Two monitors can be useful when you are doing "what if" graphical analysis. With two monitors you don't have to keep toggling back and forth between the spreadsheet and the graph, so it's much easier to see what's going on.

247 **Trick:** You can leave empty rows and columns in your data ranges to create more space in your graphs.

This trick depends on the fact that 1-2-3 will not include in graphs cells that are blank or contain ERR or NA. This feature is useful in situations where your graph would otherwise be too crowded.

For example, Figure 140 shows interest rate data; we have deliberately left certain rows blank. Figure 141 shows a macro that contains all the /Graph command input necessary to create the graph shown in Figure 142. Note that we included blank rows in both the A range and the A Data Labels specification. This graph uses the A range values themselves as data labels, so we chose "Neither" in the Format option.

	I	J	K	L	M
41	Interest Movements for February 1983				
42					
43	Date	Fed Funds Rate		LIBOR	
44					
45	01-Feb	8.13		9.56	
46					
47	03-Feb	8.15		9.50	
48	06-Feb	8.25		9.38	
49	08-Feb	8.63		9.31	
50	10-Feb	8.38		9.25	
51	11-Feb	8.56		9.25	
52					
53	12-Feb	8.57		9.13	
54	13-Feb	8.31		9.13	
55	14-Feb	8.38		9.06	
56	15-Feb	8.56		9.13	
57	16-Feb	8.42		8.88	
58	17-Feb	8.31		8.91	
59					

Figure 140

	I	J	K	L	M	N	O
61	\L	/grg				Reset graph definition	
62		tl				Type: Line	
63		aJ44. J54~				Set A range	
64		xI44. I54~				Set X-axis range	
65		o				Options	
66		daJ44. J54~				Set a data labels range	
67		c				Center data labels	
68		q				Quit data labels	
69		fan				Format A range--Neither	
70		q				Quit format	
71		tfInterest Movements...~				Title, First	
72		q				Quit options	
73		v				View	
74							

Figure 141

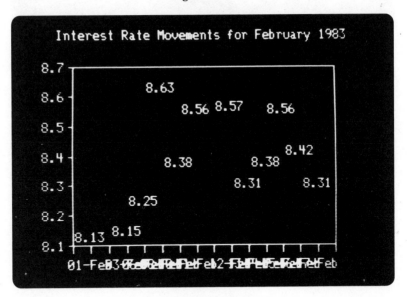

Figure 142

The graph in Figure 142 has space before the first data point, after the last, and between several pairs of data points because of the empty rows in our source data range.

Figure 143 shows the same graph without these empty rows. (This example is a variation of one used in *Using 1-2-3*.) Note the overlapping labels for data points close in value. Note also that without a blank row at the beginning and end of the data range, the labels overlap the borders.

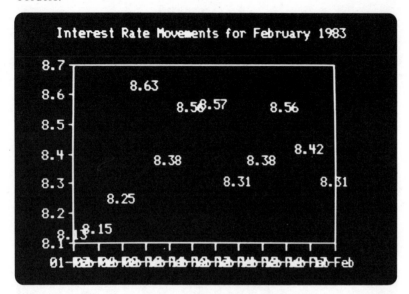

Figure 143

If we use /Graph Save to save the graph in Figure 143 and then print it with **Print Graph**, the overlapping-labels problem goes away. See the printed version in Figure 144. This illustrates the fact that the printed graph never looks exactly like the one that you see on the screen.

We still have a crowding problem in this graph; the X-axis labels overlap and are unreadable. We'll deal with this problem under the next Tip.

Labeling

248 **Tip:** You can use the /Graph Options Scale Skip command to skip labels on the X-axis and avoid overlapping labels.

This Tip takes care of the problem we had in the example of the previous Tip. (See Figures 142 and 143.) If we execute a /Graph Options Scale Skip and supply a skip factor of 3, only every third X-axis label is displayed, and we have readable labels. (See Figure 145.) Unfortunately,

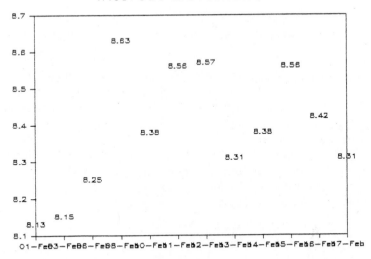

Figure 144

this method is entirely satisfactory only when the X-axis labels are continuous. If the labels are not continuous, we're not sure which data points go with which skipped labels. (This is actually the case in our example because some days are not present. See Figure 140.)

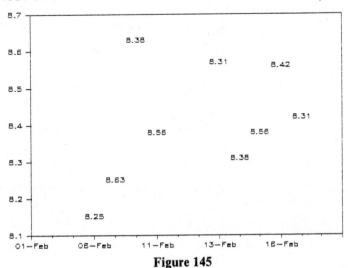

Figure 145

249 **Tip:** You can create "floating labels" by including a fake data range in your worksheet and choosing the **F**ormat **N**either option for that range.

Figure 146 shows a graph with what are sometimes called *floating labels*, the "QTR1," "QTR2," etc., at the top of the graph. These labels are floating because they have no data values with them. In this case we use floating labels to produce a second set of X-axis labels. Figure 147 shows the worksheet data from which this graph came. Note that K149..N149 contains the labels that end up floating. K150..N150 contain the "fake" data that determine the vertical positioning of the labels on the graph; because all these values are set at 115,000, the labels appear in line with the 115,000 point on the Y-axis.

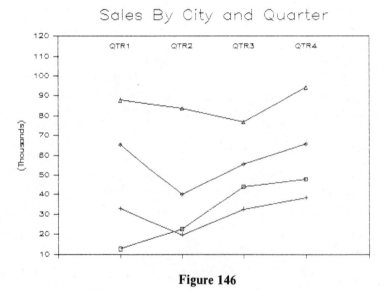

Figure 146

To produce these results,

1. Supply the fake data as an extra data range, in this case, range E, J150..O150.

2. Specify **N**either for the **F**ormat option for the E data range. This ensures that the actual data points and the lines connecting them will not appear on the graph.

```
        I       J       K       L       M       N       O       P
141
142             SALES BY CITY AND QUARTER
143
144             Jan-Mar Apr-Jun Jul-Sep Oct-Dec         Average
145   Dallas     65500   40100   55600   66000           56800
146   SF         87900   83900   77050   94300           85788
147   LA         12660   22590   44100   47900           31813
148   Den        33000   19800   32700   38600           31025
149             QTR1    QTR2    QTR3    QTR4
150             115000  115000  115000  115000
```

Figure 147

3. Use the **O**ptions **D**ata-**L**abels command to specify the range of the labels you want to float for data range E, in this case, J149..O149.

You can use this technique to place special notes almost anywhere you want on a graph. Location depends primarily on the size of the values you give to the fake data. You can also further control the positioning by what you specify for Alignment when you define the labels. In Figure 146 we used Center alignment. Figure 148 shows two variations. In the first variation we used Left alignment, so the labels are skewed to the left. In the second variation we changed the middle two fake numbers (in cells L150 and M150) to 100,000 in order to display the two middle labels lower than the other labels.

250 **Trap:** If you don't sort the X-range data supplied to an XY graph and you choose **F**ormat **L**ines, you'll end up with a mess.

For an XY graph, 1-2-3 connects the data points with lines based on the order in which the data points appear in the source area of the worksheet. If these data points are not sorted, the lines create a tangled mess. For example, the XY graph in Figure 149 uses the data in Figure 147 and plots first-quarter sales along the X-axis against average sales for all quarters along the Y-axis. The lines connect strangely because the X-axis data is not sorted.

If we sort the table on the first-quarter data field, the worksheet looks like Figure 150. This produces the graph in Figure 151, which is the graph we want.

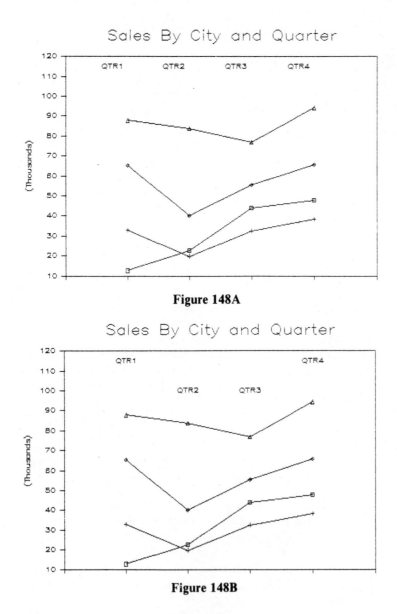

Figure 148A

Figure 148B

Figure 152 shows a macro that generates the graph in Figure 151. Note that range names are often used instead of cell addresses. We'll explain the reason for this under the next Tip.

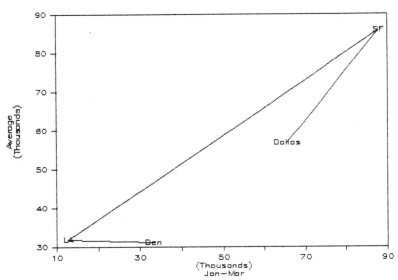

Figure 149

	I	J	K	L	M	N	O	P
141								
142			SALES BY CITY AND QUARTER					
143								
144			Jan-Mar	Apr-Jun	Jul-Sep	Oct-Dec		Average
145	LA		12660	22590	44100	47900		31813
146	Den		33000	19800	32700	38600		31025
147	Dallas		65500	40100	55600	66000		56800
148	SF		87900	83900	77050	94300		85788
149			QTR1	QTR2	QTR3	QTR4		
150			115000	115000	115000	115000		

Figure 150

251 **Tip:** If you use range names where possible in a graph definition, it is easier to make changes without actually altering the definition.

Figure 152 is a macro showing all the parameters necessary to create the graph in Figure 151. Note that we specified the following range names

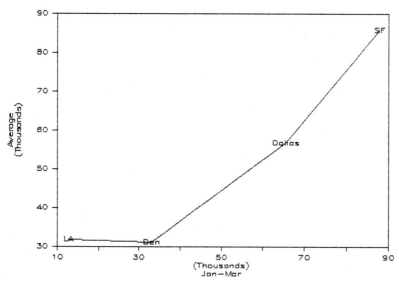

Figure 151

as parameters: "QTR1_DATA," "AVE_DATA," "TITLE,"
"X_TITLE," "Y_TITLE." Using named ranges makes the macro more
generalized, so you can modify the graph without changing the graph

	I	J	K	L	M	N
161	\X	/grg		Graph reset entire graph		
162		tx		Graph type: XY		
163		xQTR1_DATA~		QTR1_DATA on X-axis		
164		aAVE_DATA~		AVE_DATA on Y-Axis		
165		o		Options		
166		fal		Format A range with lines		
167		q		Quit format		
168		tf\TITLE~		First title: range named TITLE		
169		tx\X_TITLE~		X title: range named X_TITLE		
170		ty\Y_TITLE~		Y title: range named Y_TITLE		
171		daI145. I148~c		Data labels for A; center labels		
172		q		Quit labels		
173		q		Quit Options		
174		v		View		

Figure 152

definition. This technique helps you create a kind of generic definition for each type of graph. You can then modify the definitions as needed.

252   Trap: The use of the X-range option can be confusing.

For all types of graphs except the XY type, the /Graph X-range option is used to specify labels. In line, bar, and stacked bar graphs, the labels appear along the X-axis; in pie graphs the labels apply to the pie slices.

The XY graph is, of course, different from the others because it has numeric value scales on both the X and Y axes. 1-2-3 therefore needed some way to specify the range of values to be plotted along the X-axis. The designers chose the X-range option for this purpose. (If you look at the macro in Figure 152, you'll see that we use the X-range option on line 3 to specify that the first-quarter data be plotted along the X-axis.) This is an unfortunate choice because it mixes several different functions and leads to confusion.

253   Tip: You can specify graph Titles by referring to a cell's contents.

You can supply a range name or a cell address in response to the prompts you get from all the suboptions of the Title option. Precede the range name or cell address with a backslash (\) so 1-2-3 can tell it is not a literal label. For example, we could specify the title for a graph created from Figure 147 by issuing the command

/Graph Options Titles First \K142

The "\K142" tells 1-2-3 to use the label in cell K142 as the first title for this graph.

The reference supplied after the "\" can, of course, be a name. In the example above, if cell K142 were named "TITLE," we could substitute "\TITLE" for "\K142." The macro in Figure 152 makes use of this technique to create several titles.

254   Trick: You can have both values and labels in the labels for a pie graph.

One limitation of 1-2-3's pie graph is that you can get only one set of labels on the graph with the X-range option. You can get either labels (as in Figure 139) or the actual values represented by each pie slice, but not both. If we had specified K9..N9—the actual values and the A range—as the X-range for the data in Figure 137, we would have had the actual values as labels.

It would be nice to get both labels and actual values on the graph so that, for instance, we'd have "Corn $27,500" as a label for the corn pie-slice. We can do this with a macro if we place the label range and the value range in consecutive columns, as in Figure 153. The macro in Figure 154 uses the /Print File command to write these two columns to the disk, and then the /File Import Text command to read them back into the next column. This procedure concatenates the label column and the value column into one column. (You can see the results in the third column of Figure 153.) We then make sure that we define the X-range for the pie graph to cover this concatenated column. It's hard to see it from Figure 153, but the label in K10, for instance, is actually the concatenated value "Cotton $149,072." The resulting graph is shown in Figure 155. (The macro depends on the fact that the cursor is resting at the top of the label column when we press {Alt} L.)

	I	J	K	L	M
10	Cotton	$149,072	Cotton	$149,072	
11	Corn	$27,500	Corn	$27,500	
12	Oats	$408,596	Oats	$408,596	
13	Barley	$387,028	Barley	$387,028	
14					
15					

Figure 153

	I	J	K	L	M	N	O	P
181	\L	/pfTEMP~r				Print temp file to disk (replace).		
182		ca				Clear all print settings.		
183		r.{end}{down}{right}~				Point out range to write.		
184		o				Options.		
185		ml0~				Margin, Left, 0.		
186		mt0~				Margin, Top, 0.		
187		mb0~				Margin, Bottom, 0.		
188		ou				Other Unformatted print.		
189		q				Quit Options.		
190		gq				Go & Quit print.		
191		{right}{right}				Move to label import area.		
192		/fitTEMP~				File import labels from disk.		
193								

Figure 154

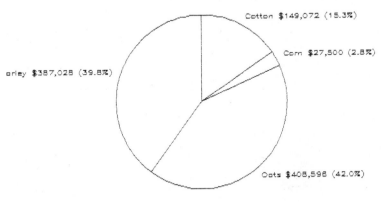

January Grain Sales

Cotton $149,072 (15.3%)

Corn $27,500 (2.8%)

orley $387,028 (39.8%)

Oats $408,598 (42.0%)

Figure 155

255 **Trap:** If your graph labels are too long, 1-2-3 truncates them.

As you can see from Figure 155, the technique shown in the previous Tip gives us the labels we want. The only problem is that our labels are too long for 1-2-3 to handle, so they are truncated. If we were able to shorten both the label and the value fields in Figure 153, we could get the full concatenated labels. (See Figure 156.)

Creating Different Kinds of Graphs

256 **Trap:** Negative values in the source data for a pie or a stacked bar graph can give misleading results.

Figure 157 shows a table that contains one net value that is negative (Corn). Figure 158 shows that 1-2-3 treats this as a positive value in a pie graph. The same thing is true of a stacked bar graph.

Obviously, the existence of a negative data item makes pie charts and stacked bar charts all but useless. This is not a problem with 1-2-3, however, but simply a characteristic of these graphs.

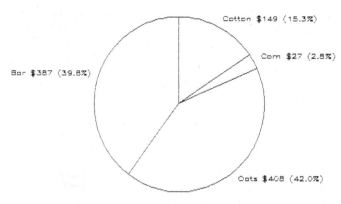

Figure 156

257 Trap: Be careful when defining the ranges for a stacked bar chart.

In 1-2-3 the various ranges in a stacked bar chart are cumulative. The total length of the stacked bar equals the sum of the lengths of the partial bars. Simple enough, right? But it is easy to become confused when defining stacked bar charts.

```
          I       J      K        L       M       N
201               January Grain Net
202               ====================
203
204               Cotton   Corn     Oats     Barley
205               -------- -------- -------- --------
206 Total Sales   $149,072 $149,072 $149,072 $149,072
207 Total Costs   $122,000 $160,000 $130,000 $100,000
208 Net            $27,072 ($10,928) $19,072  $49,072
209
```

Figure 157

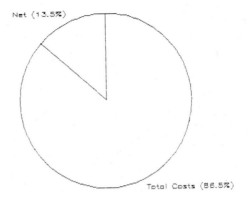

Figure 158

For example, suppose you are defining a stacked bar chart from the following worksheet:

	A	B	C	D
1	Sales	$12,652	$13,943	$15,933
2	CGS	$10,231	$11,832	$10,921
3		-------	-------	-------
4	Gross Margin	$2,421	$2,111	$5,012
5		=======	=======	=======

You want the graph to show the two components of Sales—CGS and Gross Margin. The correct A range for this graph is B2..D2, and the right B range is B4..D4; but many users define the ranges incorrectly as B1..D1 for A, and B2..D2 for B. Remember that you want to graph the components of the total of CGS and Gross Margin. The total of these two, "Sales," will be represented by the combined lengths of the two bars.

258 Trap: The difference between a line graph and an XY graph is very subtle.

XY graphs are sometimes called scatter plots. Although XY graphs are similar to line graphs, they are different in some important ways. First, in XY graphs the X labels are more than simple hash marks on the X axis. These labels are actually the X-axis scale. This means that unlike all other 1-2-3 graphs, which can be created with a single data range, an XY graph requires two ranges—an A range and an X range.

Second, in an XY chart two different data points can share the same X-axis value. This is impossible in a line graph.

Third, XY plots and line graphs are normally used to illustrate different kinds of information. Line graphs diagram time-series data. XY graphs, on the other hand, illustrate the relationships between different attributes of the data items, for instance, the relationship between age and income or between educational achievement and salary.

259   Tip: When 1-2-3's automatic scaling is inadequate, you can adjust the scale manually with **/G**raph **O**ptions **S**cale.

Figure 160 shows a graph based on the data in Figure 159. 1-2-3 scaled this graph by its default automatic scaling. But what if you want a different scale? Suppose, for instance, that you think the net loss of "Corn" is really pretty small—that it could be a great deal larger—and you plan to compare this graph with others where you need a larger negative scale. You can adjust the scale yourself by choosing **M**anual under **/G**raph **O**ptions **S**cale and adjusting both the upper and lower limits. Figure 161 shows the result of such an adjustment. (Compare with Figure 160.)

If you use the Manual option, remember that you must adjust both the lower and upper limits manually.

```
          I       J       K        L         M         N
201                   January Grain Net
202                   ====================
203
204                   Cotton   Corn      Oats      Barley
205                   --------  --------  --------  --------
206  Total Sales      $240,000 $135,000 $170,000 $143,000
207  Total Costs      $122,000 $160,000 $130,000 $100,000
208  Net              $118,000 ($25,000) $40,000  $43,000
209
```

Figure 159

260   Trap: If you use Manual adjustment, you must take care not to cut off some of your data by making the scales too small.

In the example in Figure 162, we cut off one of the data points by making the upper limit too low. If you use Manual adjustment, be careful to avoid doing this. (Compare Figure 162 with Figure 161.)

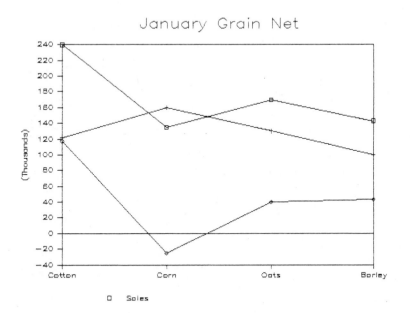

Figure 160

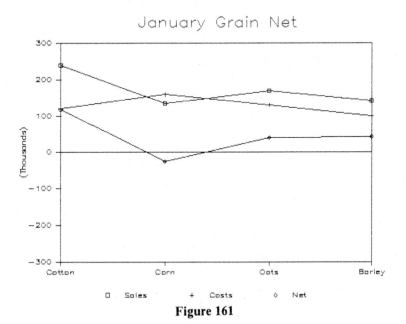

Figure 161

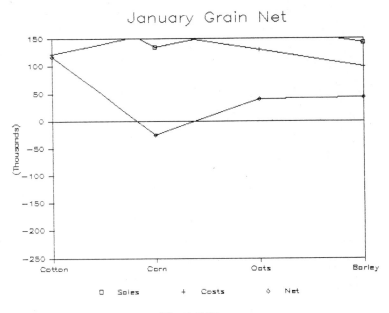

Figure 162

261 **Trap:** Whenever the numbers in the data range for a line, bar, XY, or stacked bar chart are greater than 1,000, 1-2-3 automatically converts the Y-axis labels into decimals and adds the label "Thousands" on the left side of the graph.

This feature is not a problem unless you are in the habit of truncating large numbers in your worksheet. For example, suppose you have created a balance sheet and income statement for a company with gross sales of over $100 million. Instead of writing the sales number as $124,945,000, you truncate it to $124,945. All other numbers in the worksheet are similarly truncated, and the message "000s omitted" is entered near the top of the worksheet. Figure 163 shows a simple worksheet of this sort.

Now suppose you want to create a stacked bar graph from this worksheet. The A range is B2..D2, and the B range is B4..D4. When you view the graph, it should look like Figure 164. Now, look at the labels on the Y axis and the legend next to those labels. The legend says "Thousands." But recall that these numbers are not thousands, but millions. The legends are not accurate.

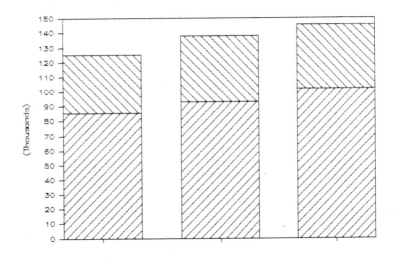

	A	B	C	D	E
1	Sales	$124,945	$137,931	$145,732	
2	Expenses	$85,623	$92,946	$101,832	
3		--------	--------	--------	
4	Profit	$39,322	$44,985	$43,900	
5		========	========	========	

Figure 163

Figure 164

262 **Trap:** On a color monitor, you may end up with confusing bar chart displays if you have more than three data ranges.

If you choose the Color option, 1-2-3 can make use of only three colors, one of which is white. All data ranges beyond the third are also shown in white. If your graph has more than three data ranges, two or more of the ranges are in white, so it is difficult to distinguish the different ranges.

Naming and Saving Graphs

263   **Tip:** To save a graph definition with a worksheet, use **/G**raph **N**ame **C**reate before you save the worksheet.

1-2-3 saves graph definitions with a worksheet if you execute /Graph Name Create after specifying all the options. When you save the worksheet, all graph definitions created in this way are saved and readily available through /Graph Name Use after you retrieve the worksheet. Don't forget to save the worksheet itself, or you will lose all the graph definitions, too.

264   **Trap:** If you **/G**raph **N**ame **U**se another graph before you name the current graph with **/G**raph **N**ame **C**reate, you'll lose the whole specification.

Unless you name your graphs, 1-2-3 can remember only one set of graph settings at a time. If you issue the /Graph Name Use command to use a named graph before you /Graph Name Create the current graph, the settings for the current graph will be lost.

265   **Trap:** If you change any parameters in the graph definition after you've issued **/G**raph **N**ame **C**reate, you must issue **C**reate again for 1-2-3 to remember the changes once the current graph is no longer the one in use.

1-2-3 does not automatically update the named version of a graph when you make changes to one or more parameters. To make those changes permanent, you must manually rename the graph with /Graph Name Create.

266   **Trap:** Remember that to save a graph permanently you must both name the graph and save the worksheet file containing the graph.

This is a mistake we've made several times. After we created or modified a graph, we stored it in the worksheet with /Graph Name Create. When the 1-2-3 session was over, though, we forgot to /File Save the worksheet containing the graph names. Because the names are stored in the worksheet and not on the disk, we lose all the named graphs in the worksheet if we forget to save it.

267   **Trap:** **/G**raph **N**ame **C**reate does not save a graph for printing or plotting.

To save a graph for output with the **Print Graph** program, you must execute the /**Graph Save** command. This command creates a special disk file with a .PIC extension. The printer or plotter uses this file to create the printed version.

Printing Graphs

268 **Tip:** If you have a number of graphs to print, you can leave the printer unattended longer if you select a group of graphs for printing all at once.

Figure 165 shows the **Print Graph Select** menu. In this example, we've selected the first three graphs for printing in a queue. Note that to select a graph for output, you must move the cursor to the line on which that graph is found and press the space bar to activate the toggle mark (#). 1-2-3 will print these graphs one after another automatically.

269 **Tip:** If you choose to print several graphs at once, be sure that you adjust the settings for the **Options Eject** and **Options Pause** commands.

The **Eject** command determines whether a form feed is sent to the printer after each graph. If **Eject** is on, each graph appears on a separate page. **Pause** tells 1-2-3 whether or not it should pause after printing each graph. If you want the printing to proceed automatically, turn this setting off.

270 **Trap:** If you do not **C**onfigure the **Print Graph** program for your output device, you will get strange results when you try to output a graph.

Figure 166 shows the **Print Graph Device Configure** menu. To configure for a device, move the cursor to the corresponding line and activate the toggle mark (#) by hitting the space bar.

271 **Tip:** You can reduce graph printing time while doing trial output of graphs by choosing a very small size for the printed graph.

Because 1-2-3 prints graphs slowly, you can waste a lot of time waiting to see if the finished version of a graph is correct. One way to overcome this problem is to use the **Option Size Manual** command to print a very

```
Copyright 1982, 1983 Lotus Development Corp.  All Rights Reserved      POINT
-----------------------------------------------------------------------------
Select graphs for output


===============================================================================
      PICTURE     DATE     TIME    SIZE
      ----------------------------------------
   #  GR0803    12-29-83    8:33   1024     [Space] toggles mark on and off
   #  GR0806    12-29-83   10:56    768     [Enter] selects marked pictures
   #  GR0807    12-29-83   11:06    768         in the order marked
      GR0808    12-29-83   11:24    768     [Escape] ignores marked pictures
                                                and returns
                                         [Home] goes to beginning of list
                                         [End] goes to end of list
                                         [Up] moves cursor up
                                         [Down] moves cursor down
                                             List scrolls if cursor moved
                                             beyond top or bottom
                                         [Graph] draws picture on screen
```

Figure 165

small graph. Because 1-2-3 has less to print when the Size is reduced, the test graph can be printed faster. After you've determined that the graph is satisfactory, return the Size to the default settings and reprint the graph.

272   Tip: Pressing {Graph} when printing allows you to preview the graph selected.

The {Graph} key works in the **P**rint **G**raph program exactly as it does in the main 1-2-3 program. Pressing {Graph} causes the current graph to be displayed on your graphics monitor. You can use the {Graph} key to preview a graph before you print it.

273   Trap: Even if you specify colors with the **/G**raph **O**ptions **C**olors command before **S**aving the graph, you must respecify any colors you want to use in the **P**rint **G**raph program.

It makes sense that if you select /**G**raph **O**ptions Color in 1-2-3 and then save that graph for printing, the graph will retain the colors. However, in 1-2-3 this is not the case. Even if the graph was saved with Color, you

```
Copyright 1982, 1983 Lotus Development Corp.  All Rights Reserved      POINT
----------------------------------------------------------------------------
Select graph output device


============================================================================

        ---------------------------------------------
        Anadex 9620A Silent Scribe Printer      [Space] bar moves mark
    #   Epson FX80 Printer, Single Density Mode [Enter] selects marked device
        Epson FX80 Printer, Double Density Mode [Escape] exits
        Epson FX80 Printer, Triple Density Mode  without changing device
        Epson FX80 Printer, Quad Density Mode   [Home] goes to beginning of list
        HP 7470A Plotter                        [End] goes to end of list
        IBM Graphics Printer, Single Density Mode [Up] moves cursor up
        IBM Graphics Printer, Double Density Mode [Down] moves cursor down
        IBM Graphics Printer, Triple Density Mode [Up] moves cursor up
        IBM Graphics Printer, Quad Density Mode   List scrolls if cursor moved
        Epson MX80 or MX100, Single Density Mode  beyond top or bottom
        Epson MX80 or MX100, Double Density Mode
        Epson MX80 or MX100, Triple Density Mode
        NEC 8023 Printer
        Okidata 82A or 83A Printer
```

Figure 166

need to respecify the colors with the **P**rint **G**raph program before printing the graph if you want color in the printed version.

274 **Tip:** You may reduce the time it takes to switch back and forth between 1-2-3 and **P**rint **G**raph by using a memory-partitioning program.

There are several programs available that patch the operating system and allow you to partition memory so that more than one program can be resident at once. This is not multitasking, so only one program can run at any one time; but you can save time if you don't have to reload every program. One such product available for the IBM PC is Memory-Shift by North American Business Systems in St. Louis, MO.

275 **Tip:** You may be able to display 1-2-3 graphs on a standard IBM monochrome display monitor.

Hercules Computer Technology in Berkeley, CA, offers an expansion board for the IBM PC that allows you to do 1-2-3 graphics in black and white on the IBM monochrome display. But you should exercise care in depending on a nonstandard feature like this. Talk to the company representatives and to people who've used the product, and ask some of these questions: Does this option have any effect on the monitor over a period of time? Could this board be incompatible with other boards I might want to put in my PC? Is the board compatible with the graphics of other programs?

13

Data Base

A data base is a specially configured part of the 1-2-3 worksheet. There is nothing special about the cells in a data base—they hold labels or numbers, just like regular 1-2-3 cells. The simplest definition of a 1-2-3 data base is *a list of information stored in a range of cells that spans at least one column and two rows.* The main thing that makes a certain part of the worksheet a data base is that you say it is a data base.

There are certain terms you need to understand before going on with this section. A *record* is an individual item in a list. For example, in the phone book, each listing (name, address, phone number) is a record. A *field* is an individual bit of data. In our phone book example, name, address, and phone are all fields. In 1-2-3 a record is a row, and a field is a column. Each record (row) is made up of one or more cells. Each cell is also a part of a field (column).

There is one other thing to mention: every field in a 1-2-3 data base must be given a unique name. All field names are entered in a single row across the top of the data base (frequently, but not necessarily, at the top of the worksheet.) All you need to do to create a 1-2-3 data base, then, is enter at least one field name in a cell and enter one piece of information in the cell just below that field name.

For more information on the fundamentals of data bases, see Chapter 11 in *Using 1-2-3* or look in the Lotus Manual.

Criteria and Criterion Ranges

276 Tip: 1-2-3 Criterion ranges allow you to search data bases for specific information.

All 1-2-3 /**D**ata **Q**uery commands and data base statistics use criterion ranges to select the records to be summed, counted, extracted, found, or deleted. In simplest form a criterion range consists of two cells. The first cell reproduces a field name from the data base being queried or analyzed. The second cell is used to enter a label or value that indicates which record you want to select.

For example, suppose that you create the data base shown in Figure 167.

	A	B	C	D	E
1	Name	Phone	Amount		
2	Smith, J.	502-555-1212	$100		
3	Jones, D.	415-555-1212	$75		
4	Caesar, J.	617-555-1212	$500		
5					
6	Name				
7	Smith, J.				

Figure 167

Now suppose you want to find all the records for J. Smith. A criterion range used by the /**D**ata **Q**uery **F**ind command to locate this record is shown in cells A6 and A7 in Figure 167. Notice that this criterion range includes the field name "Name." This header tells the program to look in the "Name" field for a record that matches the contents of cell A7. When used with the /**D**ata **F**ind command, this criterion locates the first record in the data base.

277 Tip: Criteria can be numbers as well as labels.

Criterion ranges can also use numbers to search for a match. For example, the criterion range

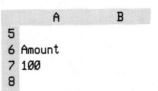

Figure 167A

translates: Select only records for which the value in the "Amount" field is equal to 100.

278 **Tip:** A good way to verbalize criterion ranges is to say "equals" between the field name and the actual criterion.

In the first example above, say, "Name equals Smith, J." In the second, say, "Amount equals 100."

Formulas

279 **Tip:** Criteria can also be formulas.

For example, the criterion range in Figure 168

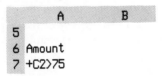

Figure 168

selects all records for which the value in the "Amount" column is greater than 75. Notice that the formula uses cell C2 as the test cell. With 1-2-3 formula criteria, the first cell in the column being tested is always used as the test cell. When you do a **F**ind or an **E**xtract or compute a sum using this criterion, 1-2-3 tests the value of every cell in column C; but the written formula refers to the first cell only.

280 **Tip:** Formula criteria do not have to be located under any particular field name.

For example, the criterion range shown in Figure 169 is identical in 1-2-3's eyes to the criterion shown in the previous Tip. It makes no difference that the formula in Figure 169 appears under the header "Name." The two criteria both return the same records.

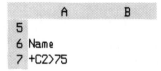

Figure 169

However, although formula criteria do not have to be entered under any particular field name, they must be entered under a legitimate field name. For example, the criterion range in Figure 170 is illegal because "Number" is not a field name in the main data base.

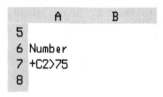

Figure 170

281 Tip: Be sure to put a plus sign (+) before criterion range formulas that begin with a cell address or range name.

This requirement is an extension of the general 1-2-3 rule for entering formulas into cells. If you enter A5>B5, 1-2-3 considers the entry a label and does not accept it as a formula criterion. As a result, you get nothing but an annoying beep when you try to activate the **Q**uery. But if you precede the entry with a plus sign, +A5>B5, you have what you want.

The same rule applies to a range name references in criteria. For example, a criterion referring to a cell named "WHLSL" should be written with a plus sign, +WHLSL>5.

282 Tip: To display the formulas used in a criterion range, format the formula cells with **/R**ange Format Text.

When you enter a formula as a criterion in a criterion range cell, 1-2-3 immediately evaluates the formula, as the program does any formula in any cell, and displays the resulting value. This feature can be confusing because it does not make obvious which formula you have entered as a criterion (although you can see the formula in the control panel if you place the cursor over the cell in question). In Figure 171 we have placed the formula +L7>5 in the criterion range cell K13. 1-2-3 has evaluated this formula as 0. Why? Because cell L7 contains the value 5. This value is not greater than 5, so the logical expression, +L7>5 evaluates as False, or 0.

```
              I         J       K       L       M       N
  1
  2
  3   ?IDGET INVENTORY
  4   ==================
  5
  6   PART#        DESCR   QTY    WHLSL   RETAIL   |
  7          123 WIDG          10   $5.00   $10.00 |
  8          345 GIDG          20  $10.00   $20.00 |<<<INPUT
  9          678 MIDG         100  $10.00   $20.00 |
 10            1 GIDG          10  $10.00   $20.00 |
 11
 12   PART#        DESCR   QTY    WHLSL   RETAIL   |
 13                          0                     |<<<CRITERION
 14                XXXX                            |
 15
 16   PART#        DESCR   QTY    WHLSL   RETAIL   |
 17                                                |
 18                                                |<<< OUTPUT
 19                                                |
 20                                                |
```

Figure 171

All this is very interesting but doesn't help us much. The way to avoid this ambiguity is to use /**R**ange Format **T**ext to display the formula rather than the result of the formula. Cell K13 will then look as it does in Figure 172, which is the result we want.

Field Names

283   Trap: The field names used in a criterion range must match exactly the corresponding field names in the data base.

Because 1-2-3 uses the field names in the criterion range to determine which fields are searched for a match, the field names in a 1-2-3 criterion range must match exactly the corresponding field names in the data base. For example, the headers "Name" and " Name" do not match because the second has a leading space; the headers "Name" and "name"

```
            I       J       K       L       M       N
  1
  2
  3  ?IDGET INVENTORY
  4  =================
  5
  6  PART#       DESCR   QTY     WHLSL   RETAIL  |
  7         123 WIDG        10  $5.00   $10.00 |
  8         345 GIDG        20  $10.00  $20.00 |<<<INPUT
  9         678 MIDG       100  $10.00  $20.00 |
 10           1 GIDG        10  $10.00  $20.00 |
 11
 12  PART#       DESCR   QTY     WHLSL   RETAIL  |
 13                     +L7>5                   |<<<CRITERION
 14             XXXX                            |
 15
 16  PART#       DESCR   QTY     WHLSL   RETAIL  |
 17                                             |
 18                                             |<<< OUTPUT
 19                                             |
 20                                             |
```

Figure 172

do not match because one starts with an uppercase letter and the other with a lowercase letter.

284 Trap: You cannot have more than 32 fields in an output or criterion range.

You can have up to 256 fields in a data base, but no more than 32 in a given output or criterion range. If you try to use more fields, you'll get a "Too many fields" message from 1-2-3.

285 Trick: If you need to extract more than 32 fields at once, you can put two output areas right next to each other.

Releases 1 and 1A of 1-2-3 limit you to a maximum of 32 fields each in the Criterion and Output ranges. If you need to extract records with more than 32 fields, you can build two Output ranges next to each other and do two separate extractions. Use /**D**ata **Q**uery **O**utput to change the Output range between queries.

There is no way, unfortunately, to create a single criterion range with more than 32 fields.

AND and OR

286 **Tip:** It's easy to create AND and OR criteria in 1-2-3.

To specify a logical AND between two or more fields in a 1-2-3 data base, put all the conditions on the same line in the range. Specify a logical OR between two or more fields by placing the criteria on different lines.

Figure 173 is an example of an AND criterion range. This set of criteria says: Select those records for which the "Name" is Smith, J. AND the "Amount" is 100.

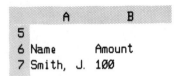

	A	B
5		
6	Name	Amount
7	Smith, J.	100

Figure 173

Figure 174 is an example of an OR criterion range. This criterion says: Select all records for which the "Name" is Smith, J. OR the "Amount" is 100. Notice that this criterion range occupies three rows, A6..B8.

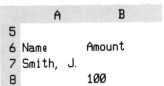

	A	B
5		
6	Name	Amount
7	Smith, J.	
8		100

Figure 174

287 **Tip:** You can use the logical #AND# and #OR# operators to create conditional criteria within a single field.

Suppose you want to create a criterion that selects all records for which the amount is either 50 or 100. How do you do it?

There are two different ways to create this kind of criterion. Figure 175 shows the first. This example uses the two-row approach presented in the last Tip to create a range that selects records for which the "Amount" is equal to 50 or 100.

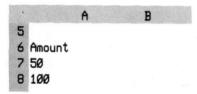

Figure 175

The second method is illustrated in Figure 176. This method combines two formulas into a single logical statement. It works just like the two-row version and selects only the records we want.

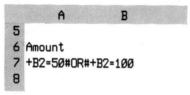

Figure 176

288   **Tip:** The fact that a formula criterion can refer to more than one row in the data base allows you to do complex queries.

Suppose we have a data base that represents the history of our departmental budget by quarter over the last two years. The input range in the left-hand part of Figure 177 shows such a data base. Note that it is sorted on Year and Quarter within Item; this sort order is critical for the type of query and retrieval we are doing. Suppose that we want to select those records for which the budgeted amount for any quarter is different from the budgeted amount for the same item for the comparable quarter in the next year. The first record in the data base meets these conditions because the budgeted amount for 1981, Quarter 1, in cell D205, is different from the budgeted amount for 1982, Quarter 1, in cell D209.

The upper-right part of Figure 177 shows a criterion range containing the formula +AMOUNT<>D209. "AMOUNT" is the range name of cell D205, and D209 obviously refers to the same "AMOUNT" field four rows down. This formula refers to two rows: the current row (row 205) and the row four rows down from it (row 209). Translated into English, this formula says: The "AMOUNT" for one quarter cannot be equal to "AMOUNT" for the next quarter.

	A	B	C	D	E	F	G	H	I
201						BUDGET BY QUARTER			
202						=================			
203	INPUT:					CRITERION:			
204	Year	Quarter	Item	Amount		Year	Quarter	Item	Amount
205	81	1	1	100		+AMOUNT<>D209			
206	81	2	1	250					
207	81	3	1	300					
208	81	4	1	1000		OUTPUT:			
209	82	1	1	200		Year	Quarter	Item	Amount
210	82	2	1	250			81	1	1	100
211	82	3	1	300			82	1	1	200
212	82	4	1	1000			82	2	1	250
213	81	1	2	100			81	2	2	350
214	81	2	2	350			81	3	2	300
215	81	3	2	300			82	1	2	100
216	81	4	2	1000			82	2	2	250
217	82	1	2	100			82	3	2	100
218	82	2	2	250			82	4	2	1000
219	82	3	2	100					
220	82	4	2	1000					

Figure 177

On the surface this appears to be what we want, but the output area in the lower-right corner of Figure 177 shows the result of a /Data Query Extract under these conditions, and the result is not quite right. The problem here is that what we put in the criterion range does not make sure that we're always comparing comparable items.

We can correct this situation by adding another formula to our criterion range. That formula is shown in Figure 178 as +ITEM=C209. This ensures that we take only those records which have been matched against the next year's record representing the same Item. The output range in Figure 178 shows the result we want. Compare these three records with the data base records in rows 209, 218, and 219, respectively, and you'll see that they do in fact satisfy the criteria we set up.

Caution: This method will work under Releases 1 and 1A only because the "ITEM" field is a number and not a label. If it were a label (as in Figure 179), we'd have the same kind of wrong result we got in Figure 177 because a label field in a formula is always considered to have the

	A	B	C	D	E	F	G	H	I
201						BUDGET BY QUARTER			
202						=================			
203	INPUT:					CRITERION:			
204	Year	Quarter		Item	Amount	Year	Quarter	Item	Amount
205	81		1	1	100	+AMOUNT<>D209	+ITEM=C209		
206	81		2	1	250				
207	81		3	1	300				
208	81		4	1	1000	OUTPUT:			
209	82		1	1	200	Year	Quarter	Item	Amount
210	82		2	1	250		81	1	1	100
211	82		3	1	300		81	2	2	350
212	82		4	1	1000		81	3	2	300
213	81		1	2	100				
214	81		2	2	350				
215	81		3	2	300				
216	81		4	2	1000				
217	82		1	2	100				
218	82		2	2	250				
219	82		3	2	100				
220	82		4	2	1000				

Figure 178

value of 0. Therefore, the formula criterion +ITEM=C209 is always true and has no effect. (See the output area in Figure 179.)

A further caution: The method in this particular example also depends on the fact that the data base is sorted on Year and Quarter within Item and on the fact that there is a record for each Item in each Quarter and each Year. If that were not the case, formulas that refer to two different rows would not do what we want.

Other Variations

289   **Tip:** You can pick up slight variations in spelling in a data base by using the wild-card characters * and ? in your criteria.

Suppose you have a data base of employees' names, and you want to extract all the Andersens. Because you know that this name is often spelled as *Anderson*, place the criterion **Anders?n** in the "Name" field of

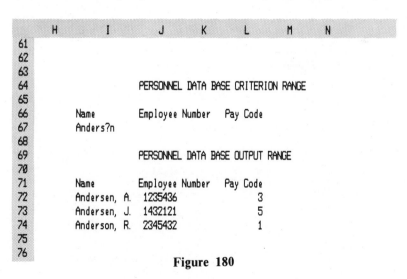

```
        A     B    C     D     E        F          G      H     I
201                          BUDGET BY QUARTER
202                          =================
203 INPUT:                    CRITERION:
204 Year Quarter Item Amount  Year          Quarter    Item  Amount
205  81       1 PAPER   100   +AMOUNT<>D209 +ITEM=C209
206  81       2 PAPER   250
207  81       3 PAPER   300
208  81       4 PAPER  1000   OUTPUT:
209  82       1 PAPER   200   Year          Quarter    Item  Amount
210  82       2 PAPER   250              81        1 PAPER    100
211  82       3 PAPER   300              82        1 PAPER    200
212  82       4 PAPER  1000              82        2 PAPER    250
213  81       1 BOOKS   100              81        2 BOOKS    350
214  81       2 BOOKS   350              81        3 BOOKS    300
215  81       3 BOOKS   300              82        1 BOOKS    100
216  81       4 BOOKS  1000              82        2 BOOKS    250
217  82       1 BOOKS   100              82        3 BOOKS    100
218  82       2 BOOKS   250              82        4 BOOKS   1000
219  82       3 BOOKS   100
220  82       4 BOOKS  1000
```

Figure 179

the criterion range. This translates: Extract all records that begin with *Anders* followed by any character followed by *n*. (See Figure 180.)

```
       H      I          J            K        L        M       N
61
62
63
64                 PERSONNEL DATA BASE CRITERION RANGE
65
66     Name        Employee Number   Pay Code
67     Anders?n
68
69                 PERSONNEL DATA BASE OUTPUT RANGE
70
71     Name        Employee Number   Pay Code
72     Andersen, A. 1235436                  3
73     Andersen, J. 1432121                  5
74     Anderson, R. 2345432                  1
75
76
```

Figure 180

The other wild-card character available to you in criteria is the asterisk (*), which means: Accept any string of characters or numbers in the rest of the field. Thus, a criterion of "Ander*" would retrieve Anders, Andersen, Anderson, Andersly, etc.

290   **Tip:** A blank criterion is the same as a wild card to 1-2-3.

To 1-2-3 an empty criterion range cell means: Accept any value. Therefore, an empty criterion range row means: AND accept any value for all fields in this row. All records in the data base satisfy the criterion range when a row in it is empty.

291   **Trap:** Make sure you leave no empty lines in your criterion range, or you may get unexpected and even disastrous results.

Sometimes you want more than one line under the field names in your criterion range so that you can create "OR tests" with several criteria. This sets up a potentially puzzling and dangerous situation. If you leave a blank row in the criterion range, 1-2-3 interprets this blank row as a wild card. Things aren't so bad when you do this with a /**D**ata **Q**uery **E**xtract, **U**nique, or **F**ind. But if you do it with a /**D**ata **Q**uery **D**elete, you'll delete all the records in your data base. That would probably result in much tearing of hair and gnashing of teeth.

292   **Trick:** To avoid this problem, put a "stopper" in every row in the criterion range.

Here's a way to prevent the possibility of accidentally deleting all records. As soon as you create a criterion range with more than one criterion line, put stoppers in at least one field in every row. These stoppers should represent values that you know you won't find in that field in the data base. Keep those stoppers there unless you have real criteria to put in that row. In Figure 172 we've used XXXX as a stopper. If you don't use this "finger-in-the-dike" technique, you may find yourself in trouble.

293   **Trap:** To work properly, a label used as a criterion must exactly match at least one label in the data base.

We've already seen that the field name used in a criterion must exactly match the corresponding field name in the data base. The same rules apply to labels used as criteria. For example, if you're looking for a record for which one field is the label "Smith", only a criterion that exactly matches that name will do the trick. " Smith" (with a leading space), "smith" (with a lowercase *s*), and "Simth" (misspelled) will not work.

294   Tip: Make sure the formulas you put in your criterion range use relative addressing for fields in the data base and absolute addressing for fields outside; otherwise, you'll get unpredictable results.

Figure 181 shows the right way to do this with a /**D**ata **Q**uery Extract. Note the absolute reference in K13 to the cell $J$21, which is outside the data base. Figure 182 shows one wrong way. Here the reference to J21 is not absolute, and the results are strange.

```
           I        J        K        L        M        N
 1
 2
 3  ?IDGET INVENTORY
 4  ==================
 5
 6  PART#        DESCR    QTY      WHLSL    RETAIL   I
 7          123 WIDG          10   $5.00   $10.00 I
 8          345 GIDG          20   $5.00   $10.00 I<<<INPUT
 9          678 MIDG         100   $5.00   $10.00 I
10            1 GIDG          10  $10.00   $20.00 I
11
12  PART#        DESCR    QTY      WHLSL    RETAIL   I
13                    +L7)$J$21                     I<<<CRITERION
14               XXXX                               I
15
16  PART#        DESCR    QTY      WHLSL    RETAIL   I
17            1 GIDG          10  $10.00   $20.00 I
18                                                  I<<< OUTPUT
19                                                  I
20                                                  I
21  MIN          $5.00
```

Figure 181

```
          I          J       K       L       M        N
1
2
3    ?IDGET INVENTORY
4    ===================
5
6    PART#       DESCR    QTY     WHLSL   RETAIL   I
7           123 WIDG      10      $5.00   $10.00 I
8           345 GIDG      20      $5.00   $10.00 I<<<INPUT
9           678 MIDG     100      $5.00   $10.00 I
10            1 GIDG      10     $10.00   $20.00 I
11
12   PART#       DESCR   QTY      WHLSL   RETAIL   I
13                      +L7>J21                   I<<<CRITERION
14               XXXX                             I
15
16   PART#       DESCR   QTY      WHLSL   RETAIL   I
17           345 GIDG      20     $5.00   $10.00 I
18             1 GIDG      10    $10.00   $20.00 I<<< OUTPUT
19                                                I
20                                                I
21   MIN         $5.00
```

Figure 182

Output Ranges

295 Tip: To set up **/D**ata **Q**uery **C**riterion and **O**utput ranges quickly,
/Copy the data base field name row.

The quickest way to set up **C**riterion and **O**utput range areas is to copy
the entire row of field names from the top of the data base to each area.
We did this to produce the criterion and output ranges shown in Figure
183.

296 Tip: The output and criterion ranges do not have to include all the
fields that are in the the data base.

It is not necessary to include all the fields in the data base in either the
criterion or the output area. Nor must you place them in the same order
as in the data base. In fact, one of the interesting uses for the Extract
command is to rearrange the order of the fields in a data base. However,

```
         I      J      K      L      M      N
 1
 2  ?IDGET INVENTORY
 3  =================
 4
 5  PART#    DESCR   QTY    WHLSL   RETAIL  I
 6           123 WIDG      10    $5.00  $10.00 I
 7           345 GIDG      20    $5.00  $10.00 I<<<INPUT
 8           678 MIDG     100    $5.00  $10.00 I
 9             1 GIDG      10   $10.00  $20.00 I
10
11  PART#    DESCR   QTY    WHLSL   RETAIL  I
12                                          I<<<CRITERION
13                                          I
14
15  PART#    DESCR   QTY    WHLSL   RETAIL  I
16                                          I
17                                          I<<< OUTPUT
18                                          I
19                                          I
20
```

Figure 183

when you want all the data base fields in all areas, you will probably find a straight copy of the entire field name row to be the simplest and quickest way to get the job done.

297 Tip: When you're using several different **Q**uery definitions on different data bases or with different criterion and output areas, save the definitions in macros.

Releases 1 and 1A of 1-2-3 have no direct way to give a name to a /**D**ata **Q**uery definition and save it as you can with a /**G**raph. You can, however, create this capability for yourself with a macro. Figure 184 shows one version of such a macro.

The \Q startup macro (activated by pressing {Alt} and Q simultaneously) activates the menu below it. This menu gives you the opportunity of choosing to **Q**uery your "Long" data base or your "Short" one. The subsidiary macros that belong to the chosen menu options set up the **I**nput, **C**riterion, and **O**utput ranges and present the main /**D**ata **Q**uery menu. This menu allows you to choose either **E**xtract, **F**ind, **U**nique, or **D**elete. With this macro you can switch between different **Q**ueries in a flash.

```
        I        J        K        L        M        N        O
41
42 \Q        /xmQ_MENU~                    Execute query menu.
43
44 Q_MENU    QUERY1   QUERY2               Query menu.
45          Long     Short
46          /xgQ1_MC~/xgQ2_MC~
47
48 Q1_MC     /dqiINPUT~                    Define all ranges for
49          cCRITERION~                   query on the Long
50          oOUTPUT~                      data base
51          {?}~/xq~                      Prompt for query option & quit.
52
53 Q2_MC     /dqiINPUT2~                   Define all ranges for
54          cCRITERION2~                  query on the Short
55          oOUTPUT2~                     data base
56          {?}~/xq~                      Prompt for query option & quit.
57
```

Figure 184

The /Data Query Commands

298 **Tip:** Avoid **/W**orksheet **D**elete by using **/D**ata **Q**uery **D**elete to delete records from a data base.

This is an alternative to the method described under a previous Tip. This approach uses the /**Data Q**uery **D**elete command to delete records. /**Data Q**uery **D**elete deletes any records in a data base that match a predefined criterion; this command has the advantage of deleting only that part of the row that's actually in the data base, thereby helping avoid accidental deletion of other information in the row.

To use the /**Data Q**uery **D**elete, first define a Criterion range, as shown at the bottom of Figure 185. Notice that we've also placed the customer number for Customer 600 in the "Customer" field in the criterion range, indicating that we want to delete all records for which the customer number is 600.

Next, execute the Input and Criterion options of /**Data Q**uery and supply the range of the data base (I65..L74) as Input and the range of the

```
      I      J      K      L      M      N      0
61
62 TELEMARKETING SYSTEM CUSTOMER DATA BASE
63 =======================================
64
65 Date     Customer Ap Sent? Inquiry? Notes
66   12-Nov   2387 y       y        Check points & call.
67   14-Nov    546 n       n
68   14-Nov    600
69   15-Nov    345 y       n
70   15-Nov    890 y       n
71   15-Nov    891 y       n
72   16-Nov     50 y       n
73   16-Nov    123 y       y        Wants 2 loans.
74   18-Nov    180 y       y
75
76
77
78 Date     Customer Ap Sent? Inquiry? Notes
79              600
80
81
```

Figure 185

criterion range (J78..J79) as the Criterion range. Finally, choose the
Delete option and confirm that choice by pressing **D** again when the
confirmation menu appears at the top of the screen. Figure 186 shows
the result.

Like the /**R**ange Erase method, /**D**ata **Q**uery **D**elete does not automatically adjust the range names in the data base. This is an unfortunate
limitation of the /**D**ata **Q**uery **D**elete command.

299 Trap: You can inadvertently delete more than you want to with
/**D**ata **Q**uery **D**elete.

As described under the previous Tip, /**D**ata **Q**uery **D**elete has the nice
feature that it deletes only that part of a row defined in the Input range.
However, the command carries its own dangers with it. Everything
depends on getting your criterion range set up corectly before you
execute the /**D**ata **Q**uery **D**elete. Unfortunately, it's easy to make
mistakes in a criterion range; and if you have mistakes in your criterion
range, you may delete the wrong records.

```
        I       J     K       L       M       N       O
  61
  62 TELEMARKETING SYSTEM CUSTOMER DATA BASE
  63 =======================================
  64
  65 Date      Customer Ap Sent? Inquiry? Notes
  66    12-Nov    2387 y         y         Check points & call.
  67    14-Nov     546 n         n
  68    15-Nov     345 y         n
  69    15-Nov     890 y         n
  70    15-Nov     891 y         n
  71    16-Nov      50 y         n
  72    16-Nov     123 y         y         Wants 2 loans.
  73    18-Nov     180 y         y
  74
  69
  75
  76
  77
  78 Date      Customer Ap Sent? Inquiry? Notes
  79               600
  80
```

Figure 186

The worst thing that can happen occurs if your criterion range
mistakenly asks for all the records in the data base when you execute the
/Data Query Delete. (This possibility gives you another reason for
keeping backup copies of all your worksheets.) This deletion happens if
any row in your criterion range is empty when you do the Delete. The
safest thing is to make sure that the criterion range you use for the
Delete has only one row below the field names row. It's pretty hard to
forget to put something in that single row.

300   **Trick:** Test your deletion criterion by doing a **/Data Query Extract**
          before you do a **/Data Query Delete**.

Once you've set up your Criterion range, along with the criteria that will
delete the proper record(s), do a /Data Query Extract. (You'll have to
define an Output range for this.) Then take a look at the records you've
extracted and make sure they are the ones you want to delete. If they
are, go ahead and do the /Data Query Delete with the same criterion
range.

301 Tip: Always back up your data base before you do a batch of **Deletes**.

It's always better to be safe than sorry, so be sure you back up your data base before you begin deleting records.

302 Trap: If the input and output areas you set up for the **/Data Query** command are too small, your results will be incomplete.

It pays to estimate carefully how many rows you'll need in both the input (original data base) and output areas for the **/Data Query** command. It's not always easy to move things around later, especially on a crowded worksheet. The best thing to do is put the area you're least sure about on the bottom so that it will have the most room to grow. If, for instance, you don't expect your original data base to grow much, but you need widely varying amounts of space for your output area, then put the output area on the bottom, as in Figure 187.

```
           I       J      K      L      M      N
 1
 2
 3  ?IDGET INVENTORY
 4  ==================
 5
 6  PART#       DESCR   QTY    WHLSL   RETAIL  |
 7        123 WIDG        10    $5.00  $10.00  |
 8        345 GIDG        20    $5.00  $10.00  |<<<INPUT
 9        678 MIDG       100    $5.00  $10.00  |
10          1 GIDG        10   $10.00  $20.00  |
11
12  PART#       DESCR   QTY    WHLSL   RETAIL  |
13              GIDG                           |<<<CRITERION
14              XXXX                           |
15
16  PART#       DESCR   QTY    WHLSL   RETAIL  |
17      345     GIDG        20    $5.00  $10.00  |
18        1     GIDG        10   $10.00  $20.00  |<<< OUTPUT
19                                             |
20                                             |
```

Figure 187

If you supply **/Data Query** with too small an output area and then execute a Unique or Extract, 1-2-3 will give you the message, "Too many records for output range," informing you that the output area is too small. After you press {Esc} to acknowledge the error, the output range will be filled with as many records as it can hold. Remember, though, that in this case you end up with an incomplete extraction. To correct this problem, increase the size of your output range and repeat the Extract or Unique.

303 Tip: To make your **/D**ata **Q**uery **E**xtracts and **U**niques as flexible as possible, you can designate a one-row output range.

1-2-3 allows you to designate an **O**utput range that consists only of the field headers in the first row of the output area. Although the range is defined by one row, the actual range is dynamic: it grows and shrinks to accommodate exactly the number of records being Extracted. This kind of output range can accommodate as many records as there are rows between the headers and the bottom of the worksheet.

For example, in Figure 187, we could create a one-row output range using the coordinates I16..M16. This range could hold as many as 2031 records, figured by subtracting the row number of the headers from the last row number, 2048.

304 Trap: The **/D**ata **Q**uery **E**xtract and **U**nique commands always erase the contents of the output range before **E**xtracting records to that range.

With normal output ranges this characteristic is not a problem. The range erased is simply the range you've specified for the output range, and the chances are small that there are any important formulas or data in this area.

With one-row output ranges, however, the area erased extends from the row immediately below the output headers to the bottom of the worksheet. Any value, formula, or label below the output headers is erased by a **/D**ata **Q**uery **E**xtract or Unique. As you can imagine, this can be disastrous. Be careful when using one-row output ranges.

305 Tip: You can use **/D**ata **Q**uery **E**xtract to eliminate fields from a data base or change their order.

It's possible to eliminate data base fields or change their order by using a combination of /Worksheet Delete Column, /Move, and /Copy. However, there are instances when /Worksheet Delete is not appropriate because you have information you want to keep in the areas above or below the data base. Furthermore, it can be a bother to do a lot of "cutting and pasting" with /Move and /Copy to change the order of fields.

One alternative is to set up an output range that has the fields you want in exactly the order you want. Then define a Criterion range with all the fields empty so that all the records in the data base meet the criteria. Finally, define your data base as the Input range and execute a /Data Query Extract. Figure 188 shows an example with all these ranges defined. Figure 189 shows the result of the /Data Query Extract. You'll probably want to do a /Range Erase on the original data base after the Extract is complete and use /Move to move the restructured data base from the output area to the original input area.

```
         I        J       K       L       M       N
 1
 2
 3  ?IDGET INVENTORY
 4  =================
 5
 6  PART#       DESCR   QTY     WHLSL   RETAIL  |
 7          123 WIDG        10  $5.00   $10.00  |
 8          345 GIDG        20  $5.00   $10.00  |<<<INPUT
 9          678 MIDG       100  $5.00   $10.00  |
10            1 GIDG        10  $10.00  $20.00  |
11
12  PART#       DESCR   QTY     WHLSL   RETAIL  |
13                                             |<<<CRITERION
14                                             |
15
16  PART#       DESCR   WHLSL   QTY     |
17                                      |
18                                      |<<< OUTPUT
19                                      |
20                                      |
```

Figure 188

306 Trap: If you want to save Extracted records, be sure to copy them to another area before you do the next retrieval.

When 1-2-3 executes a new Extract or Unique, the program first erases what is in the output area. If you want to keep a set of Extracted records, /Copy them to a different area before you do another Extract or Unique.

```
           I     J     K     L     M     N
  1
  2
  3  ?IDGET INVENTORY
  4  =================
  5
  6  PART#      DESCR   QTY     WHLSL   RETAIL   |
  7         123 WIDG      10    $5.00   $10.00 |
  8         345 GIDG      20    $5.00   $10.00 |<<<INPUT
  9         678 MIDG     100    $5.00   $10.00 |
 10           1 GIDG      10   $10.00   $20.00 |
 11
 12  PART#      DESCR   QTY     WHLSL   RETAIL   |
 13                                             |<<<CRITERION
 14                                             |
 15
 16  PART#      DESCR  WHLSL    QTY      |
 17         123 WIDG   $5.00      10 |
 18         345 GIDG   $5.00      20 |<<< OUTPUT
 19         678 MIDG   $5.00     100 |
 20           1 GIDG  $10.00      10 |
```

Figure 189

307   **Tip:** **/D**ata **Q**uery **F**ind is the best way to access quickly a record in
a data base.

To find a record with **/D**ata **Q**uery **F**ind, you must know something
about the record you want to Find, for example, the entry for that
record in the "Name" field. If you have this information, you can create
a criterion range that will allow you to Find the record. If, for instance,
you've placed *Chaplin* in the "Name" field of a criterion range, the
execution of a **/D**ata **Q**uery **F**ind will bring the cursor to the first
Chaplin in the data base.

After you have reviewed this entry, you can find out if there are other
records in the data base that match the criterion. Pressing ↓ moves the
cursor to the next match if more matches exist. You can continue to
press ↓ to view additional matches. Pressing ↑ allows you to move back
up through the matches you have already reviewed. {Home} takes you
back to the first match; {End} takes you to the last.

308 **Tip:** Use a partial field value followed by an asterisk to speed up the /Data Query Find and minimize misspellings.

When you're doing a **Find** on a long field value, often the first few characters of the value can identify what you want. For instance, if you're looking for R. Anderson in the data base in Figure 180, you don't have to enter the full name **Anderson, R.** in the criterion range. The entry **And*** will probably be enough. If this doesn't get the record you want immediately, pressing the ↓ cursor key a few times will probably take you to the one you want within seconds. This way, you minimize data entry time and also lessen the chances of misspellings.

309 **Trap:** The /Data Query Find does not allow you to edit a record after the record is found.

It's hard to believe, but it's true. The /Data Query Find command can locate a record, but it does not allow the record to be altered in any way. In fact, when you're in the Find mode, the keyboard is essentially disabled.

310 **Tip:** To edit a particular record in a large data base, use /Data Query Find to discover the address; then use {GoTo} to move to the address.

If you want to edit a record, use /Data Query Find to locate that record in the data base. Then quit from the /Data Query command and use the {GoTo} key to go directly to that record.

311 **Trap:** The /Data Query Unique command can be confusing.

The /Data Query Unique command Extracts records from an input range based on the criteria in a criterion range and also makes sure that no two records in the output range are identical.

There's a tendency to try to use /Data Query Unique to do a different kind of job, but it won't work. Here's an example. Suppose you want to Extract only the first WIDG record from the input area in Figure 190. It seems as if /Data Query Unique might do that, but when you execute it, you get what's shown in Figure 191.

As the figures show, you got both WIDG records instead of just the first one, which is all that you wanted. These two records are not 100% identical (the entry in the "Retail" field is different in each record), so

```
           I        J        K       L        M        N
 1
 2
 3  ?IDGET INVENTORY
 4  =================
 5
 6  PART#       DESCR    QTY     WHLSL    RETAIL   |
 7          123 WIDG       10    $5.00   $10.00   |
 8          345 GIDG       20    $5.00   $10.00   |<<<INPUT
 9          678 MIDG      100    $5.00   $10.00   |
10          456 WIDG       10   $10.00   $20.00   |
11
12  PART#       DESCR    QTY     WHLSL    RETAIL   |
13              WIDG                              |<<<CRITERION
14
15  PART#       DESCR    QTY     WHLSL    RETAIL   |
16                                               |
17                                               |<<< OUTPUT
18                                               |
19                                               |
20
```

Figure 190

```
           I        J        K       L        M        N
 1
 2
 3  ?IDGET INVENTORY
 4  =================
 5
 6  PART#       DESCR    QTY     WHLSL    RETAIL   |
 7          123 WIDG       10    $5.00   $10.00   |
 8          345 GIDG       20    $5.00   $10.00   |<<<INPUT
 9          678 MIDG      100    $5.00   $10.00   |
10          456 WIDG       10   $10.00   $20.00   |
11
12  PART#       DESCR    QTY     WHLSL    RETAIL   |
13              WIDG                              |<<<CRITERION
14
15  PART#       DESCR    QTY     WHLSL    RETAIL   |
16          123 WIDG       10    $5.00   $10.00   |
17          456 WIDG       10   $10.00   $20.00   |<<<OUTPUT
18                                               |
19                                               |
20
```

Figure 191

each is "unique" so far as the /**D**ata **Q**uery Unique command is concerned.

312   Tip: To repeat a **Q**uery with variations, change any criterion range cells and press the {Query} key.

1-2-3 remembers the last set of /**D**ata **Q**uery parameters specified, and the {Query} key reexecutes the last **Q**uery type with the remembered parameters. By changing any or all of the criteria in the criterion range before you press the {Query} key, you can vary the results of the **Q**uery operation. This capability allows you to do a quick "what if" analysis with queries. For instance, you could ask, "What if I extracted all the salespeople who grossed more than $100,000 in 1983?" or "What if I extracted all who grossed more than $100,000 in both 1982 and 1983?"

Multiple Data Bases

313   Tip: You may want to stack your data base and associated areas on top of each other.

Often you have several different areas associated with a data base: the data base itself, a criterion range (used by the /**D**ata **Q**uery command and data base statistical functions), and an output range (used by /**D**ata **Q**uery).

Because all these areas often have the same number of columns and corresponding column widths, it is convenient to stack them on top of each other. See Figure 187 for an example. (The comments on the right show which range is which.)

314   Tip: You may want to put multiple data bases next to each other.

What about the case where you need two or more data bases in memory at once? The chances are that they have different numbers of columns and different column widths, so you probably want the areas for the second data base beside those for the first, rather than having them stacked on top of each other.

Another advantage of this approach is that you have space below each data base for expansion. If both data bases use output ranges, putting the data bases side by side instead of on top of each other will prevent the top output range from accidentally overwriting and erasing the lower data base, criterion range, and output range.

315 **Tip:** If you need to use **/W**orksheet **I**nsert and/or **D**elete on data
bases and you have more than one, place each new data base
diagonally below the preceding one.

We suggested under the previous Tip that it's often a good idea to place
the areas for a second data base next to those for the first. However, if
you locate them so that the two data bases have some rows in common
(as in Figure 192) and then try to use **/W**orksheet **I**nsert or **D**elete on
either one, you affect the other adversely.

```
           A         B         C         D         E         F         G
 1
 2
 3    WHOLESALE DATA BASE                    RETAIL DATA BASE
 4    ===================                    ================
 5
 6    WhPART#  WHLSL      |                   RtPART#  RETAIL    |
 7        123   $75.00 |                              $100.00 |
 8        345  $500.00 |<wINPUT                     $1,000.00 |<rINPUT
 9        678  $800.00 |                           $15,000.00 |
10          1   $10.00 |                              $20.00 |
11
12    WhPART#  WHLSL      |                   RtPART#  RETAIL    |
13                     |<wCRITERION                            |<rCRITERION
14                     |                                       |
15
16    WhPART#  WHLSL      |                   RtPART#  RETAIL    |
17                     |                                       |
18                     |<wOUTPUT                               |<rOUTPUT
19                     |                                       |
20                     |                                       |
```

Figure 192

You can avoid this problem by placing the two data bases diagonally.
(See Figure 193 for an example.) This practice creates a certain amount
of "dead" space in your active area, both to the right of the first data
base and below it. Because 1-2-3 uses some memory for every cell in the
active area whether there's anything in it or not, this method also eats up
some memory; this may or may not be a problem, depending on how
much memory you have available.

```
        A      B       C      D     E      F      G
1
2
3   WHOLESALE DATA BASE
4   ==================
5
6   WhPART#  WHLSL   |
7       123  $75.00 |
8       345 $500.00 |<wINPUT
9       678 $800.00 |
10        1  $10.00 |
11
12  WhPART#  WHLSL   |
13                  |<wCRITERION
14                  |
15
16  WhPART#  WHLSL   |
17                  |
18                  |<wOUTPUT
19                  |
20                  |
21                              RETAIL DATA BASE
22                              ================
23
24
25                              RtPART#  RETAIL   |
26                                      $100.00 |
27                                    $1,000.00 |<rINPUT
28                                   $15,000.00 |
29                                       $20.00 |
30
31                              RtPART#  RETAIL   |
32                                              |<rCRITERION
33                                              |
34
35                              RtPART#  RETAIL   |
36                                              |
37                                              |<rOUTPUT
38                                              |
39                                              |
40
41
```

Figure 193

Another possible approach is to place the two data bases in parallel and then temporarily Copy the one in which you need to Insert or Delete to some safe location, for example, below and to the right of the lower-right corner of the current active area. Do the Insert or Delete there and then Copy the data base back. The disadvantage of this method is that it is a bother and, with a large data base, takes time; this practice also increases the size of the current active area and therefore uses extra memory.

The Insert and Delete Commands

316 Tip: Avoid /Worksheet Insert and Delete where possible when working with data bases.

As we've suggested under several previous Tips, Inserts and Deletes are dangerous in situations where you have other important data outside the area in which you're doing the Inserts or Deletes. These commands operate on entire rows and columns, extending throughout the worksheet.

317 Tip: Avoid /Worksheet Insert by adding new records to the end of the data base and sorting.

The /Worksheet Insert command is dangerous because it inserts an empty line that extends the entire width of the worksheet. Areas of the worksheet not visible on the screen can be damaged by a careless /Worksheet Insert command. For example, inserting a row in the middle of a macro will cause problems because an empty cell always stops a macro.

If the record you're adding to a data base belongs in a particular position, you can usually simulate an Insert by first adding the record at the end of the data base and then Sorting the data base so that the record ends up in the correct position.

For example, suppose you want to add a record to a customer data base that's part of a telemarketing system, the data base is sorted on Customer within Date, and you want to add the record and have it inserted at the proper position in the data base. Figure 194 shows the data base with the new record, a record for November 14 for Customer no. 600, added at the bottom. Figure 195 shows the same data base after it has been Sorted using the /Data Sort command. The Data range for the Sort is I66..M74. Cell I66 (Date) is the Primary key, and cell J66 (Customer) is the Secondary key.

```
        I        J        K        L        M        N

61
62  TELEMARKETING SYSTEM CUSTOMER DATA BASE
63  ==========================================

64
65  Date     Customer Ap Sent? Inquiry? Notes
66   12-Nov    2387 y        y          Check points & call.
67   14-Nov     546 n        n
68   15-Nov     345 y        n
69   15-Nov     890 y        n
70   15-Nov     891 y        n
71   16-Nov      50 y        n
72   16-Nov     123 y        y          Wants 2 loans.
73   18-Nov     180 y        y
74   14-Nov     600
75
```

Figure 194

```
        I        J        K        L        M        N

61
62  TELEMARKETING SYSTEM CUSTOMER DATA BASE
63  ==========================================

64
65  Date     Customer Ap Sent? Inquiry? Notes
66   12-Nov    2387 y        y          Check points & call.
67   14-Nov     546 n        n
68   14-Nov     600
69   15-Nov     345 y        n
70   15-Nov     890 y        n
71   15-Nov     891 y        n
72   16-Nov      50 y        n
73   16-Nov     123 y        y          Wants 2 loans.
74   18-Nov     180 y        y
75
```

Figure 195

318   Trap: Adding rows at the bottom of the data base and then **S**orting does not alter the range names and data range definitions as **/W**orksheet **I**nsert **R**ow would.

The problem with the approach shown in the previous Tip is that the method does not automatically update any range names in the model. If you have given the data base a range name (perhaps for use by a macro), you must redefine that range name to include any new records. This is not only a bother; it's easy to overlook something in doing it. When you use the /Worksheet Insert method, 1-2-3 redefines affected range names for you automatically.

319   Tip: If you must use **/W**orksheet **I**nsert to add to a data base, control the command with a macro.

One good reason to use /Worksheet Insert is that when you Insert a record in the middle of a range, the command automatically expands the range name definitions of any named ranges into which you've made an insertion. This can be very handy. If you have to worry about whether your range name definitions are up-to-date, you may lose track of something somewhere.

If you control /Worksheet Insert with a macro, you can minimize the chances of problems. You can make sure the cursor is in roughly the right area, ask for confirmation of the Insert, and force the insertion of only one line at a time.

Figure 196 shows a simple Insert macro. Note that it assumes that protection is enabled when the macro starts. Because you can't Insert with protection enabled, the macro disables protection before the Insert and reenables it afterwards. Keeping protection enabled is one way of making it unlikely that someone will inadvertently do an Insert without its being under macro control.

This same macro can also be modified to delete records.

320   Tip: You can avoid **/W**orksheet **D**elete by using **/R**ange **E**rase and **S**orting down the empty records.

/Worksheet Delete, like /Worksheet Insert, is dangerous. It's too easy to delete unintentionally a row that looks blank but contains something important just off the screen.

One alternate way of removing a record from a data base is to do the following:

```
            I        J        K        L        M        N        O
  101
  102 \I       /xmINS_MENU~              Execute insert menu.
  103
  104 INS_MENU INSERT   DON'T            Insert menu.
  105          Ins row. No-don't!
  106          /xgINS~  /xgDONT~
  107
  108 INS      /wgpd                     Disable protection for insert.
  109          /wir~                     Insert row.
  110          /wgpe                     Enable protection again.
  111          /xq~                      Quit.
  112
  113 DONT     /xq~                      No insert, so quit.
  114
```

Figure 196

1. Use the /**R**ange **E**rase command to erase (not delete) the records you wish to remove. (See Figure 197.)

2. Sort the whole data base on the chosen Sort field. Specify the entire data base as the sort range. Use a descending Sort. This will put all the empty records at the end of the data base, where they can be used to enter new information. Figure 198 shows the same data base presented in Figure 195, after both records for November 14 have been erased and the data base sorted on date, first descending and then ascending.

321 Trap: If the data base contains ranges names that describe a portion of the data base, using /**R**ange **E**rase causes trouble.

The method shown in the previous Tip will probably work fine unless you have range names in the data base that describe only portions of the data base. In this example we have assigned the range name "NOV15" to all the records for November 15. Before the Sort the November 15 records are in rows 69 through 71, the range associated with the range name "NOV15" (Figure 195). After the Sort the November 15 records have shifted to rows 67 through 69 (Figure 198), but the "NOV15" range name is still associated with rows 69 through 71. As a result we no longer have the rows for this date identified properly.

```
         I        J        K        L      M       N
61
62  TELEMARKETING SYSTEM CUSTOMER DATA BASE
63  =======================================
64
65  Date      Customer Ap Sent? Inquiry? Notes
66    12-Nov     2387 y        y           Check points & call.
67
68
69    15-Nov      345 y        n
70    15-Nov      890 y        n
71    15-Nov      891 y        n
72    16-Nov       50 y        n
73    16-Nov      123 y        y           Wants 2 loans.
74    18-Nov      180 y        y
75
```

Figure 197

```
         I        J        K        L      M       N
61
62  TELEMARKETING SYSTEM CUSTOMER DATA BASE
63  =======================================
64
65  Date      Customer Ap Sent? Inquiry? Notes
66    12-Nov     2387 y        y           Check points & call.
67    15-Nov      345 y        n
68    15-Nov      890 y        n
69    15-Nov      891 y        n
70    16-Nov       50 y        n
71    16-Nov      123 y        y           Wants 2 loans.
72    18-Nov      180 y        y
73
74
```

Figure 198

The /Data Sort Command

322 **Tip:** You can use **/D**ata **S**ort to **S**ort ranges that are not data bases.

Because the Sort command is a subcommand under **/D**ata, it is easy to assume that you can Sort only a data base that has been formally defined as such. This "formal" definition is essential if you wish to use the /**D**ata **Q**uery command, but it is not necessary for /**D**ata **S**ort. Any column or set of columns can be Sorted by 1-2-3.

323 Trap: When Sorting a data base, do not include the field names row as part of the sort range.

If you include the row containing the field names of a data base in the range to be sorted, that row will be sorted, too, and may end up in a different position. It is unlikely that you want that.

324 Tip: Make sure you understand the sort order rules that the /**D**ata **S**ort command follows.

The results of an ascending sort, top to bottom, are as follows:

1. Empty (blank) cells first.

2. Label cells in ASCII order ignoring the alignment prefix. See the Appendix on "Printer Control Codes" in the 1-2-3 Manual for a list of the ASCII codes. Note that a SPACE (a label cell with nothing but spaces) comes before numeric labels, which come before uppercase letter labels, which come before lowercase letter labels.

3. Numbers and formula values in numeric order.

A descending sort will follow the opposite order.

Figure 199 shows a data base before an ascending sort on Customer. You can't tell by looking, but there's a difference between what's in L8 and what's in L10. Cell L8 contains a label of spaces, and cell L10 is empty; you'll see that these two cells sort differently. Also notice that the 1235 in cell L13 is a numeric label (left-justified), whereas the 1234 in L5 is a number; these two will sort differently, too.

Figure 200 shows the same data base after the sort. Look carefully at the "Customer" field in every row, and you'll see that 1-2-3 followed the rules exactly.

325 Trap: Spaces at the beginning or end of a label entry affect its sort order.

Look at record number 8 in Figure 199, which shows the data base before the sort on Customer, and Figure 200, which shows the same data base after the sort. Note that record 8 sorted before record 2

```
        I      J      K        L       M       N       O       P
1   TELEMARKETING SYSTEM CUSTOMER DATA BASE
2   =======================================
3
4   Mark    Record# Date    Customer Quantity Price   Amount  Item#
5             1     13-Nov    1234      10    249.00  2490.00      2
6             2     13-Nov  jones, j     5     10.00    50.00    123
7             3     13-Nov     891        0     0.00     0.00     45
8             4     15-Nov              22     10.00   220.00    123
9             5     15-Nov     891      20  PR12        246.00     12
10            6     16-Nov                0  PR12          0.00     12
11            7     16-Nov  JONES, J      5     5.55    27.75     22
12            8     16-Nov   jones, j     2     2.00     4.00    143
13            9     16-Nov  1235          2     2.00     4.00    143
14
15
16
17
18
19
20                          PR12        12.30
```

Figure 199

```
        I      J      K        L       M       N       O       P
1   TELEMARKETING SYSTEM CUSTOMER DATA BASE
2   =======================================
3
4   Mark    Record# Date    Customer Quantity Price   Amount  Item#
5             6     16-Nov                0  PR12          0.00     12
6             4     15-Nov              22     10.00   220.00    123
7             8     16-Nov   jones, j     2     2.00     4.00    143
8             9     16-Nov  1235          2     2.00     4.00    143
9             7     16-Nov  JONES, J      5     5.55    27.75     22
10            2     13-Nov  jones, j      5     10.00    50.00    123
11            5     15-Nov     891      20  PR12        246.00     12
12            3     13-Nov     891        0     0.00     0.00     45
13            1     13-Nov    1234      10    249.00  2490.00      2
14
15
16
17
18
19
20                          PR12        12.30
```

Figure 200

because of the leading space before *jones* in the "Customer" field of the former. Remember that because SPACE has the lowest ASCII value, labels that begin with spaces will always fall before labels beginning with a letter in a sorted data base.

326 **Trap:** If you mix lowercase and uppercase letters in the same field, you may get confusing results.

In Figures 199 and 200 notice that record 7 sorted before record 2 because of the difference in case. Remember that, given two labels that are almost identical but one begins with an uppercase letter and the other begins with a lowercase letter, 1-2-3 always puts first the label beginning with the uppercase letter.

327 **Tip:** To "undo" a sort and restore the original order, use an "original record number" field.

Note that the data base shown in Figure 199 has a "Record#" field. This field is included because we know that we want to be able to sort the data base several different ways and then get it back to its original order. The original order may have been the order of original data entry and may be important because it's the order of some other document.

Because we have this original "Record#" field, we can always get back to the original order simply by sorting, ascending on that field as the primary key.

328 **Tip:** You can sometimes sort a data base on more than two keys by doing two consecutive sorts.

The /Data Sort command permits a maximum of two sort keys on a single execution of the /Data Sort Go command. If you want to sort on more than two keys, this is what you should be able to do:

1. Pick the *most minor* key and sort on that one first. For instance, if you want to sort on "Amount" within "Date" within "Customer," "Amount" is the most minor key; so first sort on that. See Figure 201 for the result, assuming you began with the data base in Figure 199.

2. Then sort on the remaining two keys, in this case "Date" and "Customer." Use "Customer" as the primary key and "Date" as the secondary key. The result in this case is correct and is shown in Figure 202.

	I	J	K	L	M	N	O	P
1	TELEMARKETING SYSTEM CUSTOMER DATA BASE							
2	===							
3								
4	Mark	Record#	Date	Customer	Quantity	Price	Amount	Item#
5		6	16-Nov		0	PR12	0.00	12
6		3	13-Nov	891	0	0.00	0.00	45
7		8	16-Nov	jones, j	2	2.00	4.00	143
8		9	16-Nov	1235	2	2.00	4.00	143
9		7	16-Nov	JONES, J	5	5.55	27.75	22
10		2	13-Nov	jones, j	5	10.00	50.00	123
11		4	15-Nov		22	10.00	220.00	123
12		5	15-Nov	891	20	PR12	246.00	12
13		1	13-Nov	1234	10	249.00	2490.00	2
14								
15								
16								
17								
18								
19								
20			PR12	12.30				

Figure 201

	I	J	K	L	M	N	O	P
1	TELEMARKETING SYSTEM CUSTOMER DATA BASE							
2	===							
3								
4	Mark	Record#	Date	Customer	Quantity	Price	Amount	Item#
5		6	16-Nov		0	PR12	0.00	12
6		4	15-Nov		22	10.00	220.00	123
7		8	16-Nov	jones, j	2	2.00	4.00	143
8		9	16-Nov	1235	2	2.00	4.00	143
9		7	16-Nov	JONES, J	5	5.55	27.75	22
10		2	13-Nov	jones, j	5	10.00	50.00	123
11		3	13-Nov	891	0	0.00	0.00	45
12		5	15-Nov	891	20	PR12	246.00	12
13		1	13-Nov	1234	10	249.00	2490.00	2
14								
15								
16								
17								
18								
19								
20			PR12	12.30				

Figure 202

This method does not always work correctly, so be sure to check your results carefully.

329   Trap: When you're doing a series of sorts, you'll usually want to reset all sort options between sorts.

The Trap here is that 1-2-3 remembers the previously specified sort range, keys, etc. Here's an example of a problem you can run into if you don't use Sort **R**eset between sorts. You first sort on Date (primary) and Customer (secondary), and you then want to sort on Amount alone. If you respecify the primary key as Amount without first doing a **R**eset, 1-2-3 will remember that the secondary key is still Customer, and the result will be a data base sorted on Customer within Amount.

330   Trap: If you're not careful, you may end up with unexpected formula adjustments as a result of a sort.

1-2-3 treats a Sort as an implicit copy as far as the distinction between absolute and relative addresses is concerned. Therefore, formulas that have moved to another row as a result of a sort have their relative addresses adjusted accordingly, but absolute addresses are not adjusted.

Figure 203 shows a data base before a sort on "Price," and Figure 204 shows the same data base after the sort. Note that the relative references in the "Amount" field have been adjusted to reflect their new row positions, but that the absolute references to the range name "$PR12" are unadjusted. This is precisely what we wanted, so we have no problem. You can get into trouble, however, if you don't follow the right rules.

The three main rules to observe in assigning formulas in a range you wish to sort are these:

1.   Use relative addresses for references to cells within the range to be sorted. This is why we made most of our references relative in the example.

2.   Use absolute addresses for references to cells outside the range you are sorting. This is why we made absolute ($PR12) our references to the range PR ("PR12" is a range name).

3.   Avoid references to other rows within the sort range; the results will be hard to predict. Because most references that

```
      I      J      K      L      M      N      O      P
42 TELEMARKETING SYSTEM CUSTOMER DATA BASE
43 =======================================
44
45 Mark      Record# Date      Customer Quantity Price    Amount
46              1   13-Nov      1234      10   249.00  +M46*N46
47              2   13-Nov JONES, J       5    10.00  +M47*N47
48              3   13-Nov       891       0     0.00  +M48*N48
49              4   15-Nov                22    10.00  +M49*N49
50              5   15-Nov       891      20 PR12    +M50*$PR12
51              6   16-Nov                 0 PR12    +M51*$PR12
52              7   16-Nov jones, j        5     5.55  +M52*N52
53              8   16-Nov jones, j        2     2.00  +M53*N53
54
55
56
57
58
59
60
61                        PR12      12.30
```

Figure 203

```
      I      J      K      L      M      N      O      P
42 TELEMARKETING SYSTEM CUSTOMER DATA BASE
43 =======================================
44
45 Mark      Record# Date      Customer Quantity Price    Amount
46              5   15-Nov       891      20 PR12    +M46*$PR12
47              6   16-Nov                 0 PR12    +M47*$PR12
48              3   13-Nov       891       0     0.00  +M48*N48
49              8   16-Nov jones, j        2     2.00  +M49*N49
50              7   16-Nov jones, j        5     5.55  +M50*N50
51              2   13-Nov JONES, J        5    10.00  +M51*N51
52              4   15-Nov                22    10.00  +M52*N52
53              1   13-Nov      1234      10   249.00  +M53*N53
54
55
56
57
58
59
60                        PR12      12.30
61
```

Figure 204

occur within a data base are between two cells in the same record (row), this restriction is not much of a problem.

Whatever you do, don't reverse rules 1 and 2, or you will adjust or fail to adjust the wrong addresses.

Data Base Statistics

331 Tip: You can use the data base statistical functions to compute statistics on a subset of the records in a data base.

The 1-2-3 data base statistical functions (such as @DSUM and @DCOUNT) resemble the standard statistical functions (such as @SUM and @COUNT). The difference is that the data base functions operate on only a subset of the records in a data base. You determine which records are included in the subset by setting up criterion ranges for the functions.

Figure 205 shows a data base that is used by a bank to keep a log of telemarketing activity on consumer loan campaigns. Figure 206 shows a criterion range (rows 103 and 104) defined for this data base. Cell L107 in Figure 206 contains an @DCOUNT that counts the number of nonblank entries in the "STATUS" column of the data base.

@DCOUNT($LOG,1,$CRIT)

This function has three parts: the data range, the offset, and the criterion range. The data range and the criterion range are like the same ranges in the /**D**ata **Q**uery command. The data range describes the data base being evaluated, and the criterion range points to the criteria that will govern the search. Because the criterion range in Figure 206 is blank, this function says: Count the number of nonblank entries in the "STATUS" column of the data base in the range J90..N100 (named "LOG"). The function evaluates to 10, the correct number of nonblank entries in the "STATUS" column in Figure 205.

Why did the function choose the "STATUS" column? Because the offset in the function, 1, told it to. The offset tells the function on which column (field) in the data base the function is to operate. Unfortunately, 1-2-3's system for numbering offsets is confusing: the first column has an offset of 0; the second column has an offset of 1, and so on. An offset of 1 tells the function to evaluate the "STATUS" column.

```
      J        K        L           M        N
 81
 82
 83  TELEMARKETING LOG
 84  ================
 85                                          DATE
 86  DATE                             2ND OR  COMMIT
 87  RESP                             OTHER   LETTER
 88  REC'D         BOX # NAME(LAST, FIRST)  LIENS?  MAILED
 89
 90  DTRCD    STATUS   DBNAME         LIENS?  DTCOMMLD
 91    01-Nov      1 BEEPER, ROBERT          25-Nov
 92    02-Nov      1 BOPPER, JOE             11-Nov
 93    01-Nov      2 TOOTER, TOOTSIE    Y
 94    05-Nov      2 DIPSEY, DOODLE     Y
 95    01-Nov      1 HANKY, PANKY            17-Nov
 96    01-Nov      1 HOLLY, TOMMY            11-Nov
 97    05-Nov      3 HOLLY, IVY         Y
 98    08-Nov      2 HOLLY, JOAN        Y    16-Nov
 99    01-Nov      2 HOLLY, ALFIE       Y
100    01-Nov      2 NASIUM, JIM        Y
101
```

Figure 205

```
      I        J        K          L            M        N
101
102
103     DTRCD    STATUS   DBNAME              LIENS?   DTCOMMLD
104
105
106
107              @DCOUNT($LOG, 1, $CRIT)
108
109                               10
```

Figure 206

Suppose you want to know the number of people who have a status of 1? First, enter the status value of 1 in the "STATUS" criterion cell in the criterion range in Figure 206. If you then press the {Calc} key to recalculate, you'll see that the @DCOUNT function has been reevaluated. The new value, 4, is the correct count of records with a status of 1.

332 Trick: If you use data base statistical functions as formulas in **/D**ata **T**ables, you can do analyses very quickly.

Using data base statistical functions in combination with data tables is one of the slickest tricks you can perform with 1-2-3. Let's continue with the example we used under the previous Tip.

Suppose you want to get a count of the number of customers with liens, separately for each date for which you received a response. The data table shown in Figure 207 does the job. This is what we did to set it up:

```
        I        J           K           L
121
122
123
124          LIEN COUNTS BY DATE
125          ===================
126                             # WITH
127          DATE                2ND OR
128          RESP                OTHER
129          REC'D                LIENS
130              @DCOUNT($LOG,3,$CRIT)
131          01-Nov                3
132          02-Nov                0
133          05-Nov                2
134          08-Nov                1
135
```

Figure 207

1. We entered all the dates we wanted to cover in the left-hand column of the data table.

2. We entered our @DCOUNT formula on the first row of the data table in K130 (Figure 207). In this case we've specified a "3" as the offset to indicate that the function should operate on the "LIENS?" field. We format this function to display as **T**ext—a good practice so we can see the exact form of the function.

3. We made sure that our criterion range was blank (as in Figure 206).

4. We executed the /**Data Table 1** command, supplying the range J130..K134 as the **Table** range and the cell J104 (the "Date Response Received" cell in the criterion range in Figure 206) as the **Input** cell.

The /**Data Table** command substitutes each date from the left-hand column of the data table sequentially into the input cell in the criterion range. The @DCOUNT formula at the top of the data table in Figure 207 is evaluated separately by 1-2-3 for each date, with the corresponding results shown in the second column of the data table under the formula. If you compare these counts to the data base in Figure 205, you'll see that they're correct.

Try a similar example yourself if you have any doubts about how all this works. It's truly magic! We can add other formulas in additional columns of the data table if we want other counts. We can also use any of the data base statistical functions this way.

333 **Tip:** You can use /**Data Query U**nique to create the input values for a data base statistical data table.

If you want to create a comprehensive summary of the SUM, COUNT, or other statistics for each record type in the data base, you can use /**Data Query Unique** to extract a list of all unique values from a data base field to an output area. The chapter on "what if" analysis shows an example of this technique.

Subtotals in Data Bases

334 **Tip:** Use subtotal divider lines and formulas that include them to create and maintain subtotals.

People are accustomed to seeing the type of subtotals shown in Figure 208, with a subtotal line before each change in the value of the primary sort field. Here our data base is sorted on Date, and we have subtotals at each change and a grand total line at the bottom. As we'll see, this situation is not as easy to produce and maintain with 1-2-3 as it should be.

Figure 209 shows the same table with Text formatting for the subtotal and total formulas. Note that each @SUM formula begins and ends

```
     I  J  K      L            M        N        O         P
1  TELEMARKETING SYSTEM CUSTOMER DATA BASE
2  ========================================
3
4  Mark Rec Date  Customer Quantity       Price    Amount       Item#
5        1  13-Nov    1234       10 249.00        2490.00   2
6        2  13-Nov jones, j       5  10.00          50.00  123
7        3  13-Nov     891        0   0.00           0.00   45
8  Sub1  4  13-Nov ================================================
9  Sub2  5  13-Nov             15              2540.00
10 Sub3  6  13-Nov ================================================
11 Sub1  7  14-Nov ================================================
12 Sub2  8  14-Nov              0                 0.00
13 Sub3  9  14-Nov ================================================
14       10 15-Nov             22  10.00         220.00  123
15       11 15-Nov     891      20  PR12          246.00   12
16 Sub1 12  15-Nov ================================================
17 Sub2 13  15-Nov             42               466.00
18 Sub3 14  15-Nov ================================================
19 Total15 *********           57              3006.00
20
```

Figure 208

with a divider row, not an actual detail data row. This allows you to use /Worksheet Insert Row to insert a row for a new date anywhere between the dividers for that date without having to adjust the subtotal and total formulas. The formulas are adjusted automatically as a result of the implicit changes made by the /Worksheet Insert command.

Figure 210 shows the same table after we've inserted a detail line for November 14 with /Worksheet Insert. Compare the formulas on rows 13 and 20 in this figure with those on rows 12 and 19, respectively, in Figure 209 to see how 1-2-3 has adjusted the cell references.

The virtue of this approach is that you never have to adjust formulas after you've set them up. There are several drawbacks, however:

1. Either you have to set up the divider lines and formulas in advance for all possible dates as we did (that's why we have lines for November 14 in Figure 209), or you have to make sure you enter the divider lines and subtotal formulas and update the totals formulas every time you start a new date.

```
      I  J   K     L        M         N     O          P
 1 TELEMARKETING SYSTEM CUSTOMER DATA BASE
 2 ========================================
 3
 4 Mark Rec  Date  Customer Quantity      Price  Amount       Item#
 5       1   13-Nov   1234        10  249.00        2490.00    2
 6       2   13-Nov jones, j       5   10.00          50.00  123
 7       3   13-Nov    891         0    0.00           0.00   45
 8 Sub1  4   13-Nov ====================================================
 9 Sub2  5   13-Nov        @SUM(M4..M8)          @SUM(O4..O8)
10 Sub3  6   13-Nov ====================================================
11 Sub1  7   14-Nov ====================================================
12 Sub2  8   14-Nov        @SUM(M10..M11)        @SUM(O10..O11)
13 Sub3  9   14-Nov ====================================================
14      10   15-Nov                  22   10.00         220.00  123
15      11   15-Nov    891           20  PR12           246.00   12
16 Sub1 12   15-Nov ====================================================
17 Sub2 13   15-Nov        @SUM(M13..M16)        @SUM(O13..O16)
18 Sub3 14   15-Nov ====================================================
19 Total15 *********     @SUM(M9+M12+M17)       @SUM(O9+O12+O17)
20
```

Figure 209

```
      I  J   K     L        M         N     O          P
 1 TELEMARKETING SYSTEM CUSTOMER DATA BASE
 2 ========================================
 3
 4 Mark Rec  Date  Customer Quantity      Price  Amount       Item#
 5       1   13-Nov   1234        10  249.00        2490.00    2
 6       2   13-Nov jones, j       5   10.00          50.00  123
 7       3   13-Nov    891         0    0.00           0.00   45
 8 Sub1  4   13-Nov ====================================================
 9 Sub2  5   13-Nov        @SUM(M4..M8)          @SUM(O4..O8)
10 Sub3  6   13-Nov ====================================================
11          14-Nov Smith, J.       10   50.00         500.00  356
12 Sub1  7   14-Nov ====================================================
13 Sub2  8   14-Nov        @SUM(M10..M12)        @SUM(O10..O12)
14 Sub3  9   14-Nov ====================================================
15      10   15-Nov                  22   10.00         220.00  123
16      11   15-Nov    891           20  PR12           246.00   12
17 Sub1 12   15-Nov ====================================================
18 Sub2 13   15-Nov        @SUM(M14..M17)        @SUM(O14..O17)
19 Sub3 14   15-Nov ====================================================
20 Total15 *********     @SUM(M9+M13+M18)       @SUM(O9+O13+O18)
```

Figure 210

This last approach depends too much on the user's having a perfect memory, so we don't recommend it.

2. You're forced to use /**Worksheet Insert** and live with its dangers.

3. You can take up a lot of extra space with divider lines.

You can write a macro to control the insertion of new lines and minimize the /**Worksheet Insert** dangers. This macro can also make sure that new divider lines are inserted for a new date and can adjust the necessary formulas. However, this is a complex macro to write, and it's wise to keep your macros simple to avoid problems.

	I	J	K	L	M	N	O	P
21	TELEMARKETING SYSTEM CUSTOMER DATA BASE							
22	==							
23								
24	Mark	Rec	Date	Customer	Quantity	Price	Amount	Item#
25		1	13-Nov	1234	10	249.00	2490.00	2
26		2	13-Nov	jones, j	5	10.00	50.00	123
27		3	13-Nov	891	0	0.00	0.00	45
28		10	15-Nov		22	10.00	220.00	123
29		11	15-Nov	891	20	100.00	2000.00	12
30								
31								
32								
33								
34								
35								
36								
37	CRITERION RANGE							
38	================							
39	Mark	Rec	Date	Customer	Quantity	Price	Amount	Item#
40								

Figure 211

Separate Subtotal Tables

335 Tip: You can create a separate table of subtotals for a data base using the /**Data Table 1** command.

People may be accustomed to seeing subtotal lines interleaved with detail lines, but it is much easier in 1-2-3 to create a separate table of subtotals using /**Data Table 1**. Figure 211 shows a data base without interleaved subtotal lines. Figure 212 shows a Data Table that produces separate subtotals and totals for this data base by date.

	I	J	K	L	M
41	TELEMARKETING SYSTEM CUSTOMER DATA BASE--SUBTOTALS				
42	==				
43					
44					
45				Quantity	Amount
46				@DSUM(INPUT, 4, CRITERION)	@DSUM(INPUT, 6, CRITERION)
47			13-Nov	15	2540
48			14-Nov	0	0
49			15-Nov	42	2220
50	TOTAL			57	4760
51					
52					
53					

Figure 212

To set up this Data Table, we took the following steps:

1.   We put the three dates for which we wanted subtotals into K47..K49 and left K50 empty.

2.   We put @DSUM formulas in the first row of the Data Table. These are the formulas that give us subtotals. (The @DSUM formulas work only because we have previously given range names to a data base named "INPUT" and a Criterion range named "CRITERION." Figure 211 shows these areas. "INPUT" covers I24..P29, and "CRITE-RION" covers I39..P40.)

3.   We defined a **Data Table 1** with a table range of K46..M50.

4.   We defined K40 (the "Date" cell in the Criterion range) as the Input Cell 1 for the Data Table.

5.   We pressed {Enter} to calculate the table.

Here is an example of the results you can produce with data base statistical functions (the @D functions) in connection with data tables. When the Data Table recalculates, it substitutes, in turn, each date from column K of the table into the "Date" cell in the Criterion range (the cell we provided as **Input Cell 1** to the **/Data Table 1** command). The two @DSUM formulas in row 46 of Figure 212 are evaluated in turn for each date, and the output values are placed in columns L and M.

We left K50 blank and included it in the Data Table range because all the records in the data base are selected when that blank cell is substituted into the "Date" field of the Criterion range. Thus, we get our grand total line on row 50.

Note that we included November 14 in the Data Table although we have no detail for it yet. The idea is to anticipate all the subtotal lines so that we don't have to reconstruct the Data Table later.

There are a couple of possible traps here.

1. It's easy to get the wrong field number as the second argument in the @DSUM function. For all these @D functions, the first field in the data base is considered field number 0; that makes "Quantity" number 4 and "Amount" number 6, as we have them.

2. It's also easy to make a mistake in getting all possible values correctly into the first column of the Data Table.

336 Tip: Use **/Data F**ill to reset the "Record Number" field quickly after new records are added to a data base.

One common use of the **/Data F**ill command is to reset the values of the "Record Number" field in a data base after records have been added and/or deleted.

Index

Assistant to the Managing Editor
Tim P. Russell

Production
Dennis R. Sheehan

Composed by Que Corporation
in Times Roman, Megaron, and Varityper Digital

Cover designed by
Cargill & Associates, Atlanta, Georgia

More Computer Knowledge from Que